The Minor Prophets

D1448614

The

Minor Prophets

their relevance
for today

edited by
IVAN STEEDS

PRECIOUS SEED PUBLICATIONS

Precious Seed Publications
P.O. Box 8,
Neath,
West Glam.
SA11 1QB

ISBN 1 871642 06 X

Printed in Great Britain by Dotesios Ltd.

Contents

KINGS AND PROPHETS OF ISRAEL AND JUDAH
following the reigns of Saul, David and Solomon

Israel		Date	Judah	
Prophets	Kings	B.C.	Kings	Prophets
	Jeroboam I		Rehoboam	
	Nadab		Abijam	
	Baasha	900	Asa	
	Elah			
	Zimri			
	Omri			
Elijah	Ahab		Jehoshaphat	
Elisha	Ahaziah			
	Joram		Jehoram	
			Ahaziah	
	Jehu		Queen Athaliah	
	Jehoahaz		Jehoash (Joash)	Joel*
	Jehoash	800	Amaziah	
Jonah	Jeroboam II		Uzziah (Azariah)	
Amos				
Hosea				
	Zachariah			
	Shallum			
	Menahem			
	Pekahiah			Isaiah
	Pekah		Jotham	Micah
			Ahaz	
	Hoshea	700	Hezekiah	
	Captivity—			Nahum*
	Assyria		Manasseh	
			Amon	
			Josiah	Zephaniah
				Jeremiah
				Habakkuk*
			Jehoahaz	
		600	Jehoiakim	
			Jehoiachin	
			Zedekiah	Ezekiel
			Captivity—	Daniel
			Babylon	Obadiah*
			(Zerubbabel)	Haggai
		500		Zechariah
			(Ezra)	
			(Nehemiah)	Malachi

*Date uncertain

Acknowledgements

ON BEHALF OF THE COMMITTEE OF 'PRECIOUS SEED' it is my pleasurable duty to acknowledge the considerable help received from a number of fellow-believers in the publication of this book. First thanks are due to all contributors to the commentary section, each busy already in the Lord's service but for this cause willing to add to their commitments. Thanks are due to Roy Hill for his valued help in planning the scale of the project, and in its design over-all. Arthur Shearman, Michael Jones, and again Roy Hill are thanked for their painstaking efforts in proof-reading, and also thanks to David Ogden for compiling a helpful bibliography. Finally, the committee express their gratitude to Anne Mortimore (photography) and Rob Penghilley (graphics) for cover-design. May I place on record that, with such support and valued contri-bution, my task in editing the book has been made a most enjoyable experience.

IVAN STEEDS
December 1992

Introduction

by IVAN STEEDS

'Men spake from God, being moved by the Holy Spirit'.
2. Pet. 1. 21 (R.V.)

HAVING RECEIVED GOD'S WORD by a process of divine communication, the prime function of the prophet was to declare that word publicly. In so doing he would 'forthtell' God's message to his contemporaries, and on occasion he might be required to 'foretell' future events, according to instruction. Prophets were bound to declare their messages without fear or favour, and regularly this led to victimisation and outright persecution by king and commoner. They were known to condemn the religious leaders of their day whenever the latter were guilty of condoning the wayward progress of a nation out of touch with God. Prophets of earlier times were inclined to speak out against individuals who had offended God, thereby drawing attention to the holiness of Almighty God, and His requirements as stated in the Law. Their messages were delivered orally, with such authority that kings trembled at their word. In later times, 8th century B.C. and thereafter, the methods if not the style used by prophets to project their messages entered a new phase. By now the nation had divided into northern and southern kingdoms, with both sub-groups consistently neglecting and rejecting Israel's God. Understandably, the messages of the prophets now extended to include the nation — their thunderous denunciations and dire warnings were directed at the entirety of the people. Again, in contrast to oral statements of their predecessors, the spoken messages of later prophets were written down in the form that we have them today. It is for this that they are sometimes referred to as the writing prophets, and the dignity, impressiveness and beauty of their writings, sometimes arranged in the form of poetry, recommend them to any reader.

Who were these men, so used by God in their own times, whose messages God has seen fit to preserve in the context of holy scripture? The answer is that they followed no regulated pattern, coming from varying circumstances of life. As men might judge, they held no special qualifications to suit them for the tasks reserved for them by God.

Evidently, they were men 'subject to like passions as we are', and their call and gifting for the task of speaking for God indicates, in a measure, the sovereignty of God in selecting His servants.

There was variety, too, in the messages they delivered, and although much common ground was adopted, there was still great variety of emphasis as they made their pronouncements. Their words were judgemental, again and again, yet not without hope! Running through their messages like a golden thread was reference to Israel's Messiah and, through Him, a glorious future. Approximately, one third of the entire text of Old Testament scripture is taken up by these prophetic writings, as 'God . . . at sundry times and in divers manners spake in time past unto the fathers by the prophets'.

And what of the twelve, the so-called Minor Prophets? It has to be said that in the estimation of some they suffer in comparison with the, so-called, Major Prophets. The sad sequel to this is that the 'Minors' are generally neglected, and their messages unappreciated. It is presumed that they hold little relevance to modern-day life, and Christian experience. This cannot be allowed, and is patently untrue!

Apart from the fact that the Minor Prophets portray significant stages in the history of Israel, and the process of divine revelation to mankind, they convey at the same time certain abiding truths that must inform and support the godly of any age. They give account of God who is sovereign over worldly affairs, so that in the end all things conspire to His glory. He is presented as God who is loving, plenteous in mercy, forgiving and ever faithful to honour His promises. He is declared to be holy, almighty, implacable in administration of justice, and awesome in His judgement upon the deserving. These prophets show mankind as hopeless and helpless in sin, increasingly out-of-touch with God, rebellious, unashamed and unrepentant. But then there is Christ 'in all the scriptures'. The Minor Prophets give glimpses of Christ that reassure us, convince us, thrill us, cause 'our heart to burn within us' as the scriptures are 'opened to us'!

Today's Christian has every reason to make a closer study of these same scriptures, and it is as a means to this end that the present volume has been put together. It is produced in the form of a commentary to assist the reader in order that he might rightly divide the word of truth, and with the help of the Holy Spirit gain true understanding of eternal verities.

CHAPTER ONE

THE PROPHECY OF
HOSEA

by JOHN RIDDLE

Introduction

HOSEA'S NAME MEANS 'SALVATION' and is probably a shorter name for Joshua or Jehoshuah. He was contemporary with Amos, Micah and Isaiah. Hosea and Amos both addressed the Northern Kingdom, but were quite different in approach. In Amos, sin is an outrage of divine law, and God commands return. In Hosea, sin is an outrage of divine love, and God pleads for return. This variation illustrates the fact that servants of God can have differing emphases in their ministry, but labour in the same sphere without collision or confusion.

The outstanding feature of this prophecy is the emphasis placed on God's love for His people. It has been aptly said that, 'the heart of God lies on the surface of Hosea's ministry'. Although Israel had failed to reciprocate God's love, and incurred divine displeasure by their infidelity to Him, He still exclaimed, 'How shall I give thee up, Ephraim? How shall I deliver thee Israel? How shall I make thee as Admah? How shall I set thee as Zeboim? Mine heart is turned within me, my repentings ('compassions' RV) are kindled together', 11. 8. Ultimately, God will say, 'I will love them freely', 14. 4.

Hosea was no mere orator. He preached out of deep conviction, and was able to do so out of his own experiences in the school of God. This is made very clear by the two main divisions of the book:

A   Chapters 1–3, Hosea's love for his unfaithful wife.
B   Chapters 4–14, God's love for His unfaithful people.

When God told Hosea to 'love a woman beloved of her friend, yet an adulteress', he was reflecting 'the love of the Lord toward the children of Israel, who look to other gods', 3. 1. The vicissitudes of his own marriage relationship taught Hosea that God deeply loved His erring people.

Since, 'Whatsoever things were written aforetime were written for our learning', we must endeavour to ascertain the message of Hosea for ourselves. First of all, there is a message to preachers. Hosea preached with deep feeling. He faithfully stated God's 'controversy (lawsuit) with the people of the land', 4. 1. But his faithfulness in exposing the guilt of Israel was accompanied by tender appeal. Preachers are all too prone to say the right thing, but to say it in entirely the wrong way. There is admirable balance in the words, 'Speaking the truth in love', Eph. 4. 15. Then, secondly, there is a message to us all. The principal charge against Israel was infidelity. When love for God diminishes, things go wrong everywhere. The Lord Jesus said, 'I have somewhat against thee, because thou hast left thy first love. Remember therefore from whence thou art fallen, and repent, and do the first works', Rev. 3. 4–5. That, surely, is the undated message of Hosea.

Hosea 1. 1–2. 1, 'Take unto thee a wife of whoredoms'

(1) The background, v. 1

Hosea lived in turbulent times. The kings of Judah named in verse 1—
Uzziah, Jotham, Ahaz, and Hezekiah—reigned between 791BC and
686BC. Jeroboam ruled Israel from 782BC to 745BC, but there is no mention of his successors, although Hosea's ministry covered their reigns as
well. A general reference is made to Zachariah, Shallum, Menahem,
Pekahiah, Pekah, and Hoshea, in 8. 4, 'They have set up kings, but not
by me'. But their names are not mentioned. The period of the so-called
'mushroom monarchs' was marked by anarchy, murder and usurp-
ation, and is dismissed altogether in Hosea 1. 1. It almost seems as if
God had no wish whatever even to recognize their existence: the grace
extended to Jeroboam II, 2 Kgs. 14. 26–27, had been exhausted.

Evidently, the opening section of the prophecy, chapters 1–3, took
place in the reign of Jeroboam II. The blood of Jezreel had not yet been
avenged, 1. 4–5, and this actually took place in the reign of his son,
Zachariah, see 2 Kgs. 10. 30, and 2 Kgs. 15. 12.

(2) The marriage, v. 2

'Go take unto thee a wife of whoredoms, and children of whoredoms:
for the land hath committed great whoredom departing from the Lord',
1. 2. Before Hosea commenced his ministry, he was instructed by God to
marry a highly undesirable woman, and in his relationship with Gomer,
he was made acutely aware of God's feelings and love for His equally
undesirable people Israel. The marriage was therefore both literal and
symbolic. Hosea conveyed the word of God with deep feelings. He
knew only too well how God felt about His people. There is all the
difference in the world between cold, clinical preaching, and preaching
that flows from deep feelings and a tender heart.

The fact that Hosea was to 'take . . . a wife of whoredoms and children
of whoredoms', indicates, clearly, what Gomer would become. If we
understand that Gomer was a harlot at the time of the marriage, we
must also understand that Hosea inherited a ready-made family!
Patently, this was not the case. The expression, 'children of whoredoms' will be explained later. M. C. UNGER comments pertinently 'It
is highly doubtful that the Lord would have commanded a holy prophet
to do what was expressly forbidden to the priests, and frowned upon for
Israel as a whole'. Hosea was warned, and therefore knew in advance,
what his wife would become, just as Jehovah Himself knew in advance

what His people would become. They would 'play the harlot', see 4. 15, etc.

(3) The children, vv. 3–9

Three children were born, and their names are invested with prophetical significance. Three stages of judgement are indicated in the names given to the children.

A) *Jezreel*. We are specifically told that 'Gomer . . . conceived, and bear him a son'. The parentage of Jezreel is undisputed. But that could not be said for the two succeeding children. It is, 'bear a daughter . . . bear a son.' The absence of 'bear him' is significant. Hence, 'children of whoredoms'.

Jezreel means, 'God scatters' and 'God sows', and this chapter elaborates both meanings. However, his name has a double significance in verse 4: it anticipated two future events;

i) 'Call his name Jezreel; for yet a little while, and I will avenge the blood of Jezreel upon the house of Jehu'. Historically, Jezreel was the place where Jehu finally destroyed the remaining representatives of the house of Ahab. Whilst he purged idolatry to a great degree, he allowed the original images established by Jeroboam I to remain, see 2 Kgs. 10. 29-31. For what he did accomplish, he was promised four generations by God, i.e. Jehoahaz, Joash (Jehoash), Jeroboam II, and Zachariah. The last of these was assassinated by Shallum. God's word, as ever, was exact. But why did God 'avenge the blood of Jezreel upon the house of Jehu', when he had been anointed for that purpose?, see 2 Kgs. 9. 1-10. The answer lies not in what Jehu did, but the ways in which he did it. D. KIDNER observes, 'The events of 2 Kings 10 are a welter of trickery, butchery and hypocrisy . . . self-interest and bloodlust were his dominant springs of conduct, and it was this that made "the blood of Jezreel" an accusing stain', cf. Isa. 10. 5-19. We should remember that, all too frequently, the right thing is done in the wrong way, with disastrous results for individuals and assemblies.

ii) 'I . . . will cause to cease the kingdom of the house of Israel. And it shall come to pass at that day, that I will break the bow of Israel in the valley of Jezreel'. The 'valley of Jezreel' was 'the great battlefield of Palestine', UNGER, see, for example, Judg. 6. 33; 1 Sam. 29. 1. Now, the same Plain of Esdraelon, where Jehu 'slew all that remained of the house of Ahab', 2 Kgs. 10. 11, would witness, not now the end of Jehu's dynasty, but the defeat of the Northern Kingdom. In other passages, 'the bow' of Israel's enemies is broken, see Hos. 2. 18 and Ps. 46. 9:

but here it is 'the bow of Israel' itself. The Assyrian did this in the reign of Pekah, 2 Kgs. 15. 27–29. In subsequent years, until the final captivity, Israel merely lingered: it was a broken nation.

B) *Lo-Ruhamah*. Her name means, 'unpitied', and she represents the second stage of divine judgement. 'I will no more have mercy on the house of Israel; but I will utterly take them away', v.6. This prophecy became history in 721BC, when the Northern Kingdom was taken into complete captivity, transported to Assyria, and its cities repopulated by colonists from the east, see 2 Kgs. 17. 'The Lord removed Israel out of his sight, as he had said by all his servants the prophets', v. 23, including Hosea.

Judah is exempted from judgement at this time. The Assyrians laid siege to Jerusalem, and God was true to His word. He saved them, but not 'by bow, nor by sword, nor by battle, by horses, nor by horsemen', v.7. Judah was saved by divine intervention. The Assyrian army was depleted by 185,000 men, see 2 Kgs. 19. 35. If one angel caused so much havoc, what would 'more than twelve legions of angels' have done? Matt. 26. 53.

C) *Lo-Ammi*. His name means, 'Not my people': he represents the third stage of judgement. 'Ye are not my people, and I will not be your God', v. 9. God had said, 'If ye will obey my voice indeed, and keep my covenant, then ye shall be a peculiar treasure unto me above all people', Exod. 19. 5–6. The absence of the name 'Israel' in verse 8, together with the obvious reference to the covenant relationship in Exodus 19, suggests that this statement refers to the entire nation, Israel and Judah. Judah had been faithful in measure, but was warned, 'Though thou Israel play the harlot, let not Judah offend', 4. 15. But Judah succumbed to idolatry as well, 'Therefore shall Israel and Ephraim fall in their iniquity; Judah shall also fall with them', 5. 5–15; 6. 4.

4) The restoration, 1. 10–2. 1

The prophecy now leaps forward, and anticipates Israel's ultimate future in the millennial kingdom. D. KIDNER puts it nicely, 'The ominous names are not God's last word. At once, as though He cannot bear to leave the matter there, He points to the far future, when everything that these names have stood for will be reversed'. These verses bring before us the nation's final blessing, when Israel and Judah will be reunited under one Head—Christ Himself. Bearing in mind the reference to the promise to Abraham in verse 10, God is evidently referring to the twelve tribes here in their entirety, 'Yet the number of the children of Israel shall be as the sand of the sea'.

The name 'Jezreel' is now invested with its other meaning. The nation, once 'scattered' among the Gentile nations, will return from captivity to be 'sown' in her own land. This is expanded in chapter 2. 14-23. The statement, 'For great shall be the day of Jezreel', is fully supported by Old Testament prophecy. But the conditions signified by the names of all three children will be reversed. 'Say ye unto your brethren, Ammi; and to your sisters, Ruhamah'. The nation will be acknowledged by God ('Ammi' means 'my people'), and will enjoy His mercy ('Ruhamah' means 'having obtained mercy'). Having worshipped lifeless gods, they will then be called 'sons of the living God'.

Hosea 1. 10, is cited in Romans 9. 26. Hosea 2. 23 is cited in Romans 9. 25. Paul quotes from Hosea 1 in support of the statement, 'And that he might make known the riches of his glory on the vessels of mercy, which he had afore prepared unto glory. Even us, whom he hath called, not of the Jews only, but also of the Gentiles'. But why appeal to a passage which refers clearly to Israel, when describing blessing for Jew and Gentile? The answer is clear: the nation had lapsed into idolatry, and God had severed connection with them: they were 'not my people', and therefore in the same position as the Gentiles. What God will do in principle when the nation is restored, He has already done in grace through the gospel.

Hosea 2. 2–23, 'I will betroth thee unto me for ever'

In chapter 1, Hosea was instructed to 'take a wife of whoredoms', and the reason immediately follows, 'For the land hath committed great whoredom, departing from the Lord'. Hosea 2 describes this 'great whoredom' in more detail. But it also describes the future blessing and restoration of Israel in more detail. Chapter 2 is therefore similar in structure to chapter 1. There is, however, a difference in approach. In chapter 1, the immediate and ultimate future of the nation is spelt out in terms of the children, whilst here it is spelt out in terms of the mother. Chapter 2 commences with the abrogation of the marriage relationship, 'She is not my wife, neither am I her husband'. Bearing in mind that God will not go back on the marriage vows, this statement can be taken to mean, 'She is no longer a wife to Me'. The chapter concludes with, 'Thou shalt call me Ishi (husband)', and the expression, 'in that day', vv. 16, 18, 21, indicates that this happy period belongs to the end-time.

The chapter therefore divides into two main sections, as follows:

1) Israel's rejection, and the reason, vv. 2–13.
2) Israel's restoration, and the reason, vv. 14–23.

In the first case, Israel's love had failed. In the second case, God's love will triumph.

(1) Israel's rejection, and the reason, vv. 2–13

The section commences, not with a command, but with a plea, 'Plead with your mother, plead'. We have already seen that Hosea could appeal to his people in this way out of deep personal experience. Israel is addressed nationally as 'your mother', and the people are addressed individually as 'her children'. The reason for Israel's rejection, is her 'whoredoms' and her 'adulteries'. The nation had been unfaithful to God, so much so that He would no longer acknowledge her whilst persisting in her sin. He therefore pleads, through Hosea, 'Let her therefore put away her whoredoms out of her sight, and her adulteries from between her breasts; lest I strip her naked, and set her as in the day that she was born, and make her as a wilderness, and set her like a dry land, and slay her with thirst'. That is, He would strip her of nationhood, and return her to original conditions of slavery.

The root cause is unfaithfulness to God, at which point we must pause and listen to James, 'Adulteresses, know ye not that friendship with the world is enmity with God? Whosoever therefore is minded to be the friend of the world is constituted enemy of God', 4. 4, JND. See also 1 John 2. 15. It is also significant that the ruin described by Jeremiah in Lamentations, was caused in exactly the same way, see 1. 2.

Notice how the charge is elaborated in verses 4–13, with emphasis on the word 'lovers'. Her 'lovers' in this particular passage are evidently the Canaanite idols; they are called 'Baalim' (plural) in verse 13. 'The gods of Canaan were largely patrons of fertility', D. KIDNER. Israel had turned to them for help in agriculture, and had become embroiled in all the debased rituals connected with Baal-worship. Obedience to God, and devotion to God, is our bulwark against spiritual and moral corruption.

i) Her determination to follow her lovers. 'I will go after my lovers, that give me my bread and my water, my wool and my flax, mine oil and my drink', v. 5. It was more than a silly mistake: it was a determined policy. 'I will go after my lovers'. More than that, it was a deliberate refusal to acknowledge the goodness and blessing of God.

His provision was credited to idols. This should promote serious thought.

First of all, we must never forget that, 'Every good gift and every perfect gift is from above, and cometh down from the Father of lights'. Secondly, we must never forget that all that we are, and have, belongs to God. He flatly contradicts their statement, 'my bread . . . water . . . wool . . . flax . . . oil . . . drink'. God insists in verse 9 that it is, 'My corn . . . wine . . . wool . . . flax'. More than that, Israel dedicated God's provision to Baal. Peter reminds us that we are to be 'good stewards of the manifold grace of God', 1 Pet. 4. 10. All spiritual ability is a divine bestowal. But we are to act as stewards in respect of everything that God gives us:

> 'Naught that I have my own I call,
> I hold it for the Giver:
> My heart, my strength, my life, my all,
> Are His, and His for ever.'

Thirdly, we must never attribute to the gods of our own intellect or ability, or to the gods of business and commerce, our blessings and provision. 'Thou shalt remember the Lord thy God: for it is he that giveth thee power to get wealth', Deut. 8. 17–18.

ii) Her disillusion with her lovers. 'She shall follow after her lovers, but she shall not overtake them', v. 7. Jeremiah described it as, 'broken cisterns, that can hold no water', 2. 13. Israel would find no lasting satisfaction in her idolatrous practices. Very much akin to the two daughters of the horseleach, Prov. 30. 15, who cry, 'Give, give', but give nothing in return.

There is something terribly casual about the statement, 'I will go and return to my first husband; for then it was better with me than now'. It is almost as if she is treating God like a safety-net. He is reduced to one of several options. There is no trace of regret for the pain she had caused, and no sorrow for the way in which she had affronted His love. She thinks she can just pick up the threads of the relationship without further ado. The Lord Jesus made it very clear indeed that something far more thorough was required, 'Remember therefore from whence thou art fallen, and repent, and do the first works', Rev. 2. 5.

iii) Her degradation before her lovers. 'And now will I discover her lewdness in the sight of her lovers', v. 10. She will be exposed before them as defiled and degraded, cf. Lam. 1. 8. The Lord Jesus taught, 'If the salt hath lost its savour, wherewith shall it be salted? It is thenceforth good for nothing, but to be cast out, and to be trodden under foot of men', Matt. 5. 13. The world has little time for people who profess one thing, and deny it in practice.

iv) Her desolation because of her lovers. 'I will also cause all her mirth to cease, her feast days . . . And I will destroy her vines and her fig trees whereof she hath said, These are my rewards that my lovers have given me', vv. 11–12. Compromise and infidelity destroy joy, and create barrenness: there is no fruit.

v) Her decoration for her lovers. 'I will visit upon her the days of Baalim, wherein she burned incense to them, and she decked herself with her earrings and her jewels, and she went after her lovers, and forgat me, saith the Lord', v. 13. That is, she made herself attractive to idols, and had no thought of being attractive to God. The New Testament has a great deal to say about this: for example, 2 Corinthians 5. 9, RV, 'Wherefore also we make it our aim, whether at home or absent, to be well-pleasing to him'.

(2) Israel's restoration, and the reason, vv. 14–23

The atmosphere of the chapter now changes completely. Divine anger gives place to divine joy. But the change is not explained by some reformation on the part of Israel, but by divine initiative. 'Therefore, behold, I will allure her . . . and speak comfortably unto her (speak tenderly to her heart)', cf. Isa. 40. 2 margin. The word 'allure' has the meaning of 'entice, woo, persuade'. God's love for His people is clear. Notice how He deals with her:

i) He takes her back to the beginning. 'I will . . . bring her into the wilderness', v. 14. Jeremiah 2. 2 explains, 'I remember thee, the kindness of thy youth, the love of thine espousals, when thou wentest after me in the wilderness', 2. 2. But this statement can be understood in the context of Revelation 12. 14, 'And to the woman were given two wings of a great eagle, that she might fly into the wilderness, into her place, where she is nourished for a time, and times, and half a time, from the face of the serpent'. It was in the inhospitable wilderness that God's people followed Him and experienced His lovingkindness. They will do so again in tribulation days.

ii) He brings her to the place of hope. 'I will give her her vineyards from thence, and the valley of Achor for a door of hope', v. 15. The valley of Achor was the place where Israel's sin was purged, and possession of the land followed, see Josh. 8, 9, cf. Isa. 65. 10. National sin will again be purged, and the land will be possessed and enjoyed.

iii) He gives her joy as a redeemed nation. 'And she shall sing there, as in the days of her youth, and as in the day when she came up out of the land of Egypt', v. 15. The reference to Exodus 15 is clear, cf. Hos. 2. 11.

iv) He acknowledges her as His wife. Israel had not long entered Canaan before idolatry reared its ugly head, and the nation became unfaithful to God. But not now, 'And it shall be at that day, saith the Lord, that thou shalt call me Ishi (my husband); and shalt call me no more Baali (my lord). For I will take away the names of Baalim out of her mouth, and they shall no more be remembered by their name', vv. 16–17. The words, 'and shalt call me no more Baali', are most significant. They represent an ancient version of the current idea that 'really all world religions are the same; we all worship the same god—some do it one way, and others do it another way—and it doesn't really matter what you call Him'. That is abhorrent to the God of heaven.

v) He undertakes her security. 'And in that day will I make a covenant for them (for their benefit) with the beasts of the field . . . and I will break the bow and the sword and the battle out of the earth, and will make them to lie down safely', v. 18, cf. v. 10. Isaiah 11. 6–9 and Isaiah 2. 4 amplify this statement.

vi) He establishes her in covenant relationship. Three times the expression occurs in verses 19–20, 'I will betroth thee unto me'. It is permanent, 'for ever'. It is perfect, 'in righteousness, and in judgement, and in lovingkindness, and in mercies'. Everything is in perfect balance—as it should be in a good marriage. It is reciprocated, 'faithfulness: and thou shalt know the Lord'. This anticipates Jeremiah 31. 31–34, 'I will put my law in their inward parts, and write it in their hearts'. God will implant faithfulness in the hearts of His people.

vii) He gives her abundant provision. Verses 21–22 trace the supply route: it starts with God Himself ('I will hear' the cry of the heavens), then it reaches the heavens ('they shall hear'—in rain and dew—the cry of the earth), then it reaches the earth ('the earth shall hear'—the cry of the crops), then it reaches the crops. But that's not where it all ends: 'And they'—the crops—'shall hear Jezreel'. That is, the crops will hear the promise cry for fulfilment. God will 'sow' (Jezreel) His people 'in the earth', and provide for them by way of the heavens, the earth and the crops. Finally, to sum it all up –

viii) He reverses her original estrangement, v. 23. Firstly, God says, 'I will sow her unto me in the earth'. 'Jezreel', once meaning 'God scatters', now means 'God sows', cf. 1. 4 and 1. 11. Secondly, God says, 'I will have mercy upon her'. 'Lo-ruhamah' becomes 'Ruhamah', cf. 1. 6 and 2. 1. Thirdly, God says, 'I will say ... thou art my people'. 'Lo-ammi' becomes 'Ammi', cf. 1. 9 with 2. 1. In that day, the regenerate nation will respond, 'Thou art my God'. Never again will she say, 'I will go after my lovers', v.5.

This verse is cited in Romans 9. 25, where Paul deals with blessing for Jew and Gentile. See note on Hosea 1. 10. It is also cited in 1 Peter 2. 10, but whilst Paul cites Hosea 1. 10 and 2. 23, Peter, writing to converted Jews, refers only to the latter, omitting reference to the former which contains the words, 'the sons (plural) of the living God'. This omission may be accounted for by the fact that in the Old Testament, Israel is called nationally, 'my son', and that Peter is using corporate terms in the passage, 'a chosen generation, a royal priesthood, an holy nation, a peculiar people'. Other explanations have been given.

Hosea 3, 'Thou shalt not play the harlot'

Chapters 1 and 2 describe the immediate and ultimate future of Israel, see 1. 2-9 with 2. 1-13, and 1. 10-11 with 2. 14-23, respectively. Chapter 3 also describes the intervening period, and demonstrates very clearly that there is no discontinuance in God's love for His people. The day has not yet dawned when God will say, 'I will betroth thee unto me for ever', 2. 19, and, 'I will love them freely', 14. 4, but God loved His people with an 'everlasting love', Jer. 31. 3. The chapter therefore commences, 'Then said the Lord unto me, Go yet ('Go again', JND: that is, 'again after', 1. 2, 'Go take unto thee'), love a woman beloved of her friend, yet an adulteress, according to the love of the Lord toward the children of Israel', v.1. Notice that it is God's love for Israel that rekindles Hosea's love for Gomer. He was to love her, 'according to' God's love for Israel. The chapter can be summarized as follows:

(1) Israel in the past, vv. 1–2

(A) The price Gomer paid for her sin

Gomer's unfaithfulness led her ultimately to slavery, possibly to the slave market: she is 'sold under sin'. Verse 1 sets out, side by side, the literal relationship between Hosea and Gomer, and the spiritual relationship between Jehovah and Israel. Hosea's experience reflected Jehovah's experience:

'Go yet, love a woman beloved of her friend, yet an adulteress'.	'According to the love of the Lord toward the children of Israel, who look to other gods and love flagons of wine'.

The complete incongruity of the situation is unmistakable. The Lord loves them: they loved raisin-cakes, which were evidently delicacies associated with religious feasts, see 2 Sam. 6. 19, 1 Chron. 16. 3 and Song of Sol. 2. 5, where 'flagons of wine' are 'raisin-cakes', JND. It is worth pausing to ask ourselves to what extent this could be true of ourselves. Does the 'love of Christ' constrain us? 2 Cor. 5. 14.

The wording of God's command is significant. Firstly, 'Go yet, love a woman', not, 'love your wife'. Gomer is described as 'an adulteress'. He was to love her without resuming the marriage relationship. Secondly, 'beloved of her friend'. Some commentators take 'friend' to mean 'paramour', but it seems more in keeping with the context and object of the passage to see reference here to Hosea himself. He is not called, 'her husband', just as she is not called, 'your wife'. He is called, 'her friend' (companion), just as she is called, 'a woman'. Cf. Jeremiah 3. 20, where 'husband' is 'friend', (JND margin). The detail of God's command must have deeply pierced Hosea. Gomer is most unwholesome, 'an adulteress', but he is to love her. If ever a man understood the depth of God's feelings to sinful people, that man must be Hosea!

B) The price Hosea paid for her redemption

Gomer is purchased for 'fifteen pieces of silver'. That is, at half the price of a gored slave, see Exod. 21. 32. The value of the nine or ten bushels of barley has also been estimated as fifteen shekels of silver. Think of the infinite price paid for Israel's deliverance. 'He was wounded for our transgressions', Isa. 53. 4–6. Think of the infinite price paid for our deliverance, see, for example, 1 Pet. 1. 18–19 and Eph. 5. 25–27. But it is not only the price that is different. Gomer was purchased, and kept, as Israel, at a distance for 'many days'. The Lord 'nourishes' and 'cherishes' His church now. The prophetic significance of the story outstrips the story itself, for whilst no specific mention is made of resumed marital relations after the 'many days', the full blessing of Israel after 'many days' is described in verse 5. We are by no means disadvantaged in this respect: the Lord Jesus will 'present it (the church) to himself a glorious church, not having spot, or wrinkle, or any such thing'.

2) Israel in the present, vv. 3–4

The present position of Israel is set out in verses 3–4. Hosea says, 'So I bought her to me'. Now, 'Thou shalt abide for me many days.' The words, 'Thou shalt not play the harlot, and thou shalt not be for a man (omit 'another'): so will I also be for thee', mean that Gomer would not enter into a relationship with any man—including Hosea, and that Hosea would not enter into a relationship with Gomer. She would be neither adulterous nor in enjoyment of conjugal rights.

This is precisely the position of Israel. Whilst she is not in communion with God, she is divinely preserved. Her national identity remains, without the existence of those things necessary to national identity. Politically, 'without a king, and without a prince'. Religiously, 'without a sacrifice, and without an image, and without an ephod, and without teraphim'.

a) The nation would not 'play the harlot'. So there is no 'image', and no 'teraphim'. The former refers to upright pillars associated with idolatry, see, for example, 1 Kgs. 14. 23, and 2 Kgs. 3. 2. The latter were household gods, see Gen. 31. 19 (rendered 'images') and 30–35. So she would be purged of idolatry. But, on the other hand:

b) The nation would not be in relation to Jehovah. So there is no 'sacrifice', and no 'ephod'. That is, no approach to God, and no revelation by God. This situation would exist for 'many days'. But not perpetually: we come now to 'the latter days', v. 5.

3) Israel in the future, v. 5

'Afterward shall the children of Israel return, and seek the Lord their God, and David their king; and shall fear the Lord and his goodness in the latter days', (JND, 'At the end of the days'). Chapter 2 told us how this will take place: 'the valley of Achor' will be 'a door of hope', v.15. This detail is omitted here, because chapter 3 emphasizes the reason for her return, that is, God's love for His people. Suffice to notice that particular reference is made to, 'David their king'. That is, the rebellious ten tribes will again recognize the throne of David, from which they had seceded. The nation will be reunited. We know that Christ will sit 'upon the throne of David, and upon his kingdom', Isa. 9. 7. The reference to David here must be read in conjunction with Jeremiah 30. 9, and Ezekiel 34. 22–24. The writer finds it difficult to escape the conclusion, particularly from the Ezekiel passage, that it will be David himself, raised from the dead, who will act as vice-regent over Israel in the millennial kingdom. However, others feel the name David is a synonym for Christ as Messianic King and His millennial reign.

Hosea 4, 'Destroyed for lack of knowledge'

In introducing the prophecy of Hosea, we noticed that the book falls into two major sections:

A) Hosea's love for his unfaithful wife, chapters 1–3
B) God's love for His unfaithful people, chapters 4–14

Chapters 1–3 illustrate Israel's spiritual adultery: chapters 4–14 describe her unfaithfulness in detail, together with her judgement and restoration. Chapter 4, which introduces the Lord's 'controversy ('lawsuit', see also 12. 2) with the inhabitants of the land', can be divided into three main paragraphs:

(1) God's charge against His people, vv. 1–3

'The Lord hath a controversy with the inhabitants of the land', because of
   A) *The absence of righteousness*, v.1. 'There is no truth, nor mercy, nor knowledge of God in the land'. As to the people personally, 'no truth'. There was an absence of faithfulness in the sense of honesty and reliability. People were not trustworthy. As to others: no 'mercy'. It is the word often rendered 'lovingkindness'. We have already met it in 2. 19. We shall meet it again in 6. 6. It is a divine characteristic that God loves to exhibit, see Micah 7. 18. As to God: no 'knowledge of God in the land'. Sin in personal life, and sin in social life, is traced to sin in spiritual life. We cannot expect to be right ourselves, and right with others, if we are not right with God. The Scriptures urge us to recognize the implications of 'having put on the new man, which according to God is created in truthful righteousness and holiness', Eph. 4. 24, JND. Bearing this in mind, the passage continues, 'Let him that stole steal no more. . . and be ye kind one to another, tenderhearted', vv. 28–32. Here is the 'truth' and 'mercy' that were so conspicuously absent in Hosea's day.
   'The knowledge of God' is not only mental acknowledgement of His will, but the practice of His will. Ezra 7. 10 illustrates, 'For Ezra had prepared his heart to seek the law of the Lord, and to do it'. The Lord Jesus did not say, 'teaching them all things', but 'teaching them to observe all things whatsoever I have commanded you', Matt. 28. 20. The true 'knowledge of God' does not subsist in information about God, but life in harmony with Him.

B) *The presence of unrighteousness*, v.2. Absence of 'knowledge of God in the land' accounts for the fearful list that follows. The New Testament says the same, see Rom. 1. 28–32. A right relationship with God is our bulwark against moral degeneracy. Remove that, and sins erupt: 'they break out'. All restraint is cast aside. The expression 'blood toucheth blood' is no understatement when we think of the violence and bloodshed of Israel's last days, read 2 Kgs. 15. 8–16. This leads to:

C) *The imminence of judgement*, v.3. 'Therefore shall the land mourn, and every one that dwelleth therein shall languish, with the beasts of the field, and with the fowls of heaven; yea, the fishes of the sea also shall be taken away'. Deuteronomy 11. 11–17 gave due warning of the famine and drought that would follow apostasy. It is a graphic picture of the spiritual barrenness that follows disobedience to the word of God.

(2) God's condemnation of the priests, vv. 4–11

A) *The responsibility they carry, vv.* 4–6. Although the people were blaming each other for the disasters, it was the priests who were particularly culpable. Verse 4, AV, reads as follows, 'Yet let no man strive, nor reprove another: for thy people are as they that strive with the priest'. This has, however, been rendered: 'Yet let no one contend, and let none accuse, for with you is my contention, O priest', Amplified Version/RSV. Whilst this rests happily in the context, it does assume some slight transmission of the Massoretic text (the standard Hebrew text). It is clear, however, that the whole section indicts the religious leadership. The gravity of the charge lies in the fact that Israel is called 'my people', vv. 6, 12.

God had said, 'there is . . . no knowledge of God in the land', v.1. Now He assigns blame, 'My people are destroyed for lack of knowledge: because thou hast rejected knowledge, I will also reject thee, thou that shalt be no priest to me', v. 6. This recalls the charge laid by the Lord Jesus, 'Woe unto you, lawyers! for ye have taken away the key of knowledge: ye entered not in yourselves, and them that were entering in ye hindered', Luke 11. 52. They were 'blind leaders of the blind', Matt. 15. 14. Notice the effect on the priest's children, 'Seeing thou hast forgotten the law of thy God, I will also forget thy children', cf. Deut. 6. 7.

We are reminded that 'the priest's lips should keep knowledge, and they should seek the law at his mouth: for he is the messenger of the Lord of hosts', Mal. 2. 7. The fact that the priests in Hosea 4 were not the authorised priests of Leviticus, does not alter the fact that God held them responsible for the miserable state of His people. They presumed to be leaders, whether priests or prophets, v. 5, and therefore incurred particular responsibility. Hence James 3. 1, 'My brethren, be not many masters (teachers), knowing that we shall receive the greater condemnation'. Let all spiritual leaders take note.

B) *The reward they incur*, vv. 7-10. 'And there shall be, like people, like priest: and I will punish them for their ways, and reward them their doings', v.9, cf. Isa. 24. 1-3. The hereditary priesthood would cease, and the reasons are spelt out in detail, 'Because thou hast rejected knowledge . . . seeing thou hast forgotten the law of thy God . . . as they were increased, so they sinned against me . . . they eat up the sin of my people, and they set their heart on their iniquity'. The words, 'they eat up the sin of my people', imply that instead of condemning sin, they delighted in it. M. C. UNGER suggests that this could be understood quite literally: they desired 'an increase in the people's sins in order that they might enjoy a good supply of choice meat'. Judgement was inevitable. Notice, 'I will also reject . . . I will also forget . . . I will change . . . I will punish'. The words, 'And there shall be, like people, like priest', indicate that the priests would not escape coming judgement because of their special position. Their sinful practices would bring total disillusion and dissatisfaction. Contrast the disappointments if we leave 'off to take heed to the Lord', with the blessings if we 'follow on to know the Lord', 6. 3.

C) *The results they produce*, vv.11-14. The section begins, 'Whoredom and wine and new wine doth take away the heart', and concludes: 'therefore the people that doth not understand shall fall'. As a result of the priest's failure, 'My people ask counsel at their stocks, and their staff declareth unto them'. Notice two things in this section:

First of all, there was religious evil. 'My people ask counsel at their stocks (wooden idols), and their staff (diviner's wand) declareth unto them . . . they sacrifice upon the tops of the mountains, and burn incense upon the hills, under oaks and poplars and elms, because the shadow thereof is good', vv.12-13. There is a strong suggestion of the occult in verse 12, see 1 Cor. 10. 20. Secondly, there was moral evil. Religious evil and moral evil are inextricably linked, cf. Rev. 2. 14 and Exod. 32. 4-6. But there is an even graver lesson. Since the men were involved in the immorality associated with idolatry, v.14, their own families would follow suit. 'Therefore your daughters shall commit whoredom, and your spouses (JND, 'daughters in law': margin 'brides') shall commit adultery'. God would not single the women out for punishment, since the menfolk were no better. How necessary to be 'an example of the believers, in word, in conversation, in charity, in spirit, in faith, in purity', 1 Tim. 4. 12.

(3) God's counsel to Judah, vv. 15–19

The sad spiritual condition of the Northern Kingdom was a warning to Judah:

A) *They were warned against hypocrisy,* v.15. 'Though thou, Israel, play the harlot, yet let not Judah offend; and come not ye unto Gilgal, neither go ye up to Beth-aven, nor swear, The Lord liveth', cf. Amos 4. 4 and 5. 5. The expression, 'the Lord liveth' was pure cant: if they had been true to their convictions, they would have said 'Baal liveth'. But it gave an air of respectability to the place. Notice the change of name: Beth-el—the house of God—had become Beth-aven—the house of vanity. Gilgal and Bethel had been places of great blessing, and immense spiritual value. Bethel recalls outstanding events in the life of Jacob, see Gen. 28. 35. Gilgal was the place of first encampment in the land, with all that was connected with entry to Canaan, see Josh. 4. 5. Joshua's headquarters were there. Gilgal stood for the possession of the land. But now . . . see 1 Kgs. 12. 33. The same story can be seen in many assemblies.

B) *They were warned against rebellion,* v. 16. 'For Israel slideth back as a backsliding heifer'. JND renders, 'Israel is refractory as an untractable heifer'. The RSV, 'Like a stubborn heifer, Israel is stubborn'. That is, like a heifer that 'throws off her yoke, and turns backward instead of going forward', UNGER. The words which follow could be construed as a question, 'Can the Lord now feed them like a lamb in a broad pasture?' But they are more likely an ironic statement predicting Israel's imminent scattering in exile by the Assyrians. The nation, once secure in its land, would now be in 'a large place'—i.e. scattered worldwide.

C) *They were warned against compromise,* vv. 17-19. 'Ephraim is joined to idols: let him alone'. This is the first of many references to Ephraim. It was the most influential of the ten tribes, and included the capital, Samaria. It therefore represents the whole nation. The force of 'joined' is 'mated'. 'Let him alone': that is, 'leave him to himself'. He is beyond correction. Don't get involved, lest you also become involved with idolatry. The New Testament is equally clear, 'Be ye not unequally yoked together with unbelievers', 2 Cor. 6. 14-17. The depth of their sinful involvement is spelt out clearly; the drunken orgy ends, harlotry begins, and the rulers love the shameful proceedings. But judgement, as irresistible as the wind, will sweep them away, cf. 8. 7.

Hosea 5. 1–6. 3, 'He hath withdrawn himself from them'

Chapter 4 ended with prediction of divine judgement. Chapter 5. 1–6. 3 now describes its cause, certainty, course, and consequences. Quite clearly, the passage extends to 6. 3, and completes the section commencing with 4. 1. The structure of the section follows the general pattern in chapters 1, 2 and 3, and ends, as they end, with divine blessing after divine chastening.

Judgement is pronounced on the religious leadership, 'Hear ye this, O priests'; on the nation generally, 'Hearken, ye house of Israel'; and on the political leadership, 'Give ye ear, O house of the king'. The inclusion of the nation at large is explained in verse 11: they 'willingly walked after the commandment (to worship idols)'. The order in which the categories are named is important. The priests are put first. As we have seen, they were not particularly culpable. The people they influenced follow: not only the nation generally, but the royal house particularly. Wrong spiritual leadership is censured, and so are the people that follow it, both small and great. The assemblies in Galatia had been invaded by false teachers. Paul censures them in the epistle, but he also reprimands those who follow them, see 1. 6.

(1) The cause of judgement, vv. 1–7a

The charge is laid in verse 1, and divine reprisal promised in verse 2. 'Ye have been a snare on Mizpah, and a net spread upon Tabor'. Whilst there is some merit in the suggestion that the 'house of the king' is addressed, it seems more likely that the entire Northern Kingdom is involved. The word 'all' in verse 2 is probable confirmation of this. The royal house is censured particularly in 7. 1–7. Hosea employs the figure of a trapper hunting game, hence the references to 'snare' and 'net'. We are not told why he refers to Mizpah and Tabor particularly, although according to Jewish tradition, these were places where people en route to the temple in Jerusalem were apprehended and murdered (M. C. UNGER). It seems more likely that they were places where the unwary became enslaved to idolatry. We must heed the warning in Romans 16, 'And by good words and fair speeches deceive the hearts of the simple'. There are still snares and nets. Notice the following:

A) Their sin is particularly obnoxious to God. The words, 'and the revolters are profound to make slaughter', are rendered by RV, 'And the revolters are gone deep in making slaughter (or 'in corruption' margin)'. See also JND. 'Revolters' has the sense of apostates.

B) Their sin will be recompensed by God. This is the sense of 'though I have been a rebuker of them all', see JND, 'but I am a rebuker of them all'.

C) Their sin is clearly known to God. 'I know Ephraim, and Israel is not hid from me'. This may be an allusion to Mizpah and Tabor, bearing in mind that the former means 'a look out' or 'watch tower', see Gen. 31. 49–50, and the latter means 'height'. Nothing is hid from God, cf. Amos 5. 12. Hosea mentions four things that God knew:

a) There was no fidelity, v. 3. 'Thou committest whoredom, and Israel is defiled'. The 'first and great commandment' had been abrogated, 'Thou shalt love the Lord thy God with all thine heart, and with all thy soul, and with all thy might', Deut. 6. 5; see, again, Jas. 4. 4.

b) There was no liberty, v. 4. 'They will not frame their doings to turn unto their God'. JND renders, 'Their doings do not allow them to return unto their God'. They were imprisoned by the grip of past deeds. Sin robs men of strength of will to obey God. Notice the expression, 'the spirit of whoredoms'. 1 Corinthians 10. 20 explains.

c) There was no humility, v. 5. 'The pride of Israel doth testify to his face', see also 7. 10. Peter reminds us that, 'God resisteth the proud, and giveth grace to the humble'. Pride is displayed in selfwill, rather than submission to God. Judah is also condemned here. This is the first of five dual references in the chapter to Ephraim and Judah, see also vv. 9–10, 12, 13, and 14. Judah's position had evidently deteriorated, cf. 1. 7; 1. 11; and 4. 15. Ezekiel 23 is an eloquent commentary on the situation.

d) There was no reality, v. 6. 'They shall go with their flocks and with their herds to seek the Lord; but they shall not find him', see also 7. 14–16, 'And they cried not unto me in their heart, when they howled upon their beds', JND, cf. Isa. 1. 15, and Prov. 1. 28. The words of the Lord Jesus must be allowed to search us all, 'Ye hypocrites! Well did Esaias prophesy of you saying, This people draweth nigh unto me with their mouth, and honoureth me with their lips: but their heart is far from me', Matt. 15. 7–8.

The results of all this are given in verses 6–7. Firstly, God had 'withdrawn himself from them'. They followed in the footsteps of Samson who 'wist not that the Lord had departed from him'. Isaiah 55 urges Israel to, 'Seek the Lord, while he may be found'. But here it is too late: God could not be found. Secondly: they had totally altered the character of the nation, 'They have dealt treacherously against the Lord: for they have begotten strange children'. That is, children without the knowledge of God. It was certainly a case of 'Lo-ammi'—'not my people'—in every sense of the term. There is a strong allusion to 1. 2; 'a wife of whoredoms, and children of whoredoms'. As we have already noticed, this was far removed from the instructions in Deuteronomy 6. 6–7. The consequences of compromise with the religious world can be frightening.

(2) The certainty of judgement, vv. 7b–11

'Ephraim shall be desolate in the day of rebuke: among the tribes of Israel have I made known that which shall surely be', v. 9. Judgement was inevitable, and it would be swift, 'Now shall a month devour them with their portions'. JND renders, 'Now shall the new moon devour them with their allotted possessions ('fields', RV)'. The most likely meaning is that it would only take one month to totally destroy the Northern Kingdom.

The significance of Gibeah, Ramah and Beth-aven (Bethel) lies in their close proximity to the border between Israel in the north and Judah in the south. The invader would penetrate to the southernmost part of Israel. Gibeah and Ramah were actually in Judah, whilst Bethel was in the north, 1 Kgs. 12. 29. Hence the alarm bells in Gibeah and Ramah, and the cry, 'Behind thee, O Benjamin!', JND. Well might Judah tremble: they were little better than their northern neighbours, see v.10. There was sin on both sides of the border. In the south, the 'princes of Judah were like them that remove the bound (landmark)'. In the north, 'Ephraim . . . willingly (RV 'was content') walked after the commandment (to worship idols)'. They became idolaters, with everything associated with it, without protest.

(3) The course of the judgement, vv. 12–14

Divine judgement was executed on both houses in two ways.

A) By internal decay. 'Therefore will I be unto Ephraim as a moth, and to the house of Judah as rottenness (dry rot—caries)'. That is, it was gradual and unseen: slow and silent. Faced with growing weakness, both houses ignored the root cause of their malaise, and turned to the Assyrian for help. 'When Ephraim saw his sickness, and Judah saw his wound, then went Ephraim to the Assyrian, and sent to king Jareb: yet could he not heal you, nor cure you of your wound'. Judah did this in the reign of Ahaz, see 2 Kgs. 16. 7. Menahem and Hoshea did the same, see 2 Kgs. 15. 19–20; and 17. 3. Hosea 7. 11 also refers to this, and the consequences are spelt out in 9. 3. It was so refreshingly different in Ezra

8. 21–22. 'King Jareb' is adjectival, meaning, 'a contentious king', JND footnote. GEORGE ADAM SMITH calls him, 'King Pick-Quarrel'!

B) By external destruction. Recourse to the Assyrians would bring divine fury, 'For I will be unto Ephraim as a lion, and as a young lion to the house of Judah'. Judgement would be sudden and visible. There would be no escape then, 'I, even I, will tear and go away; I will take away, and none shall rescue him', v.14.

(4) The consequences of the judgement, 5. 15–6. 3

The object of discipline is restoration, 5. 15, and a tender appeal follows in chapter 6. 1–3. It is made by Hosea, and was, undoubtedly, a bona fide appeal to the nation at the time, cf. Acts 3. 19–20. The sad fact remains that it was disregarded then, but it clearly anticipates the future when it will not be disregarded. Verse 3 clearly agrees with other passages which describe the return of Messiah.

The present position is described in 5. 15, 'I will go and return to my place'. God no longer pleads with His people: He ceases to act as a husband toward them, which is precisely the position described in chapter 3. But the purpose of divine discipline will be achieved: God withdraws His care for Israel, but only 'till they acknowledge their offence, and seek my face; in their affliction they will seek me early', cf. 3. 5. This anticipates the ultimate affliction of the nation, described as 'the time of Jacob's trouble', Jer. 30. 7. God will say, 'Why criest thou for thine affliction? Thy sorrow is incurable for the multitude of thine iniquity: because thy sins were increased, I have done these things unto thee'. But He will hear their cry, 'For I will restore health unto thee, and I will heal thee of thy wounds, saith the Lord', Jer. 30. 15–17. In this connection, we must notice:

A) *Recognition of divine chastening*, 6. 1. Previously, Israel had looked elsewhere: but the Assyrians could not 'heal . . . nor cure', 5. 13. Now they say, 'Come, and let us return unto the Lord (not 'king Jareb'): for he hath torn, and he will heal us; he hath smitten, and he will bind us up'.

B) *Resurrection of national life*, 6. 2. 'After two days will he revive us: in the third day he will raise us up, and we shall live in his sight'. The Lord Jesus 'rose again the third day according to the Scriptures', 1 Cor. 15: 4. The reference to 'two days' and 'the third day', is significant when compared with Psalm 90. 4 and 2 Peter 3. 8. Whilst, undoubtedly, Psalm 90 emphasizes the timelessness of God, it does appear that the words cited by Peter have additional significance, and apply to Hosea 6. Israel, the ten tribes, went into captivity in 721BC: Judah followed in 606BC, and a remnant returned seventy years later. National life was finally destroyed by the Romans, and for approaching two thousand years, (two prophetic days, the 'many days' of 3. 4,) the 'whole house of Israel' has been 'dry bones', Ezek. 37. But the third prophetic day will come, and the nation will 'live in his sight'. The Millennial day will dawn, and it will be said, 'This is the day which the Lord hath made', Psa. 118. 24.

C) *Return of the Lord*, 6. 3. 'His going forth ... he shall come'. The nation will then, 'know the Lord', Jer. 31. 34. See JND, 'And we shall know—we shall follow on to know Jehovah'. Malachi 4. 2 and Psalm 72. 6 amplify the beautiful description of the Lord's return with its attendant blessings, 'His going forth is prepared as the morning; and he shall come unto us as the rain, as the latter and former rain unto the earth'.

Hosea 6. 4–11, 'Your goodness is as a morning cloud'

The previous section of the book ended with two beautiful pictures of the way in which the Lord will return to His people. First, 'His going forth is prepared as the morning'. Second, 'He shall come unto us as the rain, as the latter and former rain unto the earth'. The former recalls Psalm 19, where the sun is described as 'a bridegroom coming out of his chamber, and rejoiceth as a strong man to run a race. His going forth is from the end of the heaven, and his circuit unto the ends of it', vv. 4–5. God's purposes are like sunrise: they are certain. The latter recalls the promise of Deuteronomy 11. 14, 'I will give you the rain of your land in his due season, the first rain and the latter rain'. God's ability to fulfil His promise is unquestionable.

The next section of this prophecy commences in sharp contrast to this. Notice, therefore, first of all:

(1) Unfulfilled promise, v. 4

Both northern and southern kingdoms are addressed, with pathos, 'O Ephraim, what shall I do unto thee? O Judah, what shall I do unto thee?' Jehovah's 'going forth is prepared as the morning', but their 'goodness is as the morning cloud'. Jehovah's coming is described as 'the rain, as the latter and former rain unto the earth', but their goodness is described as 'the early dew'. It is all summed up in the words, 'it goeth away'. After early promise, their goodness proved impermanent and transitory.

The word 'goodness' (translated 'mercy' in verse 6), has the idea of 'lovingkindness'. It is so rendered in 2. 19. It is employed by Jeremiah in describing, as here, the transitory nature of Israel's devotion to God, 'I remember thee, the kindness of thy youth, the love of thine espousals', Jer. 2. 2. But that first love had been dissipated, 'as a morning cloud, and as the early dew'. They had not continued to reciprocate God's love for them. In the language of verse 7, they had 'transgressed the covenant' and 'dealt treacherously'. Or, to use earlier language, 'the land hath committed great whoredom, departing from the Lord', 1. 2

Centuries later, the Lord Jesus was obliged to say, 'I have somewhat against thee, because thou hast left thy first love', Rev. 2. 4. Can we still sing –

'My Saviour, I love Thee,
I know Thou art mine'?

But God had not allowed the matter to rest. This is implied in His words, 'O Ephraim, what shall I do unto thee?' We therefore notice next:

(2) Uncompromising preaching, vv. 5–6

A) The strength of the preaching, v. 5. God did not employ platitudes. The preaching was incisive, and intended to touch the conscience. 'Therefore have I hewed them by the prophets; I have slain them by the words of my mouth'. He faithfully exposed their sin.

B) The clarity of the preaching, v. 5. 'Thy judgements are as the light that goeth forth'. It was unmistakable and without ambiguity. This also suggests the equity and purity of His judgements.

C) The purpose of the preaching, v. 6. 'For I desired mercy, and not sacrifice; and the knowledge of God more than burnt offerings'. Bearing in mind that 'mercy' is lovingkindness, rendered 'goodness' in verse 4, it is clear that the preaching was intended to restore God's people to their original relationship with Him. The fact remains however that a right relationship with God will mean a right relationship with our fellowmen, and Hosea 6. 6 is twice cited by the Lord Jesus in this way, see Matt. 9. 12-13, and 12. 7. On both occasions, the Pharisees are reproved: they insisted on ceremonial niceties, and utterly failed to practice 'the weightier matters of the law, judgement, mercy, and faith', Matt. 23. 23. 'Sacrifices' and 'burnt offerings' are only meaningful when they express true devotion. Else they are meaningless: worse—they are offensive to God. We too must beware. There is nothing worse than people, and assemblies, who glory in their orthodox position, but

apparently forget the need to 'be . . . kind one to another, tenderhearted, forgiving one another, even as God for Christ's sake hath forgiven
you', Eph. 4. 32. Empty ritual is no substitute for true piety. For
additional proof, read 1 Samuel 15. 22, Isaiah 1. 12–17, Amos 5. 21–24,
and Micah 6. 6–8.

But, alas, the preaching was to no avail.

(3) Unrepentant people, vv. 7–11

Verse 7 is elsewhere rendered, 'But they, like Adam, have transgressed
the covenant', RV/JND, cf. Rom. 5. 14. Some argue for Adam as a place,
see Josh. 3. 16, although this requires an alteration in the text. We have
already noted the transitory nature of Israel's devotion to God, v.4, and
verse 7 traces the history of human weakness back to its origin, cf. Job
31. 33. That same weakness was seen again in Israel. When presented
with the covenant, the people 'answered together, and said, All that the
Lord hath spoken we will do', Exod. 19. 5–8. The first two clauses of the
covenant said, 'Thou shalt have no other gods before me. Thou shalt not
make unto thee any graven image . . . for I the Lord thy God am a jealous
God'. He is jealous of the affections of His people, Exod. 20. 3–5. Hosea
chapters 1–3 present this covenant in terms of the marriage relationship,
and display Israel's failure in fidelity to God as stated here, 'But they like
men (Adam) have transgressed the covenant: there have they dealt
treacherously against me'. Failure in their covenant relationship with
God brought fearful results both locally and nationally.

A) Locally, vv. 8–9. 'Gilead (on the east of Jordan) is a city of them that
work iniquity, and is polluted with blood', v. 8, JND, 'It is tracked with
blood' with margin, 'full of bloodmarks'. Shechem is named in verse 9,
although it is obscured in the AV rendering. See JND/RV, 'And as
troops of robbers wait for a man, so the company of priests murder in the
way toward Shechem' (on the west of Jordan). Whilst we cannot now
ascertain the precise significance of the references to Gilead and Shechem, or to Tabor and Mizpah, 5. 1, they would have been readily
understood at the time. The abiding lesson lies in the fact that God knew
precisely what was happening at each location. The Lord Jesus still
says, in each local situation, 'I know thy works', Rev. 2. 2, etc.

B) Nationally, vv. 10–11. 'A little leaven (locally) leaveneth the whole
lump (nationally)'. The overall situation is summed up in verse 10, 'I
have seen an horrible thing in the house of Israel: there is the whoredom
of Ephraim, Israel is defiled'. Notice the words, 'I have seen'. Whether

locally or nationally, 'all things are naked and opened unto the eyes of him with whom we have to do', Heb. 4. 13.

Judah has not escaped infection, 'Also, O Judah, he hath set a harvest for thee'. The law of sowing and reaping is everywhere in Scripture, see Gal. 6. 7-8. Judah had 'run with them (Israel) to the same sink of corruption', 1 Pet. 4. 4, JND, and proved the accuracy of 1 Corinthians 15: 33, that, 'evil company doth corrupt good manners', RV.

Hosea 7. 1-16, 'They consider not . . . that I remember'

'King and Country', vv. 1-2

Hosea has given us a fairly comprehensive tour of Israel's country districts: Gilgal and Bethaven, 4. 15; Mizpah and Tabor, 5. 1; Gilead and Shechem, 6. 8-9. In fact, we have travelled from south to north, and then from east to west. We come now to the capital city, to the heart of the nation, and then to the king himself. The chapter commences by embracing the nation at large, then Ephraim, most prominent of the ten tribes, and finally, Samaria, the royal city. Sin lies at the heart of the nation, 'When I returned (would return) the captivity of my people, when I would have healed Israel, then the iniquity of Ephraim was discovered, and the wickedness of Samaria', 6. 11-7. 1.

The general wickedness of the capital is described in verse 1, 'For they commit falsehood; and the thief cometh in, and the troop of robbers spoileth without'. Society was permeated by deception and lies. People were not secure at home, and not secure in the streets. This has a familiar ring. Society has not changed since Hosea's day. The words that follow are equally true of the twentieth century, 'And they consider not in their hearts that I remember all their wickedness: now their own doings have beset them about; they are before my face', v. 2. We should never forget the name given to God by Hagar, 'Thou God seest me', Gen. 16. 13-14.

Corrupt society did not have far to look for its lead; just as far as the palace. King and court were utterly debased. The balance of the chapter divides into two main sections:

(1) Depravity at court, vv. 3-7

There are three references to king and court in this passage, and the figure of a baker's oven is used in each case:

A) The impurity of the court, vv. 3–4

'They make the king glad with their wickedness, and the princes with their lies'; Rom. 1. 32 paints the same picture. The following verse describes the progress and process of evil, and makes the first of three references to the baker's oven. 'They are all adulterers, as an oven heated by the baker, who ceaseth from raising after he hath kneaded the dough, until it be leavened', v. 4. This describes an oven whose fire is banked up, and needs no immediate attention after fermentation begins. The process proceeds in gentle heat. Moral leaven works in the same way: evil is quietly imagined and anticipated. The picture gallery of the mind must be clean, else we will become corrupted by what D. KIDNER aptly calls 'self-propagating passion'. Notice the words, 'until it be leavened'. They recall the Lord's teaching, Matt. 13. 33, and Paul's teaching in 1 Corinthians 5. 6–8 and Galatians 5. 9. Whether moral or doctrinal, leaven works silently and unseen, but with complete effectiveness.

B) The intrigue of the court, vv. 5–6a

It is the anniversary of the king's enthronement, 'The day of our king'. The day is spent in drunkenness and ribaldry. It takes little imagination to visualize the scene. 'In the day of our king the princes have made him sick with bottles of wine; he stretched out his hand with scorners'. But worse follows. The night is given to plotting and intrigue. Now we have the second reference to the baker's oven, 'For they have made ready their heart like an oven, whiles they lie in wait: their baker sleepeth all the night'. Some translate, 'all night their anger smoulders', see also RV margin.

C) The incontinence of the court, vv. 6b–7

The third reference to the baker's oven. We left it smouldering overnight: now, 'in the morning it burneth as a flaming fire. They are all hot as an oven, and have devoured their judges; all their kings are fallen: there is none among them that calleth unto me'. Evil was unrestrained. This aptly describes the mayhem of the period. As D. KIDNER succinctly observes, 'Of the six men who reigned in those thirty years, four were assassins, and only one died in his own bed'. Not one of them turned to God at any time.

If the court was so fearfully evil, it is hardly surprising that the nation followed suit:

(2) Decline in the country, vv. 8–16

This is described under four graphic figures of speech:

A) 'A cake not turned', v. 8

'Ephraim, he hath mixed himself among the people; Ephraim is a cake not turned', v. 8. GEORGE ADAM SMITH is regularly quoted here, 'How better describe half-fed people, a half-cultured society, a half-lived religion, a half-hearted policy, than by a half-baked scone'. In other words, Ephraim was 'neither one thing or another'. It trafficked with Assyria, see 2 Kgs. 15. 19–20; Isa. 7. 2; and Egypt, 2 Kgs 17. 4, whilst retaining some kind of nominal allegiance to Jehovah, see v. 14. But Ephraim was unpalatable to its allies, and unpalatable to God, cf. Matt. 5. 13 and Rev. 3. 15–16. We ignore the lesson at our spiritual peril.

B) 'Gray hairs . . . here and there upon him', vv. 9–10

Whilst the nation thought itself to be in the prime of life, it was unconsciously degenerating. Hence the repetition of, 'he knoweth not'. Compromise with the world ('he hath mixed himself among the people') will bring spiritual weakness and decline. We may have a temporary sense of progress and achievement, but the inevitable result is not power, but weakness. The sad case of Samson stresses the lesson, 'I will go out as at other times before, and shake myself. And he wist not that the Lord was departed from him', Judg. 16. 20. The very fact that they were proud of themselves, see also 5. 5, proclaimed their decline. If we conclude that we are spiritually strong, we are actually weak and vulnerable. 'Wherefore let him that thinketh he standeth, take heed lest he fall', 1 Cor. 10. 12. Ephraim had no sense of need, and therefore 'they do not return unto the Lord their God, nor seek him for all this'.

C) 'A silly dove without heart', vv. 11–15

'Ephraim also is like a silly (open to deception) dove without heart (senseless): they call to Egypt, they go to Assyria'. Ephraim is described in this way for the following reasons:
    i) Their behaviour was senseless because it was useless, vv. 11–12. 'They call to Egypt, they go to Assyria'. Their 'shuttle diplomacy' is illustrated in 2 Kings 17. 1–4. They attempted to avert a crisis by making an alliance elsewhere, only to find that the very God they had ignored and forgotten was waiting with His net. They looked south-west, and

north-east, but they forgot to look up. Such conduct was intolerable to God, 'I will chastise them, as their congregation hath heard'.

iii) Their behaviour was senseless because it was lawless, vv. 13–14. Notice the repeated words, 'against me' in verses 13–15. This is emphasized particularly in verse 13, where we have two contrasting expressions, 'Woe unto them! for they have fled from me: destruction unto them! because they have transgressed against me'. Their attitude belied their words, v. 14.

iv) Their behaviour was senseless because it was thankless, v. 15. It was an insult to God's love and care for them in the past. More is said about this in chapter 11, see Isa. 1. 2.

D) 'A deceitful bow', v. 16

'They return, but not to the Most High: they are like a deceitful bow'. That is, there is nothing dependable about them. See Psalm 78, 'They . . . turned back, and dealt unfaithfully like their fathers: they were turned aside (they turned, twisted) like a deceitful bow', vv. 56–58.

Their 'rage' (angry insolence) would be requited by the sword, and their downfall would be greeted by the derision of their would-be allies in Egypt. The present world is no different. No wonder Paul wrote 'Give none occasion to the adversary to speak reproachfully', 1 Tim. 5. 14.

Hosea 8. 1–14, 'They have sown . . . they shall reap'

Sowing and Reaping

'They have sown the wind, and they shall reap the whirlwind'. These words lie at the heart of the chapter, and dictate its character. There are six references to sowing and reaping:

(1) They would reap the consequences of false profession, vv. 1–3

These verses are summed up in the language of Titus 1. 16, 'they profess that they know God; but in works they deny him'. The profession in Hosea's day sounded very grand indeed, 'Israel shall cry unto me, My God, we know thee', v. 2. The RV emphasizes the strength of their claim, 'My God, we Israel know thee'. They traded on their relationship with God as expressed in Amos 3. 2, 'You only have I known of all the families of the earth'. The balance of this verse stresses the responsibility attaching to that relationship, 'therefore I will punish you for all your iniquities'. Hosea uses three expressions to demonstrate the emptiness of their claim:

i) 'They have transgressed my covenant', v. 1. 'Covenant' describes their basic relationship with God. In Hosea, it is 'as binding and intimate as a marriage', D. KIDNER, see comments on 6. 7.

ii) 'They have . . . trespassed against my law', v. 1. 'Law' describes the principles which made that relationship harmonious and effective.

iii) 'They have . . . cast off . . . good', v. 3. 'Good' describes the benefits arising from 'covenant' and 'law'. If they had been maintained, their quality of life would have been 'good' in every sense— spiritually, morally and physically. Sadly, they had rejected 'covenant', 'law', and 'good': they did not know God at all, 'Israel (who said, 'we know thee') hath cast off the thing that is good', v. 3. Their actions belied their words.

The Jews in the New Testament were little different. They too claimed a special relationship. See John 8, 'Abraham is our father . . . we have one Father, even God', vv. 39, 41. In both cases, the Lord Jesus invalidated their claim, 'If ye were Abraham's children, ye would do the works of Abraham . . . If God were your Father, ye would love me', vv. 39, 42. But the New Testament will not allow us to distance ourselves too far from Hosea 8 or John 9. 'He that saith, I know him, and keepeth not his commandments, is a liar, and the truth is not in him,' 1 John 2. 4.

They would reap the whirlwind, 'Set the trumpet to thy mouth. He shall come as an eagle against the house of the Lord . . . the enemy shall pursue him', vv. 1, 3. The expression, 'house of the Lord', can be understood as 'household of the Lord'. That, after all, was what they professed to be.

(2) They would reap the consequences of false leadership, v. 4a

'They have set up kings, but not by me: they have made princes, and I knew it not'. This refers, not only to the last kings of Israel, but to the history of the Northern Kingdom generally. Jehu was an exception, see 2 Kgs. 12. 16–19. Samaria rivalled Jerusalem. But not for ever, see 3. 5, 'Afterward shall the children of Israel return, and seek the Lord their God, and David their king'.

God Himself had established the throne of David, see, for example, 2 Sam. 7. 16, just as He had chosen the princes, in Numbers 2. New Testament appointments are no different. See Acts 20. 28, 'the flock, over (in) the which the Holy Ghost hath made you overseers'. Woe to Israel with its self-appointed leaders, and woe to the assembly that substitutes its own choice for God's choice, 'Except the Lord build the house, they labour in vain that build it,' Ps. 127. 1.

(3) They would reap the consequences of false gods, vv. 4b–7

'Of their silver and their gold have they made them idols, that they may be cut off'. A fourfold description of idolatry follows:

i) The helplessness of their idolatry. The words, 'thy calf, O Samaria, hath cast thee off', indicate its complete inability to help, cf. 1 Kgs. 18. 26, 'O Baal, hear us. But there was no voice, nor any that answered'.

ii) The hopelessness of their idolatry. God had endeavoured to teach them that idols were impotent, but they refused to learn. He despaired over His people, 'Mine anger is kindled against them: how long will it be ere they attain to innocency, JND, 'purity'?'

iii) The seriousness of their idolatry. 'For from Israel was it also'. This is a terrible indictment: the calf had not been imposed on them by a foreign power: it emanated from Israel itself, see 1 Kgs. 12. 27–29.

iv) The thoughtlessness of their idolatry. It was utterly stupid, 'The workman made it; therefore it is not God', see 13. 2, and the repeated words, 'which he had made', in 1 Kgs. 12. 32–33, cf. Isa. 40. 18–20; 44. 9; 44. 20, etc. Notice the way in which Galatians 4. 8 refers to idolatry.

Israel had 'sown the wind', which 'denotes devoting effort to vanity', UNGER: they would 'reap the whirlwind', that is, far more than they had sown. Their trusted calf would be 'broken to pieces', but more—their crops would fail, and anything that was produced would be stripped by the invader, cf. 2. 3. The teaching of Galatians 6. 7–8 cannot be ignored.

(4) They would reap the consequences of false allies, vv. 8–10

'Israel is swallowed up: now shall they be among the Gentiles as a vessel wherein is no pleasure'. 'A crock that no one wants', *Jerusalem Bible*. H. A. IRONSIDE comments, 'This describes in one verse their history over two thousand years. Driven out of their land, scattered among all nations, they have been as a vessel in which God could take no delight'. To which we add, a vessel in which nobody took delight.

The reason follows, 'For they are gone up to Assyria, a wild ass alone by himself: Ephraim hath hired lovers', cf. 7. 11; read James 4. 4. The untameable and obstinate 'wild ass' is an apt description of Israel. But their alliances would prove disastrous, 'Yea, though they have hired among the nations, now will I gather them, and they shall sorrow a little for the burden of the king of princes', v. 10. This has been rendered,

'They will begin to waste away under the oppression (a king of princes)'. The Assyrian began to domi? Menahem, see 2 Kgs. 15. 19–20, and his dominatio the reign of Hoshea, see 2 Kgs. 17.

The lesson is clear: if we sow alliance with the whirlwind of domination by the world.

(5) They would reap the consequences of false religion, vv. 11–13

Religion proliferated, but it was totally unacceptable to God. The reason is given in verse 12, 'I have written to him the great things of my law, but they were counted as a strange thing'. In the South, Isaiah censured Judah in the same way: he describes the 'great things' of God's law as follows, 'Learn to do well, seek judgement, relieve the oppressed, judge the fatherless, plead for the widow', 1. 11–17, cf. Mic. 6. 6–8. The Lord Jesus called the 'great things' of God's law, 'the weightier matters of the law', and defined them as 'judgement, mercy, and faith', Matt. 23. 23. We too must be careful not to have 'a form of godliness, but denying the power thereof', 2 Tim. 3. 5.

But even the mechanics of their religion were wrong. First, God had prescribed that sacrifices were to be offered at Jerusalem alone, see Deut. 12. 5–6; 13–14. But Ephraim had made 'many altars'. Second, they were procedurally wrong, 'They sacrifice flesh ... and eat it'. Their religion was really self-indulgence. Their sacrifices were just 'flesh': not offerings to God.

The whirlwind follows, 'Now will he remember their iniquity, and visit their sins: they shall return to Egypt'. Although, unlike Judah, scripture does not record any return to Egypt on the part of Israel, there seems little reason to interpret the statement other than literally, see note on 9. 6, and 11. 5.

(6) They would reap the consequences of false security, v. 14

'For Israel hath forgotten his Maker, and buildeth temples; and Judah hath multiplied fenced cities.' In the North, they looked for security through religion: in the South, they trusted in tangible defences. But in both cases, God was ignored.

The whirlwind follows: 'But I will send a fire upon his cities, and it shall devour the palaces thereof'. The Assyrians overran Israel, and captured all Judah's fortified cities except Jerusalem, see 2 Kgs. 18. 13. The Assyrian invasion of Judah was routed by God Himself, see com-

...it on 1. 7, but the Assyrians were eventually followed by the Babylonians, and then it was a different story.

Hosea 9. 1–17, 'Their glory shall fly away'

The final verse of this chapter sums up its message, 'My God will cast them away because they did not hearken unto him; and they shall be wanderers among the nations', v. 17. The misery of captivity and exile is emphasized, 'Rejoice not, O Israel, for joy, as other people ... woe also to them when I depart from them!', vv.1, 12. Three reasons are given for Israel's misery:

(1) They had rejected the love of God, vv. 1–6

'Thou hast gone a whoring from thy God'. Every word must have pierced Hosea's heart, since it reflected his own painful experience, 'Go, take unto thee a wife of whoredoms', 1. 2. The chapter commences by emphasizing the infidelity of God's people, with its warning for us, 'Love not the world, neither the things that are in the world. If any man love the world, the love of (love for) the Father is not in him', 1 John 2. 15. The consequences of their infidelity are now spelt out in terms of lost joy:

A) *No joy in the land*, vv. 1–2. 'Thou hast loved a reward upon every cornfloor. The floor and the winepress shall not feed them, and the new wine shall fail in her'. This recalls Israel's language in 2. 5, 'I will go after my lovers, that give me my bread and my water, my wool and my flax, mine oil and my drink'. She attributed her supplies to Baal, in exchange for worship. But Baal would fail them: there would be no harlot's reward. God saw to that in chapter 2, 'Therefore will I return, and take away my corn ... and my wine ...', v. 9. This is repeated here: 'the floor and the winepress shall not feed them'. The Lord Jesus taught that true joy is connected with obedience, see John 15. 9–11.

B) *No joy in captivity*, vv. 3–6. God now emphasizes the enormity of their loss through captivity. In chapter 2, the failure of idolatry prompted Israel to say, 'I will go, and return to my first husband; for then was it better with me than now', v. 7. But it was to no avail then, and it is to no avail here: any desire for God is frustrated. As chapter 3 explains, Israel would worship neither idols, nor Jehovah. Their infidelity would incur a fourfold loss:

i) Loss of inheritance in 'the Lord's land', v. 3. 'They shall not dwell in the Lord's land'. There is a certain emphasis on 'The Lord's land': they had treated it as 'Baal's land'. The very nations whose favour they courted, 7. 11; 8. 9, would become their captors. Disobedience has robbed many a child of God of enjoyment of their spiritual inheritance, and made them eat 'unclean things', cf. Dan. 1. 8.

ii) Loss of joy and worship in 'offerings to the Lord', v. 4. They would not be in a position to offer to the Lord. First of all, because they were not in the right place, and therefore sacrifices would not 'be pleasing unto him'. Secondly, because such sacrifices would be 'as the bread of mourners'. This is explained by Deuteronomy 26. 12–14, where people, ceremonially unclean by their association with death, were excluded from offering to God. Israel, surrounded by the defilement of heathen Assyria, would be in the same position.

iii) Loss of access to 'the house of the Lord', v. 4. The words, 'their bread for their soul shall not come into the house of the Lord', are better rendered, 'for their bread shall be for themselves (for their appetite); it shall not come into the house of the Jehovah', JND. Uncleanliness still distances children of God from the house of God.

iv) Loss of fellowship at the 'feast of the Lord', v. 5. 'What will ye do in the solemn day, and in the day of the feast of the Lord?', cf. Hos. 2. 11, 'I will also cause all her mirth to cease, her feast days, her new moons, and her sabbaths, and all her solemn feasts'. These were occasions of fellowship with God, and with one another, 'Whither the tribes go up', Ps. 122. 4.

The solemn lessons for ourselves in these verses are clearly expressed by H. A. IRONSIDE, 'The very recollections of past joys, of hours and days when the soul delighted in God and found precious food in his word, but make all the more cheerless the restless, unhappy experiences of the backslider in heart as he becomes filled with his own devices'. There is a note of terrible finality in verse 6, 'For, lo, they are gone because of destruction: Egypt shall gather them up, Memphis shall bury them: the pleasant places for their silver, nettles shall possess them: thorns shall be in their tabernacles'. The references to Egypt may allude to Hoshea's alliance with 'So, king of Egypt', 2 Kgs. 17. 4, and could therefore imply that the alliance would be the cause of their captivity. But however we understand the reference, the lesson for ourselves is clear: compromise with the world will mean that we will be ultimately buried, 'swallowed up', 8. 8, by the world.

(2) They had reviled the servants of God, vv. 7–9

The second reason for Israel's misery is introduced by the statements, 'The days of visitation are come, the days of recompense are come'.

Divine judgement is expressed impersonally, whereas in verse 9, it is expressed personally. 'He will visit their sins'. They would only realize the relevance and reality of God's word when it was too late, 'Israel shall know it', cf. Zech. 1. 6. Sadly, they did not recognize it at the time. The reasons for 'visitation' and 'recompense' follow. Notice:

i) What God called His servants. 'The prophet . . . the spiritual man (RV, 'the man that hath the Spirit') . . . the watchman of Ephraim', that is, assuming the rendering, 'The prophet is the watchman of Ephraim', cf. Ezek. 33. 1-9. See 1 Corinthians 4. 1.

ii) What Israel called His servants. 'Fool . . . mad', cf. Acts 26. 24, 2 Cor. 10. 10. But there was worse: D. KIDNER puts it as follows: they attempted 'to entangle and compromise the speaker ("the fowler's snare")' and treated him to 'the special venom of religious disdain ("hatred in the house of his God")'.

Rejection of the word of God opens the door to fearful sin. This is the sense of the words that follow, 'they have deeply corrupted themselves, as in the days of Gibeah', see also 10. 9. This cites the sad story in Judges 19–21. It has been aptly described as 'the abominable atrocity of Gibeah', UNGER. It resulted in the near extinction of Benjamin: Israel's sin would result in national disaster.

(3) They had reversed the pleasure of God, vv. 10–17

The third reason for Israel's misery: early promise had been dashed. Notice:

A) *God's initial delight in them,* v. 10. 'I found Israel like grapes in the wilderness; I saw your fathers as the first-ripe in the fig tree at her first time'. This eloquently expresses God's delight and anticipation. UNGER puts it nicely, 'At first Israel was a delight to the Lord, like luscious grapes or first-ripe figs are to a hungry and thirsty traveller', cf. Matt. 21. 18–19; 33–41. There was now nothing for God, see 10. 1.

B) *God's subsequent disappointment in them,* v. 10. 'But they went to Baal-peor, and separated themselves unto that shame; and their abominations were according as they loved'. They 'became detestable like the thing they loved', RSV. This cites Numbers 25. In Balaam's four parables, Numbers 23–24, God described His people, as here, in beautiful language, see, for example, Num. 24. 5–6. This was immediately followed by the chilling words, 'And Israel abode in Shittim, and the people began to commit whoredom with the daughters of Moab . . . and Israel joined himself unto Baal-peor', 25. 1-3.

C) *God's eventual destruction of them,* vv. 11–17. As in Numbers 25, so here, 'The anger of the Lord was kindled against Israel'. Its effect is spelt out in detail:

i) There would be no children, vv. 11-14. 'Ephraim, their glory shall fly away like a bird, from the birth, and from the womb, and from the conception'. The significance of this statement lies in the meaning of 'Ephraim', see Gen. 41. 52, 'For God hath caused me to be fruitful in the land of my affliction'. But now, Ephraim would be fruitful no longer, see also 13. 15. 'Their glory' refers, in context, to their children. The nation would be reduced either through slaughter, v.13, or barrenness, v.14. This prediction is all the more significant when we remember that the most abominable fertility rites were associated with Baal-worship. For Tyre, see Ezek. 26-28. It was ultimately destroyed in spite of its position and beauty, and Ephraim's pleasant situation would not prevent fearful carnage either. However, more recent translations render verse 13 differently: for example, 'Ephraim's sons, as I have seen, are destined for a prey', RSV.

ii) There would be no love, vv.15-16. 'All their wickedness is in Gilgal: for there I hated them: for the wickedness of their doings I will drive them out of mine house, I will love them no more: all their princes are revolters'. The words, 'I will love them no more', do not mean that He had ceased to love them and would never do so again, see 11. 8; 14. 4. They imply the cessation of the marriage relationship. Hence, 'I will drive them out of mine house'. They would no longer enjoy God's love and provision. Hosea's own experience in chapters 1-3 illustrates the meaning of this verse. For Gilgal, see 4. 15 and Amos 4. 4. The place, with most sacred associations in the past, was now evidently notorious for idolatry.

iii) There would be no home, v. 17. 'My God will cast them away, because they did not hearken unto him: and they shall be wanderers among the nations', see Deut. 28. 63-68.

The lessons for ourselves are clear: disobedience and disloyalty to Christ, will rob us of spiritual fruitfulness, rob us of enjoyment of God's love, and rob us of the security and stability of our God-given citizenship. No wonder we read, 'Woe also to them when I depart from them!', v. 12.

Hosea 10. 1-15, 'Israel is an empty vine'

Previous chapters have built up a picture of Israel's coming captivity: they are derided at the end of chapter 7, devoured at the end of chapter 8, and dispossessed at the end of chapter 9. Now, they are demeaned by the yoke of slavery, 'I will make Ephraim to ride; Judah shall plough, and Jacob shall break his clods', v.11. Three reasons are given:

(1) God found them unfruitful, vv. 1–13

Israel had originally brought some pleasure to God, 'I found Israel like grapes in the wilderness', 9. 10. But there was nothing for God now, 'Israel is an empty vine, he bringeth forth fruit unto himself'.

The vine is a familiar picture of Israel, see Psa. 80. 8–16; Isa. 5. 1–7; Ezek. 15. GESENIUS states that the Hebrew root for 'empty', is used here intransitively, and means 'to be poured out, to be spread wide, used of a spreading tree'. Hence 'unpruned' (JND), 'luxuriant' (RV), and 'a spreading vine' (NIV), which is well illustrated in Psalm 80. 8–11. Israel had enjoyed some prosperity during the reign of Jeroboam II, see 2 Kgs. 14. 23–29; note v. 27 particularly, 'the Lord . . . saved them by the hand of Jeroboam'. But God had not been honoured, and worse, idolatry had flourished. The improvement in national life had been attributed to idols, and every effort was made to secure their future patronage: hence, 'according to the multitude of his fruit he hath increased the altars; according to the goodness of his land they have made goodly images (pillars)'.

Any comment on these verses would be incomplete without reference to the Lord Jesus. Israel failed to bring pleasure to God. The Lord Jesus is 'the true vine'. Our privilege, on earth, as branches 'abiding in the vine', is to bring forth fruit for God's pleasure, 'Herein is my Father glorified in that ye bear much fruit', John 15. 1–8.

Although Israel cried, 'My God, we know thee', 8. 2, it was false profession. They paid lip-service to Jehovah, but they gave their allegiance to Baal: 'their heart is divided', v. 2. They failed to 'cleave unto the Lord' with 'purpose of heart', Acts 12. 23. They were 'double-minded', and therefore 'unstable' in all their ways, Jas. 1. 8. It is impossible to have a divided heart, and walk with God. God must have all: He will tolerate no rival: hence, He finds them 'guilty' (AV 'faulty'), and will 'break down their altars' and 'spoil their images'. For the last three years of its history, Samaria was under siege and without a king. Hoshea had been captured and imprisoned by the Assyrians. This dire situation wrung from Samaria the cry, 'We have no king, because we feared not the Lord: what then should a king do to us?', v. 3. Human leadership would be totally ineffective without a right relationship with God.

(2) Men found them unfaithful, vv. 4–8

Israel had certainly become 'a cake not turned', 7. 8. They were unpalatable to God in verses 1-3, and unpalatable to Assyria in verses 4-8. 'They speak (mere) words, swearing falsely in making a covenant', JND. The reference to Assyria in verse 6, identifies the king 'cut off' in verses 7 and 15, as Hoshea. The expression 'swearing falsely in making a covenant' must therefore refer to 2 Kings 17. 3-4, where Hoshea's agreement to pay tribute to Assyria was violated by his alliance with Egypt. In consequence, Israel was invaded and conquered, but the underlying reason was Israel's long-standing rebellion against God, see 2 Kgs. 17. 7-23. His judgement, carried out by the Assyrian, would carpet the land with death: it would resemble 'hemlock (a poisonous weed) in the furrows of the field'. The land would be desolate:

A) *Empty shrines*, vv. 5-6. No calves. Notice the sad commentary on the spiritual state of God's people: 'the inhabitants of Samaria shall fear because of the calves of Bethaven', see note on 4. 15. They 'feared not the Lord', v. 3, and had no concern for His glory: but they feared, mourned, and had every concern for the glory of their lost calves. Chapter 8. 6 suggests that king Jareb, see 5. 13, was not too impressed with his present. So much for their calf-worship: no wonder 'Ephraim shall receive shame, and Israel shall be ashamed of his own counsel'.

B) *Empty throne*, v. 7. No king: he would be 'cut off as the foam (some render 'twigs' or 'chips') upon the water'. Hoshea was left helpless when 'the king of Assyria shut him up, and bound him in prison', 2 Kgs. 17. 4.

C) *Empty altars*, v. 8. No worshippers. 'The high places also of Aven, the sin of Israel, see 1 Kgs. 12. 28-33, shall be destroyed; the thorn and the thistle shall come up on their altars'.

The horror of invasion and massacre is graphically expressed in the words, 'And they shall say to the mountains, Cover us; and to the hills, Fall on us'. The Assyrians treated prisoners of war monstrously. The Lord Jesus cited this verse in speaking to the 'daughters of Jerusalem', Luke 23. 30, and it is cited again in Revelation 6. 16. The sheer terror caused by the Assyrians and the Romans, is a pale reflection of the universal terror which will be caused by the 'wrath of the Lamb'.

(3) History found them unrighteous, vv. 9–15

Israel's long-standing sin is stressed by the words, 'O Israel, thou hast sinned from the days of Gibeah', see 8. 9; Judg. 18. 20. This implies that 'the nation had persisted in sin, and had not advanced beyond their early wicked condition', UNGER. The fearful sin of Benjamin at that time was judged by God. Although twice defeated, the other tribes ultimately triumphed, and almost completely destroyed Benjamin. 'There they (the other tribes) stood: the battle in Gibeah against the children of iniquity did not overtake them'. Foreign nations would now come against the spiritual successors of Benjamin. 'At my pleasure will I chasten them; and the peoples shall be assembled against them (the ten tribes, just as the tribes themselves had once assembled against Benjamin) when they are bound (RV margin 'yoked') for their two iniquities', JND. Their 'two iniquities' are not here identified, and have been variously interpreted. Jeremiah 2. 13 could provide the answer: 'For my people have committed two evils'. God now illustrates the course of divine chastisement by referring in four ways to agricultural work with 'bound' or 'yoked' animals.

A) *The work they loved doing*, v. 11. 'Ephraim is as an heifer that is taught, and loveth to tread out the corn'. It was comparatively light work, and the beast was fed and provisioned, see Deut. 25. 4. Similarly, God had blessed His people in the past, and provided amply for them.

B) *The work they would be doing*, v. 11. 'But I passed over upon her fair neck (i.e., put a yoke upon her neck): I will make Ephraim to ride (JND 'draw': RV 'I will set a rider on Ephraim'); Judah shall plough, and Jacob shall break his clods'. Light work now gives place to laborious toil and the discipline of the yoke. This describes the bondage imposed by captivity. The passage also anticipates the ultimate downfall of Judah, bringing the entire nation into captivity; hence, 'Jacob shall break his clods'.

C) *The work they should be doing*, v. 12. 'Sow to yourselves in righteousness, reap in mercy; break up your fallow ground: for it is time to seek the Lord, till he come and rain righteousness upon you', see also Jeremiah 4. 3. As UNGER observes, this involved 'repentance toward God', and required 'more than scratching the surface'. KIDNER is worth quoting in full here: 'The expression "fallow ground" was extraordinarily well suited to describe a people doubly impervious to the good seed of the word of God, both by the tangled growth of worldly notions and preoccupations which had taken hold of them, and by the hard crust beneath it all, of wills and attitudes never broken into penitence'. If we have hardened our hearts in any way to the word of God, it is also, for us, 'time to seek the Lord'. There was little time left for Israel, and perhaps little time left before we 'appear before the judgement seat of Christ; that every one may receive the things done in his body', 2 Cor. 5. 10.

D) The work they had been doing, v. 13. 'Ye have ploughed wickedness, ye have reaped iniquity: ye have eaten the fruit of lies'. The chilling words that follow are introduced by 'therefore'. The horrors of a previous military campaign under Shalmaneser (Shalman for short) would be repeated. They had 'sown the wind': now they would 'reap the whirlwind', 8. 7.

Hosea 11. 1–11, 'How shall I give thee up?'

The atmosphere of the book now changes. Whilst Israel had offended and rejected God's love, and would reap judgement of the greatest severity, God's love for His people had not altered. The comment of J. N. DARBY in connection with Lamentations, is applicable here, 'He loves that which He is obliged to smite, and is obliged to smite that which He loves'. The nation would be restored, not out of dogged determination to honour ancient promises, but because God loved His people.

(1) God's love for them in their redemption, vv. 1–4

First of all, God recalls His love for them in national infancy. 'When Israel was a child, then I loved him, and called my son out of Egypt'. God's relationship with His people rested on His love for them. Deuteronomy 7 explains, 'The Lord did not set his love upon you, nor choose you, because ye were more in number than any people . . .but because the Lord loved you', vv. 6–7; cf. Isa. 63. 9; Jer. 31. 3; Mal. 1. 2–3. God's love was expressed in four ways:

A) *In love, He called them.* 'I . . .called my son out of Egypt'. God chose Israel out of His love for them, and the time came for Him to implement His sovereign choice. Cf. Romans 8. 30, 'whom he did predestinate, them he also called . . .'. God's love for His people gave them a unique status, 'My son'. They were, in fact, God's firstborn son, see Exod. 4. 22. As such, they were doubly-privileged, Deut. 21. 15–17, and doubly-responsible, Isa. 40. 2.

The Lord Jesus, not the church, is the true Israel. This is made clear from the New Testament quotation of verse 1 in Matthew 2. 14–15. Israel is called 'My son'. The Lord Jesus is called 'My Son', Heb. 1. 5: but more than that, He is called 'My beloved Son', Matt. 3. 17, etc. In order to escape death by the sword, the Lord Jesus also found refuge in Egypt. Israel returned from Egypt to its own land in order to fulfil its calling.

The Lord Jesus also returned from Egypt to His own land ('Thy land, O Immanuel', Isa. 8. 8) in order to fulfil God's purposes. This is not an exaggerated comparison: Matthew is precise; 'that it might be fulfilled which was spoken of the Lord by the prophet saying, Out of Egypt have I called my Son'.

B) *In love, He taught them.* 'I taught Ephraim also to go, taking them by their arms'. God displayed His love for Israel in 'coaxing and supporting the child's first staggering steps; picking him up when he tires or tumbles', KIDNER. Exodus 14 describes the tottering child by the Red Sea, and the way in which God took 'them by the arms' in reassurance and deliverance. He taught them to trust in Him.

C) *In love, He drew them.* 'I drew them with cords ... with bands of love'. The 'cords' here are not 'the ropes and halters by which dumb cattle are led', UNGER, but 'cords of compassion with the bands of love', RSV. Israel reciprocated His love in guiding them through the desert, 'I remember thee, the kindness of thy youth, the love of thine espousals, when thou wentest after me in the wilderness', Jer. 2. 2.

D) *In love, He fed them.* 'I was to them as they that take off the yoke on their jaws, and I laid meat unto them'. GEORGE ADAM SMITH sees here, 'the team of draught oxen surmounting the steep road', followed by rest and refreshment at its summit. God did not overdrive His people; they came, for example, to Elim with its 'twelve wells of water, and threescore and ten palm trees', Exod. 15. 27. He provided the manna, Exod. 16.

But the child grew up, and became rebellious. God's love was not reciprocated. They rejected His word. 'As they (the prophets) called them, so they went from them', v.2. God's tender support and help was unrecognized: 'they knew not that I healed them', v. 3. H. A. IRONSIDE writes as follows, 'What saint but will see in words so lovely the story of his own deliverance from sin and Satan, when first brought to the knowledge of Christ ... let us challenge our hearts as to what return we have made to love so deep and tender'.

(2) God's love for them in their rebellion, vv. 5–9

God's love for the nation in its infancy had not diminished, even in the face of their rebellion and backsliding:

A) *The consequences of their backsliding, vv. 5–7.* 'He shall not return into the land of Egypt, but the Assyrian shall be his king'. This is a most significant statement. God would not reverse the redemption of His people. He did not do it then, and He does not do it now. One consequence of alliance with Egypt was that some would return there, 9. 3: we know from Jeremiah 41-44, that refugees from Judah did so. But there would be no national return to Egypt. God would use the Assyrian, as He did in connection with Judah, as 'the rod of mine anger', Isa. 10. 5. Three reasons are given:

i) 'They refused to return'. That is, return to God, see v. 3: God had spoken to them, He had made His word clear, but they had consciously rejected it.

ii) They preferred 'their own counsels'. This refers particularly to their penchant for unholy alliances, see 10. 6.

iii) They were 'bent to backsliding from me'. Their deliberate policy, 'bent', is illustrated by the words which follow: 'though they (the prophets) called them to the Most High, none at all would exalt him'. The saddest part of it all is that they were God's people, 'My people are bent to backsliding from me', cf. Jer. 2. 13.

B) *The continuity of God's love*, vv.8-9. Jeremiah exclaimed, 'It is of the Lord's mercies that we are not consumed, because his compassions fail not', Lam. 3. 22, and this is the atmosphere of verses 8-9. God says four times in verse 8, 'How shall I?', and three times in verse 9, 'I will not'. We cannot miss the depth of divine feeling expressed in these words.

The enormity of Israel's sin merited judgement akin to the destruction of Admah and Zeboim (companion cities to Sodom and Gomorrah), Deut. 29. 23. But although 'the sword shall abide on his cities, and shall consume his branches, and devour them', the love of God for His people did not permit their total rejection and annihilation. 'Mine heart is turned within me, my repentings ('compassions' RV) are kindled together'. God's anger was tempered by His compassion. This is not the language of impulse and emotion, but of deep unchangeable love. The strength of God's determination to preserve, rather than destroy, His people is expressed in the words, 'For I am God, and not man; the Holy One in the midst of thee'. God's love was not fickle and unreliable: He would not abandon the people whom He had chosen in love, even though they deserved destruction, cf. Isa. 49. 14-16.

(3) God's love for them in their restoration, vv. 10-11

In proof of what He has said, God now anticipates the future blessing of His people, as a result of which, 'They shall walk after the Lord'.

i) *Reawakening*. 'He shall roar like a lion'. The lion's roar signals imminent judgement, see Jer. 25. 30-38; Joel 3. 16; Amos 1. 2; and

Amos 3. 8. It anticipates here the judicial hand of God in tribulation days, which will be recognized as 'the day of the Lord'.

ii) *Regathering*. 'The children shall tremble from the west. They shall tremble as a bird out of Egypt, and as a dove out of the land of Assyria'. That is, they will come from all points of the compass, cf. 7. 11–12; see Isa. 60. 8.

iii) *Resettlement*. 'I will place them in their houses, saith the Lord', cf. Ezek. 36. 11, 'I will settle you after your old estates, and will do better unto you than at your beginnings', v. 11.

Note: the competent authorities tell us that in the Hebrew Bible, the last verse in chapter 11, is the first verse in chapter 12.

Hosea 11. 12–12. 14, 'The Lord will punish Jacob'

After reaffirming His love for erring Israel in chapter 11. 1–11, God resumes His lawsuit ('controversy', 4. 1) against Israel in the concluding verse, with particular reference to alliances with foreign powers. If only they would learn, like Jacob centuries before, that power does not lie in subtlety and deceit, but in submission and dependence on God! He appeals to them on this basis in verse 6.

(1) Perversity before God, 11. 12–12. 2

Both kingdoms are censured by God. The context favours the translation, 'And Judah is unruly against God, even against the faithful Holy One', 11. 12 RSV. See JND/RV margin. GESENIUS states that the Hebrew word rendered 'ruleth' (AV), was 'used of beasts which have broken the yoke, and wander freely'. In any case, it seems unlikely that 'Judah yet ruleth with God, and is faithful with the saints', whilst 'the Lord also hath a controversy with Judah', 12. 2.

Their double-dealing with God, 'lies...deceit', 11. 12, was matched by double-dealing with foreign powers, 12. 1. Chapter 8. 11–13 illustrates the former, and 2 Kings 17. 4 explains the latter. It is therefore clear, firstly, that lack of integrity with God will lessen integrity with our fellow men. It is also made clear, secondly, that the policy of alliance with foreign powers, and for us, 'the friendship of the world', was both futile ('Ephraim feedeth on wind'), and perilous ('followeth after the east wind'). The 'east wind' is identified in 13. 15, where clear reference is made to the Assyrian destruction of Samaria. Israel would certainly prove to its cost, that the 'east wind'

was 'the hot, destructive sirocco from the scorching desert', UNGER;
see also Ezek. 19. 12.

(2) Power with God, 12. 3–6

God now addresses both Ephraim and Judah together, as 'Jacob'. The
reason is clear: the nation had endeavoured to achieve security by diplomacy and double-dealing, by 'lies' and 'deceit'. In his early history,
Jacob displayed these very characteristics, but turned, in later life, from
his duplicity to complete dependence on God. This great event in
Jacob's life is now recalled, and made the ground of an appeal, 'Therefore (in view of Jacob's experience) turn thou to thy God', v.6. Reference is made to Jacob's babyhood, and to his manhood:

A) *'In the womb he took his brother by the heel'*, RV. Jacob means,
'taking hold of the heel', Gen. 25. 26; see GESENIUS' *Lexicon*, and 'for
years his dealings with his fellows were to confirm all that was sinister in
the name, as one who steals up from behind to outwit and overreach
you', KIDNER. In this respect, he was a picture of his descendants in
Hosea's day, as they endeavoured to achieve security by diplomacy and
alliance. But God looked for a change in His people, in exactly the same
way that Jacob became Israel. So:

B) *'In his manhood (AV 'strength') he had power with God'*, RV.
Reference is made to Peniel, Gen. 32. 24–32, and to Bethel, Gen. 28.
11–12: that is, in reverse chronological order.

i) God gave power to Jacob at Peniel. 'Yea he had power ('he strove',
RV: 'he wrestled' JND) over the angel, and prevailed' and became Israel
('for as a prince hast thou power with God, and has prevailed'), by
crying, 'I will not let thee go, except thou bless me'. Jacob did not
become Israel by resisting God ('there wrestled a man with him'), but by
dependence on Him. In the language of the New Testament, 'My grace
is sufficient for thee: for my strength is made perfect in weakness',
2 Cor. 12. 9. Israel and Judah desperately needed to learn the lesson,
and so do we. (For the identity of the angel, see Exod. 3. 2–4; Judg. 6.
20–22; Judg. 13. 17–22; Isa. 63. 9, Rev. 10. 1, etc).

ii) God made promises to Jacob at Bethel. 'He found him in Bethel,
and there he spake with us'. The plural indicates that the promises were
made, not to one man only, but also to his descendants. We have
noticed how Jacob became a 'prince with God', but what was God's
interest in Jacob in the first place? Although he was a fugitive, fleeing
because of deceit, Jacob was none the less the subject of divine
promises, which were directly confirmed to him at Bethel. But before he

could realize those promises, he had to learn dependence on God. The lesson is now clear: God's people, as Jacob, were in receipt of divine promises, which could only be enjoyed once they, too, had learned dependence on God alone. The people, who had made 'a covenant with the Assyrians' and supplied oil to Egypt (probably as a bribe), are now therefore urged, 'Turn thou to thy God, keep mercy and judgement, and wait on thy God continually'. He was perfectly able to protect and sustain them: He is 'the Lord God of hosts: the Lord is his memorial ('name')'. The title, 'Lord God of hosts', conveys His immense resources, see Dan. 4. 35, etc. He was infinitely stronger than Assyria or Egypt.

(3) Prosperity without God, 12. 7–9

But, as H. A. IRONSIDE observes, 'the nation was following the first ways of their father'. God, who had called them to 'keep mercy and judgement, and wait on thy God continually' had to say, 'He is a merchant', 'a Canaanite', cf. Zech. 14. 21. The words, 'balances of deceit' and 'loveth to oppress (defraud)', v. 7, tell us about their business transactions, see also Amos 8. 4–6. Whilst they were quite confident that they could baffle the Fraud Squad of the day, v. 8, God was perfectly aware of their deceit. They were His people, and He would correct them, 'But I am the Lord thy God from the land of Egypt; I will yet again make thee to dwell in tents, as in the days of the solemn feasts', v. 9, JND. At first glance, this appears to refer to the millennial kingdom, but the context demands otherwise: their deceit would be rewarded by dispossession of the land, and they would become, again, a wandering people without permanent dwelling. Hence the words, 'in tabernacles as in the days of the solemn feasts', not, 'in tabernacles in the days of the solemn feasts'. Peter describes his readers as 'sojourners of the dispersion', 1 Pet. 1. 1, RV.

(4) Prophets from God, 12. 10–14

The final paragraph of this chapter emphasizes, again (see 6. 5 and 9. 7–8), that God had warned His people about the consequences of their sin and wickedness. There are two sub-paragraphs, both of which stress the divinely-given authority of the prophets, and the consequences of ignoring them:

A) *The prophets generally*, vv.10–12. They were men in receipt of God's word. 'I have also spoken to the prophets', JND. Hebrews 1. 1 is a good commentary on verse 10, 'God who at sundry times and in divers manners spake in time past unto the fathers by the prophets'. Notice the source of their ministry, 'I have . . . I have': the variety in their ministry; 'visions . . . similitudes (parables)': the forthrightness of their ministry, 'Is there iniquity in Gilead . . . they sacrifice bullocks in Gilgal'. There was nothing neutral about their preaching; they got down to detail.

This is followed by a fourth, and rather unexpected, reference to Jacob, 'And Jacob fled into the country of Syria ('Aram', RV), and Israel served for a wife, and for a wife he kept sheep', see Gen. 29. So, in a chapter which draws lessons from the life of Jacob, God cites his history again to illustrate the consequences of their lies and deceit, witnessed by their sacrifices and altars. For his deceit, Jacob was out of the land, and engaged in long and laborious toil. It would not be long before Israel followed suit.

B) *A prophet particularly*, vv.13–14. The solemn consequences of rejecting the word of God, are stressed again. The value and importance of the prophetic office is emphasized by the fact that Moses is not mentioned by name, 'By a prophet the Lord brought Israel out of Egypt, and by a prophet was he preserved'. It was not so much who Moses was, but what Moses was, cf. 1 Cor. 3. 5. The awful crime of rejecting the prophetic word follows, 'Ephraim hath provoked to anger most bitterly: therefore shall his blood be left upon him, and his reproach shall his Lord return unto him', RV. It is still perilous for sinners and saints to reject God's word.

Hosea 13. 1–16, 'Thou hast destroyed thyself'

As D. KIDNER observes, 'This is the climax of Hosea's prophecies of doom, but not the climax of the book. That distinction is reserved for the next chapter'. Hosea 13 ends on the most chilling note of all. There are four main paragraphs:

(1) Increasing sin, vv. 1–3

Pride and self-assertion open the door to fearful sin. No wonder that Peter wrote, 'God resisteth the proud, and giveth grace to the humble. Humble yourselves therefore under the mighty hand of God, that he may exalt you in due time', 1 Pet. 5. 5-6. Ephraim achieved eminence in

Israel through Joshua, see Num. 13. 8. It was Ephraim's most glorious son who charged the nation with idolatry, and urged them to 'fear the Lord, and serve Him in sincerity', Josh. 24. 14–28. Another son of Ephraim, Jeroboam, 1 Kgs. 11. 26, RV, introduced idol worship. Some fifty years later, Ahab 'went and served Baal, and worshipped him', 1 Kgs. 16. 31–32. Hosea describes the result as follows, 'When he offended in Baal, he died'. 2 Kings 9. 7–10 explains the meaning. But the nation failed to learn the lesson, 'And now they sin more and more'. They deliberately transgressed the first and second commandments, and exhibited gross stupidity, 'Let the men that sacrifice kiss the calves'. Human beings, the crowning glory of God's creation, were kissing calves! It was sinful in the first place, and bizarre in the second.

Hosea employs four figures to describe the cessation of national life, 'the morning cloud . . . the early dew . . . the chaff . . . the smoke out of the chimney'. All are irretrievably lost, and it is worth noting that Israel, unlike Judah, was never restored. Like the house of Ahab, the nation would die.

(2) Incontestable rights, vv. 4–8

God asserts His interest in the affairs of His people. This had been displayed in their deliverance from Egypt, vv. 4–5, and would be displayed again in their deliverance to their enemies, vv. 5–8. God had redeemed and preserved His people: He therefore had every right to punish their disobedience and unthankfulness. The assembly at Corinth learnt the same lesson to their cost, see 1 Cor. 11. 29–31. So did Ananias and Sapphira. We, too, must never forget the rights of the same God who says, 'No God but me . . . no Saviour beside me'. Like Israel, we have been delivered from bondage, preserved and provisioned in this wilderness-world, and brought into a wonderful inheritance: 'according to their pasture, so were they filled'. But then, 'they were filled, and their heart was exalted'. Like Uzziah, who was 'marvellously helped, till he was strong. But when he was strong, his heart was lifted up to his destruction', 2 Chron. 26. 15–16, cf. 1 Sam. 15. 17. How much we all need to 'speak trembling', v.1.

The references to 'lion . . . leopard . . . bear . . . wild beast', are undoubtedly employed to emphasize the severity of pending judgement. But, at the same time, they could have specific prophetic significance, cf. Dan. 7. 1–7.

(3) Infinite grace, vv. 9–14

God's infinite grace comes at the end of the paragraph, although the AV rendering suggests that it comes at the beginning as well. However, the RV reads, 'It is thy destruction, O Israel, that thou art against me, against thy help. Where now is thy king, that he may save thee in all thy cities?' This is supported by J. N. DARBY. We know that Hosea was in prison for the last three years of Israel's existence, see 2 Kgs. 17. 4–6, and this seems to be the most likely allusion in the question, 'Where now is thy king?' The failure of Samuel's sons, and the desire to emulate surrounding nations, engendered the request, 'make us a king'. But they gave another reason, 'that our king may judge us, and go out before us, and fight our battles'. There was now no king to do anything. So much for human leadership without recourse to 'the King of kings'. God gave them 'a king in mine anger', with the words, 'they have rejected me that I should not reign over them', 1 Sam. 8. Their first king was certainly removed in God's wrath, and so was the last king of Israel, together with the last king of Judah, see 2 Kgs. 25. 7. But the throne of David will not be empty for ever: the Lord Jesus will sit 'upon the throne of David, and upon his kingdom, to order it, and to establish it with judgement and with justice, from henceforth even for ever', Isa. 9. 7.

Pending judgement has been graphically described in verses 7–9. Now Hosea employs different language. Its certainty is emphasized in verse 12, where the words, 'bound up . . . hid', are used in the sense of Romans 2. 5, 'treasurest up unto thyself wrath against the day of wrath'. The words, 'The sorrows of a travailing woman shall come upon him', recall Jeremiah 30. 6–7, and 1 Thessalonians 5. 3, which refer to the sufferings of Israel in the Great Tribulation. Hezekiah explains Hosea 13. 13 for us: 'This day is a day of trouble . . . for the children are come to the birth, and there is not strength to bring forth', 2 Kgs. 19. 3. But Hezekiah prayed to God, and the threat of fatal birth was averted. Having passed through the coming tribulation, God's people will be 'saved out of it'. But although Hosea had cried, 'It is time to seek the Lord', 10. 12, Ephraim stayed 'long in the place of the breaking forth of children'. That is, instead of deliverance by seeking God, the nation, by delaying, would never see the light of day. UNGER writes, 'If he waited much longer, he would be like a child whose mother had no strength to bring it to birth, and who remains so long in the passage from the womb that it runs the risk of death.'

But suddenly the picture changes: death gives place to life. 'I will ransom them from the power of the grave; I will redeem them from

death: O death, I will be thy plagues; O grave, I will be thy destruction',
v.14. This verse is, of course, cited by Paul interrogatively, as rendered
by RV and JND, in 1 Corinthians 15. 55. In the New Testament setting, it
refers to the resurrection of individual believers, but in Hosea, it refers to
national resurrection. This is demanded by the context, cf. Ezek. 37.
1-14. Isaiah 26. 16–19 are parallel to Hosea 13. 13–14, and Daniel 12. 2,
often understood with reference to individual Israelites, more likely
anticipates national restoration. The basis on which the nation will ultimately be restored is clearly stated in the words, 'I will ransom . . . I will
redeem'. All blessing, in every age, individual or national, rests upon
the redemptive work of Christ. Although national destruction stared
Israel in the face, 'the Lord's unchanging purpose to restore Israel was
once more reiterated in the very vortex of the maelstrom of sin that was
about to hurl the nation into ruin', H. A. IRONSIDE. God's purpose for
His people would not alter, and the words, 'repentance shall be hid
from mine eyes', recall the language of Romans 11. 29 in connection
with Israel, 'for the gifts and calling of God are without repentance'. But
the millennial blessing of Israel was then far distant: the storm of divine
judgement was about to break.

(4) Inevitable judgement, vv. 15–16

Joseph named his second son Ephraim, 'For God hath caused me to be
fruitful in the land of my affliction', Gen. 41. 52. But not now: Ephraim
would cease to be fruitful, both materially, v.15, and in progeny, v.16.
We have already encountered 'the east wind', see 12. 1. The Assyrians
achieved notoriety by their cruelty and barbarity. But behind Assyria lay
the hand of God: it was 'an east wind . . . the wind of the Lord'. But the
hand that judged, is the hand that will restore, as the final chapter will
prove.

Hosea 14. 1–9, 'Return unto the Lord thy God'

The preceding chapters of Hosea leave us in no doubt about the
justice of God's 'controversy' with His people, 4. 1. There is no
doubt, either, that although the guilt of the nation could not be
excused, God retained His original love for them. This is emphasized
particularly in chapter 11, let alone in the analogy of Hosea's own
relationship with Gomer, and now underlies the tender appeal with

which the prophecy terminates: 'I will heal their backsliding, I will love them freely', v. 4.

The chapter is both a bona fide appeal to Israel at the time, and a description of ultimate national blessing following repentance. Since, however, it is addressed to people 'bent to backsliding', its application to ourselves is very clear. What is God's attitude to the backsliding Christian? The chapter reveals the heart of God.

(1) The return, vv. 1–3

This section of the chapter sets out the pathway which the backslider must take in returning to God:

A) *Depth of Conviction*. There must be recognition of previous failure and decline, 'O Israel, return unto the Lord thy God: for thou hast fallen by thine iniquity'. Previous chapters, with their searching messages, may have illuminated areas of weakness and deficiency in our lives. Perhaps we have heard the Saviour say, 'I have somewhat against thee'. None of us is immune from the danger of backsliding.

B) *Desire for Cleansing*. Conviction of sin is followed by confession, and desire for forgiveness and cleansing, 'Say unto him, Take away all iniquity, and receive us graciously ('accept that which is good', RV and JND margin): so will we render the calves of our lips', v. 2. There had been a great deal of lip-service, and a great deal of religious ceremony, but now there must be reality. 'That which is good' is described in Psalm 51 as follows, 'For thou desirest not sacrifice; else would I give it . . . the sacrifices of God are a broken spirit: a broken and a contrite heart, O God, thou wilt not despise', vv.16–17. The word 'render' is the 'term used for paying one's vows (e.g. Ps. 116. 14) in due gratitude for answered prayer', KIDNER. Here, thanksgiving after cleansing. The verse is cited Hebrews 13. 15, 'By him therefore let us offer the sacrifice of praise continually, that is, the fruit of our lips, giving thanks to his name'.

C) *Display of Confidence*. 'In thee the fatherless findeth mercy', v. 3. This recalls the birth of both Lo-ruhamah ('I will no more have mercy upon the house of Israel'), and Lo-ammi ('for ye are not my people, and I will not be your God'), 1. 6–9. But it must be said that God's mercy is only displayed when there are 'fruits meet for repentance', Matt. 3. 8. No more recourse to Assyria or Egypt with its horses, see Isa. 31. 1; S. of S. 1. 9, and no more idolatry. 'Neither will we say any more to the works of our hands, Ye are our gods', see 1 John 1. 9.

(2) The reception, vv. 4–5

If verses 1–3 describe the mind and heart necessary for restoration after backsliding, then verses 4–5 describe the grace and kindness of God. The expression, 'I will', occurs three times:

1) 'I will heal their backsliding'. God had said, 'My people are bent to backsliding from me', 11. 7. He now announces His willingness to restore. At the same time, we must not forget that backsliding involves spiritual loss. Abram was brought back to 'the place where his tent (and altar) had been at the beginning', Gen. 13. 3–4, and Israel was ultimately brought back to Kadesh-Barnea, Num. 20. 1, but not without loss of fellowship with God in the first place, and fearful loss of personnel and time in the second. But God remains intent on the highest good of His people, even though Israel had looked elsewhere for help in the past, 'When Ephraim saw his sickness, and Judah saw his wound, then went Ephraim to the Assyrian, and sent to king Jareb, yet could he not heal you, nor cure you of your wound', 5. 13, cf. 6. 1.

But this is not all. We might be tempted to feel that having once, or more, allowed our affections to be weaned away from God, any restoration can only be, at the very best, recovery of an inferior place in His love. Not so: the passage continues:

2) 'I will love them freely'. There is nothing grudging about God's welcome. It recalls the welcome given to the son in Luke 15, for whilst the parable is often used effectively in gospel preaching, it is worth using it as an illustration of the restoration of a backsliding Christian. The welcome amounted to far more than readmission to the house as 'one of the hired servants': the father said, 'bring forth the best robe and put it on him'.

This particular verse is, of course, characteristic of Hosea's ministry, which was to shew God's love for His erring people. Nothing will bring our heavenly Father greater pleasure, should we backslide, than to make us feel again the warmth of His love toward us.

3) 'I will be as the dew unto Israel'. Isaac spoke of 'the dew of heaven from above', Gen. 27. 39. It is looked upon as a blessing – a refreshment sent from God – and withheld in punishment when the conduct of His people merited judgement. The summer dew is most copious in Israel, and aids greatly in the cultivation of the land. Israel's goodness has been described 'as the early dew, it goeth away', 6. 4. This verse describes the blessing of God abiding on His people restored after backsliding: they are not precluded from divine blessing.

The characteristics of the restored backslider are now outlined, and emphasize the abundance of divine grace:

(3) The result, vv. 5–9

1) 'He shall grow (literally 'blossom') as the lily'. Solomon refers to the same species: 'As the lily among thorns, so is my love among the daughters', S. of S. 2. 2. Israel's moral and spiritual identification with her neighbours had made her anything but beautiful, but the nation will 'worship the Lord in the beauty of holiness', Ps. 29. 2. We, too, have the privilege of such worship.

2) 'And cast forth his roots as Lebanon'. The picture is now stability. The stability of a tree depends, of course, on its roots: no less the stability of the Christian. Psalm 1. 1–3 and Psalm 92. 12–13 make a good Old Testament commentary on the subject. The New Testament has the following to say: 'That Christ might dwell in your hearts by faith; that ye, being rooted and grounded in love', Eph. 3. 17. 'As ye have therefore received Christ Jesus the Lord, so walk in him; rooted and built up in him', Col. 2. 6–7. A root is a God-given device that links supply with need. The phrase 'cast forth his roots as Lebanon', must be taken in conjunction with the next:

3) 'His branches shall spread'. That is, as opposed to 11. 6, 'And the sword shall abide on his cities, and shall consume his branches'. Now it is expansion. If we ensure that our spiritual roots, that is, the unseen life of prayer, reading, study, and fellowship with God, are developing, then we can be certain that our public life and testimony will grow too, cf. Isa. 37. 31; notice Job 29. 19.

4) 'His beauty shall be as the olive tree'. The olive tree speaks of witness. See Zechariah 4 and Revelation 11. 3–4, 'And I will give power unto my two witnesses . . . these are the two olive trees, and the two candlesticks standing before the God of the earth'.

5) 'His smell as Lebanon'. Cedar is an odiferous wood, and aromatic shrubs grow extensively in the area; hence the reference, cf. S. of S. 4. 11, 'the smell of thy garments is like the smell of Lebanon'. Paul describes the practical fellowship of the assembly at Philippi as, 'an odour of a sweet smell, a sacrifice acceptable, well-pleasing to God'.

6) 'They that dwell under his shadow shall return'. Better, 'they shall return and sit under his shadow', JND. This implies nearness, cf. S. of S. 2. 3, 'I sat down under his shadow with great delight'. To be within a person's shadow necessitates nearness to them. Previously, Israel had dwelt under the shadow of idolatry, 'They sacrifice upon the tops of the mountains, and burn incense upon the hills, under oaks and poplars and elms, because the shadow thereof is good', 4. 13.

7) 'They shall revive as the corn, and grow ('blossom', RV) as the

vine'. This indicates fruitfulness', see 2. 22. Both recall millennial blessings, see Ps. 72. 16, Mic. 4. 4.

8) 'The scent thereof (the blossoming vine) shall be as the wine of
Lebanon'. The word rendered 'scent' is more correctly 'memorial' or
'renown'. 'The nation's fame in millennial blessing, is compared to the
wine of Lebanon, which was celebrated for its aroma, flavour, and
medicinal properties', UNGER. The nation will be known for its unique
character: Christians should be known in the same way.

J. N. DARBY, and other writers of his period, suggest that verse 8 gives
a conversation between Ephraim and God, as follows:

> Ephraim: 'What have I to do any more with idols?'
> God: 'I have heard him and observed him'.
> Ephraim: 'I am like a green fir tree'.
> God: 'From me is thy fruit found'.

Their attitude to idolatry is now reversed. Once it was said, 'Ephraim is
joined to idols: let him alone', 4. 17. Now, 'What have I to do any more
with idols?' Reference is made to the evergreen fir, rather than to a
deciduous tree. This emphasizes the consistency and continuity of the
nation. See, again, Psalm 92. 12–14, 'they shall still bring forth fruit in
old age; they shall be fat and flourishing (AV 'green')'. This happy
condition will not be produced by natural genius. God says, 'From me is
thy fruit found'. Once, 'an empty vine, he bringeth forth fruit unto
himself', 10. 1. Galatians 5 specifically states that 'the fruit of the Spirit
is . . .'. The Lord Jesus emphasized that, 'as the branch cannot bear fruit
of itself, except it abide in the vine; no more can ye, except ye abide in
me. I am the vine, ye are the branches: He that abideth in me, and I in
him, the same bringeth forth much fruit: for without me ye can do
nothing'.

If, in any measure, we have backslidden, there is possibility of wonderful restoration. We must heed the final encouragement, and warning, of the prophecy:

> 'Who is wise, and he shall understand these things? Prudent, and he
> shall know them? For the ways of the Lord are right, and the just shall
> walk in them: but the transgressors shall fall therein'.

CHAPTER TWO

THE PROPHECY OF
JOEL

by DENIS CLAPHAM

INTRODUCTION

1. Introduction, 1.1

Concerning the prophet Joel ('Jehovah is God') himself we know only as
much as the first verse of his prophecy tells us. The same can also be said of
his father Pethuel. God has not seen fit to inform us when they lived,
although some would tell us that it was before the captivity of Judah,
while others that it was after the return from their exile. But such differing
views can leave us speculating about what is not revealed, and it is not a
wise thing for us to do that. There is no indication as to who reigned in
Jerusalem at the time, nor whether there were any other contemporary
prophets, either in Judah or Israel. The references to Zion, 2.1, 15, 32;
3.16, 17, 21; and Jerusalem, 2.32; 3.1, 16, 17, 18, 20; and to the children of
Judah and Jerusalem, 3.6, 8, 19, probably indicate that his home was in or
near Jerusalem. He was familiar with the temple and its services, and
with the priests and their ministry, 1.9, 13, 14, 16; 2.14, 17; 3.18. Of the
unprecedented locust invasion in successive years which completely
devastated the land and occasioned the writing of this prophet's message
there is no other allusion elsewhere in holy scripture, nor, as far as we
know, is any reference made to them in secular writings or records.

All of this might seem unhelpful to those who would prefer to read this
little book in its historical setting, but, obviously, God's message in it is
not intended to be restricted by such considerations. It is not for us to
supplement or diminish the sacred word. What is God-breathed, 2 Tim.
3.16, was written by a holy man of God, 'who spoke as he was moved by
the Holy Spirit', 2 Pet. 1.21. That is the chief thing, as we are simply told,
it was 'the word of the Lord that came to Joel', 1.1. As such, its message,
though originally meant for the people of Judah and Jerusalem in Joel's
day, looks on to the overwhelming terrors of that still future, great and
terrible day of the Lord, which is referred to five times, 1.15; 2.1, 11, 31;
3.14, and which will be for those, whether of Israel or of other nations on
the earth during that dreadful era when divine judgements will cul-
minate in the revelation of the Son of Man, the Lord from heaven.

2. Description of the Devastation, 1.2–12

Being well versed in the law of the Lord the prophet wastes no time in
speaking of the instrument with which the Lord had chosen to afflict and
humble His people, in His effort to recall them to the worship of Himself. We may well wonder how God's people could have completely
forgotten the first commandment, 'Thou shalt have no other gods

before me', Exod. 20.3. It seems they ceased to fear the Lord their God and no longer cared that He was a jealous God, visiting the iniquity of the fathers upon the children unto the third and fourth generation, Exod. 20.5. They ought, surely, to have remembered the solemn declaration of Moses, to be pronounced by the priests and the Levites on the day Israel formally became the people of God, when they passed over Jordan into the land and set up the plastered stones in mount Ebal! Had not Moses then said, that to hear, and to observe, and to do all the Lord's commandments would bring them many temporal blessings; but failure to hearken and to observe to do His commandments and statutes would as surely bring down awful curses upon them? Deut. 28.1, 2, 15. Among the curses he foretold was, 'Thou shalt carry much seed out into the field, and shalt gather but little in; for the locust shall consume it', v. 38. And again, 'All thy trees and fruit of thy land shall the locust consume', v. 42.

'Hath this been in your days, or even in the days of your fathers?' v. 2, is the challenge issued to the old men and all the inhabitants of the ravaged land of Judah in this, the first of four questions Joel asks. The others occur at 1.16; 2.11 and 2.14.

In the days of their forefathers' slavery, before the Lord had brought them out of Egypt, Israel had witnessed an unparalleled plague of locusts which was sent as a judgement from the Lord upon the Egyptians, 'For they covered the face of the whole earth, so that the land was darkened: and they did eat every herb of the land, and all the fruit of the trees which the hail had left: and there remained not any green thing in the trees, or in the herbs of the field, through all the land of Egypt', Exod. 10.15. Now, because of their own iniquities, the same Lord, their God, had sent locusts in successive waves as an invading army on Judah: first the palmerworm, then the locust, then the cankerworm and then the caterpillar, v. 4. They were veritably a nation of insects, 'strong and without number, whose teeth are the teeth of a lion, and he hath the cheek teeth of a great lion', v. 6. By means of such invincible hordes He had destroyed every tree and all the crops, vv. 10–12. This instrument of terrifying destruction from the hand of the Lord was sent to soften and prepare their hearts for the prophet's call to repentance, to weep and howl. The drunkards and drinkers of wine are roused from their stupor, v. 5, and the husbandmen and vinedressers whose businesses have failed are called upon to consider the cause, v. 11.

What is even more lamentable to the prophet than the denial to the people of their luxuries and necessities, is the fact that the meat (grain) offering and the drink offering were cut off from the house of the Lord,

v. 9. So serious a matter was the people's failure to respond to the Lord's goodness, by offering to Him when they were well able to do so, that the Lord had taken from them every one of those things of which He should have received His portion. We need to understand that such offerings foreshadowed the Messiah and His offering of Himself, just as did those in Leviticus 1-7. Since Christ alone among men by His perfect obedience would bring untold pleasure and complete satisfaction, i.e. 'a savour of rest', to the heart of God, for the people to rob God of what spoke of Christ amounted to a refusal on their part to recognize what the Lord most appreciated. Nothing could more fully express their evil heart of unbelief. Joel alludes to these offerings at 1.9, 13, 16 and 2.14.

3. Call to Mourn and Fast, 1.13-20

It was now the turn for the priests, the ministers of the altar, to hear what the prophet had to say directly to them, and to be told by him that they must take the lead and set an example in repentance. This was surely most fitting, for in view of the withholding of the meat (grain) and drink offerings, which they were responsible for presenting on behalf of the people, they ought to have been the first to recognize why the Lord was judging His people, v. 13. Not only were they, therefore, called upon to 'lie all night in sackcloth', unseen by any other eye than God's, they were also required to 'sanctify a fast', by gathering all the people in the land, even the most ancient and revered, to the house of the Lord their God to 'cry unto the Lord' in words which it seems probable the prophet would put into their mouths as a suitable expression of their true contrition, vv. 15-20.

Joel being the one man in touch with God in the situation, and the word of the Lord being in his mouth, it would be entirely reasonable that he should be granted suitable words with which to frame what is somewhat like a short, penitential psalm for the people, if they would use it. It begins with a cry, 'Alas, for the day! for the day of the Lord is at hand, and as a destruction from the Almighty shall it come', v. 15. It then continues by rehearsing the sorrowful state that the land is presently in. And while the prophet sees a judgement upon the people in the catastrophic events that have wasted the countryside, destroying everything that grew, even causing the domestic cattle to wander around in the fields, perplexed and bewildered, v. 18, he is also given to predict an apocalyptic day of judgement yet to be, more dark and foreboding than anything this world has ever known, v. 15.

From other Old Testament prophecies, and from what we now have in the New Testament, we know that the day of the Lord will be an extended period of time when God will humble all nations, and judge everything that is offensive to Himself and to His Son, with a view to establishing His kingdom on earth in righteousness. Not until then will His will be done on earth as it is in heaven. Those in our day who mistakenly believe that it is part of their commission to restore the kingdom and establish a world-wide Christian dominion, would do well to recognise that this is something which has been entrusted to the Son of Man, and that He will accomplish it at His coming with power and great glory.

Many details of this ultimate 'day of the Lord' are disclosed in the last of all biblical prophecies, the Book of the Revelation of Jesus Christ, chapters 6-19. But even from Joel's short prophecy we can gather the following: (i) It will come as a destruction from the Almighty, 1.15; (ii) So great and terrible will it be that the question is raised, 'who can abide it'? 2.11; (iii) It will be marked by portents in the heavens and in the earth, 2.30, 31; (iv) Then will the nations of the earth be brought to the valley of decision to be smitten in battle by the Lord, 3.9-14.

4. The Lord's Army Pictured, 2.1-11

This section opens with a call for the trumpet to be blown in Zion and an alarm to be sounded, and it reminds us of what is written in Numbers 10.1-10. The silver trumpets were used originally for the calling together of the assembly, and for the journeyings of the camps of Israel. Then, when oppressed by an enemy, the priests were to blow an alarm that they might be remembered before the Lord and saved by Him. This was to be an ordinance for ever throughout their generations.

The trumpet call in Zion, v. 1, would probably indicate that the ravages caused by the locusts in the fields and countryside were about to be felt in a more threatening way in the towns and villages. In the light of the peril which was now literally on their doorsteps, the prophet calls upon all the inhabitants of the land to tremble. None was exempt from the call to repent, for the judgement was upon every one without exception because of their wilful disobedience to God's word, of which as a nation they had been made the special custodians, Rom. 3.2.

The description given here of the locust plague is unsurpassed for its graphic imagery. It seems to depict a day's march of the myriads of

invading insect forces, from the first light of early morning spread upon
the mountains, v. 2, to the time when the stars appear, but withdraw
their shining because the clouds of locusts blot them out, v. 10. They are
pictured as the dawn's rays overspreading the mountains, and as a
raging fire in the burning heat of the day that leaves a land, once so
fertile that it could be likened to the garden of Eden, as bare, scorched
earth covered with ashes when the fire has passed, v. 3. These invaders
of the land are likened to war-horses in full charge with the noise of
battle in their nostrils. The sound of rumbling chariots, and the crackling
of a raging fire devouring stubble can be heard as they run ahead and
scale every obstacle they encounter. Nothing puts them out of step or
causes them to break ranks. They are divinely disciplined, for after all
they are the Lord's army, v. 11. They cause terror and anguish among
the inhabitants of the land, while accompanying, ominous signs of
heaven's displeasure give further warning of the day of the Lord. Let
everyone that will not worship and obey God beware, the wrath of God
may be long delayed, but Joel's message is plain, the wrath will come,
and who is there who knows not the Saviour, who can escape it?

We suggest that all of this should be read, if possible, in a version
setting the lines in metrical parallelism in order to gain more of its
impact. See the *Newberry Bible*, large type handy reference edition; *The
Revised Authorised Version*; the *NASB* reference edition, or similar.

5. Spare Thy People, O Lord, 2.12–17

Here, for the one and only time in Joel's prophecy, we hear the phrase,
so common among the prophets, 'saith the Lord'. That is not to say that
the rest of the prophecy is any less the word of the Lord, for we have
noted in the introduction that the whole book constitutes 'The word of
the Lord that came to Joel'.

Perhaps what is intended here is that we should note the importance
of this particular section which concludes the first part of the prophecy,
from 1.1–2.17, and brings to its culmination the impassioned appeal of
the prophet to make the people aware of the cause of their dire trouble.
Above all, he desires to call them back to God whom they have forsaken:
'yet even now, saith the Lord, turn ye unto Me with all your heart . . .
rend your heart . . . and turn unto the Lord your God', vv. 12, 13.

In spite of God's severity, the evidence of His displeasure with His
people, what He says of Himself in the days of the last of the Old
Testament prophets is always true, namely, 'I am the Lord, I change

not, therefore ye sons of Jacob are not consumed'. And this being so, Joel is able to appeal to them once more on the ground that their God 'is gracious and merciful, slow to anger, and of great kindness, and repenteth him of the evil', v. 13. This final appeal echoes the words of Moses, 'When thou art in tribulation, and all these things are come upon thee . . . if thou turn to the Lord thy God, and shalt be obedient to his voice: (for the Lord thy God is a merciful God;) he will not forsake thee, neither destroy thee, nor forget the covenant with thy fathers which he swore unto them', Deut. 4.30, 31. God is predictable. He is always consistent with Himself and His word. His people can surely count upon Him to 'return and repent, and leave a blessing behind him', v. 14, if they will but respond to His call, issued here for the last time in its fullest terms. First the drunkards and drinkers of wine had been addressed, 1.5; then the husbandmen and vinedressers were singled out, 1.11; the priests were then called upon to lament and howl, 1.13, and to gather the elders and all the inhabitants of the land to a solemn assembly, 1.14; and, finally, the whole of the people, as a sanctified congregation, even the elders, children, babes, bridegroom and bride are summoned.

In particular, the priests are instructed to weep between the porch and the altar, that is, in the very precincts of the temple, and to say on behalf of the congregation, 'Spare thy people, O Lord, and give not thine heritage to reproach, that the heathen should rule over them. Wherefore should they say among thy people, where is their God?' vv. 15–17.

The supreme concern of the Lord's people should always be the Lord's honour. For if His own people, whom He has separated unto Himself, and for whom He has done such great things, become subjugated to the heathen, (i.e. overwhelmed by the world), it could justly be said of them, 'Where is their God?' And that would not only be a reproach to the people, but a blasphemous expression of contempt for their God. Hence the people's cry from the heart was to be, 'Spare thy people, O Lord', that once more His mighty works on behalf of His people might become the occasion of His fear coming upon the nations of the earth, as it had done long before on Egypt, Eden, Moab and the Canaanites.

How great, too, the need for all Christians today to walk worthily of their calling, having been separated by the cross of Christ from this present evil world, and being alive unto God as those who have been raised from among the dead. If we seek not the things which are above where Christ sits on the right hand of God it may even be said of us that we have a name that we live, and yet are dead, Rev. 3.1. What a terrible indictment! Yet this is how a worldly church is addressed by Him who has the seven spirits of God, and the seven stars, Rev. 3.1–6, and who still walks in the midst of the seven golden lampstands, i.e. the churches.

6. The Great Reversal of Events, 2.18–27

Another has written, 'Here occurs the peripeteia of the book. Hitherto it has been a description of the calamity, and an eager call to repentance. Now – the fast day has doubtless been held – we are told how Jehovah intervened, heard, forgave and opened up a wonderful prospect of judgement and deliverance'. The RV does a great service by marking this, and by putting the verbs in verses 18 and 19 into the past tense.

We have reached at last, therefore, the watershed of the book. After reviewing the old dried up watercourse, as it were, we are now about to follow 'a river, the streams whereof shall make glad the city of God', Ps. 46.4. 'Then, (i.e. after true repentance for unspecified sins had been shown by a people humbled under God's mighty hand) was the Lord jealous for his land, and had pity on His people. And the Lord answered and said unto his people', vv. 18, 19, 26, RV. There then follows what the Lord had to say, though not to the prophet or to the priests, but directly to His people, vv. 18, 19, 26, 27. This is followed by comforting words to the land, v. 21; to the beasts of the field, v. 22; and lastly, to the children of Zion, v. 23.

Frequently in scripture we find God making unconditional promises. It was so in the case of Abram as recorded in Genesis 12.2, 3; 13.15–17; 17.6–8; and also of Moses. Again, it is true with reference to the new covenant which the Lord will make with the house of Israel and with the house of Judah, as foretold in Jeremiah 31.31–34 and Hebrews 8.8–12. Here, through Joel He does the same, 'Behold I will send you corn and wine, and oil, and ye shall be satisfied therewith; . . . . and I will remove far off from you the northern army', (lit. the northerner) vv. 19, 20; and I will 'restore to you the years that the locust hath eaten', v. 25. In the near future the Lord promised to undo all the damage recently done by the locusts, and send the people corn, oil and wine to their hearts' content. In the reference to 'the northerner', v. 20, the prophet, looking beyond the locust invasion of the land, sees a future aggressor who will attack from the north, cf. Jer. 1.13; Zeph. 2.13. Now, unless we are ready to compare scripture with scripture, and bear in mind the words of 2 Peter 1.20, 'that no prophecy of the scripture is of any private interpretation', i.e. is self-interpreting, but rather is dependent on the Holy Spirit's intent in the whole range of prophecy; we shall often fail to grasp a point that is made, for want of seeing its relationship to the prophetic word as a whole.

In his book, *Prophetic Profile* (published by Precious Seed, 1992) G. B. FYFE writes about this 'northerner', pointing out that he goes under several names or titles in the scriptures, viz.

a He is called the 'Assyrian' in Isaiah 10; Micah 5, etc.
b He is termed the 'King of the fierce countenance', Daniel 8.23-25.
c He is 'the little horn', Daniel 8.9, but not the 'little horn' of Daniel 7.8 who foreshadows the Roman dictator.
d He is the 'King of the North', Daniel 11.40.

Although he will be a greater scourge of the land and people in a coming day than the locusts had been in Joel's day, the Lord will remove and destroy him, and make his end to be only a very unsavoury memory. As the Lord's appointed instrument of chastisement it is said, 'he hath done great things', a past tense indicating the certainty of what he will accomplish in a future day. But his things will be eclipsed by the wondrous things the Lord will yet do that His people will never again have cause to be ashamed, vv. 26, 27.

In the paragraph verses 21-27 the prophet is so full of faith and confidence in what he believes the Lord will yet do for His people that he exults in a wonderfully triumphant outburst of praise, calling upon the people to fear no more, but to be glad and rejoice, and to praise the name of the Lord their God, who will reverse their evil circumstances and bless them with the greatest of blessings, even His presence in their midst – Jehovah Shammah of Leviticus 26.3-12.

7. 'It shall come to pass afterward', 2.28-32

In the Hebrew scriptures verses 28-32 form a third chapter.

We come now to the well known passage concerning the outpouring of the Spirit which is quoted in the New Testament, first by the apostle Peter on the day of Pentecost, Acts 2.17-21, and then in part by the apostle Paul in his letter to the saints in Rome some twenty-five or so years later, Rom. 10.13. That this scripture was not fulfilled in all its details in apostolic times, nor has been even up to this present time, need not trouble us. The prophetic word frequently contains Messianic passages which have an initial, partial fulfilment, and a long-delayed complete realization. For example, when the Lord Jesus read from Isaiah 61 in the synagogue in Nazareth, what was fulfilled that day caused Him to conclude His reading part way through a verse. 'The day of vengeance of our God' had not then come; but come it finally will, for the scripture cannot be broken. Similarly, in Isaiah's minutely detailed Messianic passage referring to Jehovah's suffering servant, 52.13–53.12, certain portions were literally fulfilled by the first appearing on earth of the Lord Jesus, viz. 52.14; 53.2–5, 7–9, 12b; while others, 'made more sure', 2 Pet. 1.19, RV, will as certainly be fulfilled to the letter at His second advent, viz. 52.13; 53.10b–12a. Then will the suffering servant (Ben-oni) be seen to be the all-conquering warrior of God's right hand (Benjamin).

'Afterward' has been translated 'in the last days', or 'in the latter days', and invariably refers to the days of the Messiah. The predicted outpouring of the Spirit no doubt found an initial fulfilment 'when the day of Pentecost was fully come', Acts 2.1; but that outpouring was not then upon all flesh, and the accompanying signs were also restricted to a partial exhibition of what will ultimately be seen to herald the coming of the Lord to Zion. At Pentecost, the early disciples in Jerusalem were in one Spirit baptized into one body, and the church of this present dispensation was brought into being, see 1 Cor. 12.13. That historical event is no more repeatable than is the crucifixion and the resurrection of our Lord. However, it is not without significance that the context in which the apostle Paul's quotation of verse 32 occurs in Romans 10.13 has to do with the great longing he had for the conversion of his brethren, his kinsmen according to the flesh who are Israelites, 9.3, 4. He points out that the righteousness of faith is available to all who believe, whether Jew or Greek, and quotes Deuteronomy 30.12–14; Isaiah 28.16 and Joel 2.32 to confirm to the Jews in particular that the gospel he preached was consistent with their own scriptures. So it is, and so it will prove to be when, in the future, 'all Israel shall be saved', Rom. 11.26, for 'whosoever shall call upon the name of the Lord shall be saved', cf. Isa. 46.13; 59.20; Obad. 17.

There was, of course in Joel's day, nothing that escaped from the hordes of locusts, 2.3, but in the great day of the Lord there will be a remnant in Mount Zion and in Jerusalem that will call upon the Name of the Lord, and He will be their deliverer. Or, as the RV translates, 'there shall be those that escape', the very word used in 2.3. So, whether the remnant in Judah, the nation of Israel, or 'whosoever', the wonderful fact is that to call by faith on the Name of the Lord will always ensure salvation. 'Let us, therefore, call upon Him while He is near'.

8. The Valley of Jehoshaphat, or Decision, 3.1-8

'For', continues that part of the prophecy which is taken up with the things which shall take place 'afterward', or 'in the last days', 2.28. The whole of chapter 3 projects our thoughts forward to still future events concerning Judah and Jerusalem, and the hostile nations with which the Lord will reckon because of their ill treatment of His people.

The Lord has always had a peculiar interest in His chosen people Israel. They have been in His mind since the scattering of mankind upon the face of the earth, Gen. 11.9, for they are His portion, the lot of His inheritance, Deut. 32.10. Having kept them as the apple of His eye, is it any marvel that He will requite their enemies for scattering them among the nations? Their destiny is to be on high above all nations of the earth, Deut. 28.1; while over them the Messiah will be the Lord's firstborn, higher than the kings of the earth, Ps. 89.27. God will not be thwarted nor allow His word to fail.

So it is that the prophet predicts what the Lord will yet do in gathering all nations, and bringing them down into the 'valley of Jehoshaphat' (Jah is judge), vv. 2, 12, or, 'the valley of decision', v. 14. As mountains symbolically suggest prospects of enlargement, exaltation and blessing, so valleys convey thoughts of humiliation, reckoning and judgement. And in this valley of reckoning the Lord will fully recompense those who have been ruthless in their heartless disregard of His people, bartering little boys and girls to procure prostitutes and intoxicants for the gratification of their sinful lusts and pleasures. Tyre and Zidon, and all the coasts of Palestine through which this sordid traffic was shipped will not escape, for the eye of the Lord misses nothing that is done on earth, whether good or evil. 'The Lord looketh from heaven; and beholdeth all the sons of men', Ps. 33.13. The desecration and plundering of the temple in Jerusalem for holy vessels and treasures for the adornment of heathen places of worship will on that day mean for the guilty peoples, as for a wicked Babylonian monarch before them, that the writing will be on the wall, 'thou art weighed in the balances and found wanting', Dan. 5.27. A swift and just recompense will be fully meted out, 'For the Lord hath spoken', v. 8. Let us also consider our ways, 'whatsoever a man soweth that shall he also reap', Gal. 6.7, and 'let the wicked forsake his way, and the unrighteous man his thoughts: and let him return unto the Lord, and he will have mercy upon him; and to our God, for he will abundantly pardon', Isa. 55.7.

9. The Nations are Challenged to do Battle, 3.9–17

The Lord Jesus said to His disciples that in the end time 'ye shall hear of wars and rumours of wars: see that ye be not troubled: for all these things must come to pass, but the end is not yet', Matt. 24.6. Such wars we are told would be the result of nations and kingdoms being in conflict with one another, 24.7. What is envisaged here by Joel is different, for it will be a great battle between the Lord Himself and 'the Gentiles', v. 9; 'all ye heathen', v. 11. It will not be a challenge thrown down by the enemies of His people, but quite the reverse, for, in a public proclamation by His own heralds, the command will be carried to the nations to meet the Lord in the place of His choosing, v. 12. There, in 'the valley of decision', v. 14, the nations are to bring their mighty men, equipped and armed to do battle. It will be a trial of strength both fierce and decisive, and in preparation for it they are told to concentrate their industries, usually devoted for peaceful purposes, into a total war machine.

In our own time have we not witnessed how nations are able to arm themselves by modern technological means with the most sophisticated weapons capable of delivering destruction by bomb or guided missile almost anywhere at will? But in that day there will be witnessed a battle between puny man and Almighty God: how totally one-sided it will be! As to the Lord's armoury, all that is said is that 'the Lord shall roar out of Zion, and utter his voice from Jerusalem', v. 16. Have we considered what awesome power there is when God speaks? At the first, did He not command light to shine out of darkness, and bring the world into being by the word of His power? At Sinai, when His voice was heard by Israel, did not the earth shake and all the people tremble? And let us not forget that the future, antichrist, called 'another beast' in Revelation 13.11, and that 'man of sin (lawlessness)' in 2 Thessalonians 2.3, to whom Satan will lend his power will be destroyed 'with the breath of his mouth', when 'the Lord Jesus shall be revealed from heaven . . . taking vengeance on them that know not God, and that obey not the gospel of our Lord Jesus Christ', 2 Thess. 1.7, 8.

However, the battle envisaged by Joel will ensure the overturn of the northern power, the Assyrian, and will prepare for the subsequent destruction of both Beast and False Prophet, and the nations they head up in the great battle of Armageddon, under the sixth bowl of Revelation 16.12–16. Well might the Psalmist have indited the second Psalm as a warning for that coming day, every word of which all men should weigh carefully, lest they 'perish from the way, when his wrath is kindled but a little'.

10. Blessing following Judgement, 3.18–21

Having introduced the future outpouring of the Spirit by the familiar prophetic expression, 'And it shall come to pass', at 2.28, on two more occasions the prophet uses the same phrase, first to assure those of Judah and Jerusalem of deliverance in that day if they 'call on the name of the Lord', 2.32; and then to forecast the certain, glorious future for Judah and the ultimate desolation of her foes, 3.18.

The Lord's purpose regarding His people on earth will surely be realized. Every promise He has made concerning them will be fulfilled. Despite their guilt, culminating in the rejection of the Messiah, He 'will cleanse their blood that he has not cleansed', v. 21, and perfect what concerns them.

Perhaps we can see, though Joel's language is poetic in the extreme and calls for restraint in its interpretation, that the once devastated heights shall again luxuriate with vines, and support its 'cattle on a thousand hills'; while the dried-up valleys and watercourses shall sparkle with flowing rivers, making the land to be what it was at the first, 'a land flowing with milk and honey'. Then will the Lord also cause a new thing to be known, for 'a fountain shall come forth of the house of the Lord, and shall water the valley of Shittim', v. 18, cf. Ezek. 47.1; Zech. 14.8. In this respect the city of the Great King will become as the garden of the Lord before sin entered and man was driven out, Gen. 2.10, a scene of unimagined delight and the source of unparalleled blessing. We should not baulk at such a transformation, though we know from its history how it has been trodden down; in that day there will be no city on earth to compare with it 'for the Lord dwelleth in Zion', v. 21. Amen.

CHAPTER THREE

THE PROPHECY OF AMOS

by BERNARD OSBORNE

Introduction

THE PROPHET WAS FROM TEKOA, just south east of Bethlehem. He came from Judah, but prophesied in Israel. He was a herdsman, 1.1, and a gatherer of sycamore fruit, 7.14. While he was pursuing his daily occupation, the Lord called him, 7.14,15. In obedience to his call he left Judah for Israel. There at Bethel he gave his message. He had been prepared in secret by God as so many of God's great men. He was not of the school of the prophets, had received no professional training, 7.14,15. God's servants are determined by the law of His choice, and not by any human succession or profession. He who took David from the sheepfolds, now chose Amos to declare His message of impending judgement.

DATE. Amos prophesied two years before the earthquake which happened in Uzziah's reign, cf. Zech.14.5. Uzziah was king of Judah. In Israel Jeroboam II was king. He prophesied around about 765 BC.

TIMES. Jeroboam's reign was one of peace and prosperity. The material prosperity had a disastrous effect upon the character of the people. They sank into a life of profligacy, luxury, cruelty and deceit. The poor were oppressed and justice was lacking. Immorality was shamelessly practised. They lived in the enjoyment of the material with very little real thought for the spiritual.

MESSAGE. One of almost unrelieved judgement and punishment. He gains their ear by proclaiming judgement against surrounding nations, knowing the readiness of men to listen to the sins and sentences of others. But they too were to be judged, and more severely than outside nations, because they had sinned against the light of God's revelation. The threats of doom are interspersed with exhortations to 'seek the Lord', and the promise of Israel's ultimate restoration comes at the end of the book, 9.11–15.

Structure

1 Prologue, 1.1,2
2 Proclamations of Judgements on the Nations, 1.3–2.16
3 Exposition of the Transgressions of Israel, 3.1–6.14.
    a) First Discourse, 3.1–15.
    b) Second Discourse, 4.1–13.
    c) Third Discourse, 5.1–6.14.
4 Visions of the Judgement of Israel, 7.1–9.10.
5 Epilogue, 9.11–15.

(1) Prologue 1.1, 2

'The words of Amos'; yet the context shows that the words were not
strictly his own, but had a divine origin. They were words which he
'saw'. The Hebrew word 'saw' is not of mere sight, but of a vision given
by God. Amos was but the human organ through whom God spoke, cf.
Jer.25.30. Amos also emphasizes his own nothingness – he was 'among
the herdsmen'.

It was in the reign of Jeroboam II, the grandson of Jehu. His kingdom
had been weak on his accession, but during his 41-year reign its territory
had been regained, and so had its prosperity, cf. 2 Kgs.14.27,28. That
prosperity did not bring the people back to God and Amos was sent to
warn them.

The earthquake referred to must have been one of great severity for it
was recalled in Zechariah's day, cf. Zech.14.5. Amos's prophecy is
dated by it.

'The words of Amos', then, but it is the Lord who 'roars from Zion and
utters His voice from Jerusalem'. He speaks from Zion, for His earthly
dwelling place was in the temple at Zion, and His power was manifested
in Jerusalem. Here was an important censure of the schismatic
sanctuaries of Israel – they were not where Jehovah had placed His
Name.

It is from Zion the Lord 'roars'. The figure of a lion was in the
prophet's mind, especially the loud cry with which a lion springs upon
its prey. In like manner the prophet implies the Lord had burst into
human affairs in judgement. It is the sound of near destruction that
Amos hears roaring from Zion. The day of reckoning had come. The roar
of judgement came only when the patience of mercy had long, but
vainly, waited for repentance and amendment of life. This is the significance of the repeated phrase 'for three transgressions and for four'. The
phrase implied that offences had multiplied, and that the measure of
guilt was full. On man's part the cup of sinfulness had been filled to the
brim, and on God's part there had been no hasty action. The first transgression well merited divine wrath, but mercy waited and watched.
God gives ample opportunity for repentance before His judgement falls.
It never falls until sin has become so complete that there is no room for
the exercise of mercy. When that is so, His judgement inevitably falls.

The Lord will also 'utter his voice'. Here is the figure of rolling
thunder, cf. Ps. 18.13; Job 36.29-32; Joel 2.11. There would be drought
which would dry up the pasturelands of Israel, even those of Carmel
itself. Little wonder the shepherd would lament, for if Carmel is to

wither through drought, the most fruitful hill in the north, what other pastures could there be left in the land? Israel appeared to be feeding in rich pastures, and all seemed outwardly well, but that was not the case. Judgement was imminent.

(2) Proclamations of Judgement upon the Nations, 1.3–2.16

To Amos God was the God of the whole world. Not Israel alone, but every nation was responsible to Him. None of the nations outside Israel and Judah had received any special revelation of God or of His law. He had never sent prophets to them. They had no scriptures, but that did not mean they were not accountable to God, cf. Rom. 1.18–20; 2.14,15. Amos presents them as nations under judgement. They were without special revelation, but not without moral accountability; they were without the law written on tables of stone, but not without the law written on their consciences. Each person has a conscience, and that is enough.

Amos did not complain about their idolatry, cf. Acts 17.30. What he complained of was their treatment of, and crimes against, fellow human beings, their brutality, their treachery, their cruelty towards them. They did not need the scriptures to tell them these things were wrong – their consciences should have done so. Here, then, the law written in the conscience is spelled out in terms of human relationships, and not merely relationships to Israel. It concerns what they have done to one another as well. In each case the formula is repeated – 'for three transgressions . . . and for four'. In His longsuffering God had waited again and again, looking for some evidence of repentance before finally dealing in wrath, but there was none. Judgement followed, and in each case the judgement was not to be revoked.

The first two nations are characterized by gross cruelty, and the general relationships of life are violated. That the second pair are brothers adds an extra dimension to their cruelty. The particular relationships of life are being violated. In the third pair cruelty was wreaked on the unborn babe, destroying thereby the future, and on a corpse, thus desecrating the past. Here violation was done to the special claims of life, the attitude of the strong to the weak.

Syria, 1.3–5

An example of the cruelty of Syria is given,' the threshing of Gilead'. The reference is probably to the atrocities perpetrated by Hazael when he invaded Gilead, cf. 2 Kgs. 8.12. It was an incredibly barbarous action of which they were guilty. Heavy threshing boards, studded with sharp pieces of basalt, were drawn over the quivering bodies of the victims. Retribution was now to come upon them. Jehovah was not merely the God of Israel. He was Sovereign of the universe, and the nations were accountable to Him for their conduct. The Syrian defences would be completely swept away and the royal line destroyed. The bar of the gate of Damascus would be broken and nothing would stop the enemy entering. They would be cut off and carried away captive, cf. 2 Kgs. 16.9.

Philistia, 1.6–8

Gaza was the southernmost Philistine city. It was a fertile spot on the edge of the desert on the trade route between Syria and Egypt, a trading centre, and pre-eminently the centre of the slave trade. Amos condemns their slave traffic. They carried away entire populations. There may be references here to raids on Israel and Judah, without excuse of war, to procure slaves for Edom, cf. 2 Chron. 21.16, 17; Joel 3.4–6. God would destroy the fortifications of Gaza, and cut off the other cities.

Phoenicia, 1.9, 10

This nation also engaged in the slave trade, 'the whole captivity' again being 'the whole people'. It also broke the covenant of brothers. This probably refers to a covenant between Hiram and Solomon, and earlier, between David and Hiram, cf. 2 Sam. 5.11; 1 Kgs. 5.1,12. Here was a relationship formed and sealed with a covenant. The slave trade was a breach of treaty obligations. The word had been given, and the word had not been kept.

Edom, 1.11, 12

Edom and Israel are frequently spoken of as 'brothers', cf. Deut. 2.4; 23.7; Obad. 10–12. Whenever Edom saw 'his brother' weak, he attacked him, cf. 2 Chron. 20.10, 11. This unbrotherly attitude, adopted too frequently by Edom, was the basis of his offence, cf. Num. 20.14–21. All through their history Edom sided with Israel's enemies, cf. 1 Sam. 14.47; 2 Sam. 8.14; 2 Chron. 21.8–10; Ps. 60.9. The perpetual and unrelenting nature of the enmity is stressed. Edom 'cast off all pity'. Edom deadened the appeal of compassion. Here was hatred nurtured in the heart.

Ammon, 1.13–15

This was a brother nation to the Moabites, cf. Gen. 19.37. To enlarge their border they made war on unborn children. Their defeat was to be utter and complete, cf. Jer. 49.1–3; Zeph. 2.9; Ezek. 25.5. Cruelty inevitably meets with retribution. Nothing moves God so much as wanton cruelty to the helpless, for it is He who is called the Father of the fatherless and the defender of the widow's cause, cf. Ps. 68.5.

Moab, 2.1–3

Moab was also a descendant of Lot. If the Ammonites were guilty of declaring war on unborn children, the Moabites were guilty of declaring war on a corpse. It was against Israel's enemy, Edom, but is nonetheless condemned by Amos as being a crime against humanity. It was commonly regarded in the ancient world as sacriligious to deny burial to anyone. The outrageous treatment adopted by the Moabites was reserved for criminals, cf. Gen. 38.24; Lev. 20.14. The day Moab opened the Edomite tomb he signed his own death warrant, 'Moab shall die', v. 2. His action was unpardonable. His prospect was hopeless. He would disappear as a power. Sin rebounds and none more so than to take revenge. It has no place in human behaviour, much less in the behaviour of God's children.

Judah, 2.4, 5

Amos included Israel and Judah among the nations. They had thought of themselves as separated in some privileged way from the other nations. Amos enforced the truth that God is reigning over all nations, and doing so upon the same principles. The greater the light, the greater the responsibility.

The charge now was not of an offence against humanity, but against God Himself. The other nations had sinned 'without law'; they had gone against the dictates of conscience. But Judah knew God as the Lord, the covenant God. They had the written law, the revelation of His will, and despised it. They forsook this for 'lies', idols which led them astray. They followed their fathers who were devoted to idols, cf. Deut. 4.3; 8.19; 11.28; 13.2,3; Jer. 2.5, 8, 23, etc. Above all nations Judah should have known the will of God and the standards He had set for man. They were the repositories of the law; the divine oracles had been entrusted to them. Yet they had rejected His law, being no longer prepared to accept that divine standards applied to their lives and conduct.

These were the people of God whom He had signally blessed, and they could turn away from Him and treat His will as of no account. It is still so. God's word has been taught, and His claims made clear, yet in general men have hardened their hearts and refused to listen to His voice. Judgement was promised, 2 Kings 25.8–9 sees the fulfilment.

Israel, 2.6–16

Having described and denounced the sins of Israel's neighbours, and probably stirred up Israel's indignation against them, Amos now comes to his main purpose, the denunciation of Israel's own sins. He lists them in verses 6–8. With what surprise Israel would have listened to Amos. Note the sins of which they were guilty—covetousness, material things taking precedence in life; indifference and oppression making them insensible to the rights of others; self importance and the unrestrained promotion of self advantage. For those sins the heathen had been condemned. Here were sins against others. They were also sins against revelation and light.

The case in verse 6 concerns the 'righteous' and the 'poor'. The word 'righteous' is used here in a forensic sense. Here is someone innocent of the charge, cf. Deut. 25.1. He was in debt through no fault of his own. 'On account of a pair of sandals', a paltry debt equivalent in worth to a pair of sandals, would not save him from bondage at the hands of an oppressive ruler. For a trifling article or debt the hardhearted creditor would sell his debtor, cf. Matt. 18.25.

The poor man cast a handful of dust on his head in token of his misery, v. 7, but the greedy landowner is after that dust, so great is his land hunger! The meek are turned aside, the humble follower of the Lord. Hindrances are placed in his way, his purposes thwarted, and all to lead him into difficulties. The turning away the meek foreshadowed the unjust judgement of Him who was the meek and lowly One; the selling of the righteous for a paltry sum foreshadowed the selling of the Holy One and Just for thirty pieces of silver.

Self gratification had become their main aim in life rather than obedience to God. God had shown mercy to this people; they did not show it to others. They did not reflect God's compassion to them. We cannot be right with God unless what He is to us provides the pattern for what we are to others.

Then there was the sin of immorality. Reverence was due from the son to the father, example from the father to the son. But now the father was an example of evil to his son. The reference has probably to do with idolatrous worship, cf. Hos. 4.14. Priestesses engaged in heathen worship, which involved temple prostitution, were yet regarded by the heathen as 'holy women'. These Canaanitish practices had been allowed to erode the distinctive standards and practices of Israel's holy religion. The word 'same' should be omitted, and then there is a further twist in the picture. Amos may well be regarding the Israelite males as womanizers, running after women, father and son. In any case, the father committed adultery, being unfaithful to his marriage vow, and the son contravened the law against fornication. They both alike transgressed the divine prohibition in the use of 'holy women' in the worship of Jehovah. They sinned against revelation, cf. Exod. 20.14; Deut. 23.17. The words 'go in' suggest 'resort to', 'betake themselves openly to' – they had lost all sense that they were disobeying the commandments of their God.

They did it to profane God's holy Name. When people do that which they know to be offensive to God, the Bible recognizes their purpose. Behind all deliberate, knowing sin there is this careless effrontery towards God. This was an open flagrant offence against God, cf. Lev. 22.32. The sins of God's people are a reproach unto Himself, cf. 2 Sam. 12.14; Ezek. 36.23; Rom. 2.24.

The money wrung from those who could not pay was spent in rioting and feasting, v. 8. Note where they did this,' in the house of their God'. They lay down beside the altar on garments taken as pledges. The large, outer garment which served as a covering at night was taken as a pledge, but was regarded as the property of the creditor, cf. Deut. 24.12, 13. It was to be returned at night for the debtor to sleep on. This was not happening. The 'condemned' refers to those 'fined' or 'mulcted'. The fine imposed was spent in buying wine which they drank in the house of their god. Extortion was carried on under the guise of religion.

The sins and ingratitude of the people were aggravated by a recital of the divine mercy, v. 9. Note here the recurrence of the personal pronoun. It emphasizes that salvation is all of God; man has contributed neither power nor merit. God had given them victory over their enemies, the Amorite, that is, the people of Canaan. Not only were they huge, but numerous, cf. Num. 13.32, 33. It was not by their own strength that Israel prevailed. It was God who defeated their foes. He had redeemed His people, v. 10, and led them in the 40 years' wanderings, even though those wanderings were the result of their rebellion. He did not forsake them. He brought them into the land of promised inheritance, and even then He did not finish with them. He not only provided for their material needs, but also for their spiritual needs. He gave prophets to them to show them His will, and Nazarites to demonstrate consecrated living. And what had they been? Slaves, unable to redeem themselves from Egypt, maintain their walk with God, or overthrow the Amorite. Their salvation was entirely of God. Their disobedience to God was inexcusable.

The response of Israel, v. 12, was to silence the prophets and seduce the Nazarites from loyalty by breaking their vow. When men set themselves deliberately to corrupt the pure, and to silence the prophets, they are ripe for God's judgement.

The Lord's reaction was that His people had forfeited His favour. The same God who redeemed them, vv. 9, 10, now says 'I will press you down'. It is the same God who speaks here as in verses 6-11. God has turned to afflict His people. He proposes to do so by an enemy much too strong for them, and before whom nothing will avail. The punishment will be comprehensive, none will escape. The mills of God grind slow, but nothing will stop them. To refuse to listen to the divine appeals and to follow (resolutely) self-chosen courses can have only one end.

(3) Exposition of the Transgressions of Israel, 3.1–6.14

From chapter 3.1 to the end of chapter 6 there are three discourses by the prophet. Each discourse begins with the words, 'Hear this word', 3.1; 4.1; 5.1.

First Discourse, 3.1–15

This is addressed to people who are steeped in religious complacency because of their inherited privileges. They boasted in the covenant relationship with Jehovah, and ignored the ethical implication, declining to live in a manner honouring to their Benefactor. Amos now states that they have misunderstood God's love. The Lord had singled Israel out for special love, bringing them from Egypt's bondage, vv. 1, 2. God was the Father of the nation. He had adopted them at the Exodus to be His son, cf. Exod. 4.22. They had been brought up out of bondage in Egypt and brought to the promised land. They knew the blessing of salvation. But not only that. 'You only have I known' taught them the privilege of election. Israel of all the nations was placed in this special relationship to Him. Israel was the only nation the Lord 'knew' in this special sense, and visited with the tokens of His friendship. Out of all the nations, He had chosen them. They were God's elect in that God had made a covenant with Abraham to be his God and the God of his descendants, cf. Gen. 17.7; Rom. 9.10–13.

There was, however, the question of their iniquities, v. 2. Having great privileges did not mean licence to live as they pleased. Christians can think the same way as they did. They know they are saved and secure, but their lives are no different from the unsaved around them. Thus Israel returned His love, after what He had done for them.

God's election of Israel was no guarantee of immunity from punishment for wrongdoing. Indeed their nearness to God called for punishment for their iniquities. Note the 'therefore', v. 2. Their privileges but increase their responsibilities and make them more accountable than their ignorant heathen neighbours. Here is a divine principle worth noting–responsibility flows from relationship. Because God had separated Israel from the nations, and had taken them into covenant relationship with Himself, they were expected to give that obedience which their favoured position demanded; otherwise they must be the special objects of His disciplinary dealing. The divine election of Israel did not ensure against punishment, but the close relationship into which the Lord had entered with Israel, broken and violated by sin, demanded a correspondingly great punishment. Israel's sins were not those of other nations. They were sins against light and love. Mercy, favour and instruction had been lavished upon them. Thus they had more to answer for; their guilt was greater, cf. Luke 12.48. So it is of the Christian. He, too, claims God as his Father. He, too, has been redeemed from bondage. He, too, has been the subject of God's electing grace, cf. Eph. 1.4. He is called to walk worthy of his exalted vocation; if he does not, he incurs the Father's displeasure, cf. Eph. 4.1; John 14.15; 1 Cor. 10.14. He cannot sin with impunity. Sin is desperately serious among the people of God. Like the Israelites the Christian may argue that if His love is so great, does holiness matter after all? Since He chose, will He not keep, come what may? Certainly God does not revoke covenants or break promises, but here we are dealing with a discipline that chastises, disciplining those who are in the family, but whose sins need the Father's loving chastisement, cf. Heb. 12.7ff. The Father requires His children to be perfect as He is perfect, cf. Matt. 5.48.

If Israel questions what is happening to them, let them remember that nothing happens without a reason. Every effect has its cause. So, communion proves agreement, v. 3; the lion roaring proves the prey taken, v. 4; the fall of a bird proves the presence of bait, v. 5; the spring of the snare proves the bird is taken, v. 5; the trumpet proves alarm, v. 6; and calamity in the city proves Jehovah. So their suffering had a reason, 'the

Lord hath done it', v. 6. It was His punishing for sin. At the same time, if they were questioning Amos's authority, why he had spoken as he did, there must be an adequate cause. There was! His message had been given him by God. The sum of the matter is found in verse 8. Jehovah has roared – therefore fear; Jehovah has spoken – therefore prophesy. If God has not spoken, then one man's guess is as good as another, but if He has spoken, as He has in His word, that at once settles everything for the one who fears Him. God has revealed His will in His word.

What had Amos been saying? Seeing two men walking together the inference would be that they had made an appointment to do so. No one would travel with a stranger alone. So if Amos had spoken the word of God, it must be because he was walking with God. His utterances were due to a divine and irresistible impulse, v. 3. The sound of a lion's roar, or a young lion's growl, had a cause. The lion had caught its prey, the young lion had its food. In both cases the sound indicated something had happened. The inference is that Amos's voice is a sign that God's judgement has come, v. 4. No bird would be caught without bait. No trap would spring up unless a bird had been caught. So when the punishment came it would not be without cause. Their iniquities were the reason, v. 5. A city is warned of impending danger by the watchman's trumpet. So the prophet's warning of coming punishment should have awakened the people of Israel out of their complacency and indifference. If disaster was about to fall upon Israel, it must be the working of God, and for good reason, v. 6. If a prophet prophesies it must be because God has inspired him. God had always sent them messengers to alert them to His actions and their required response. Amos was one such messenger. He had been instructed of God in His purpose, and they ought to obey his message. People fear at the roar of a lion, but Amos had heard the voice of God. He must speak. He knew what judgement held for Israel. He would not be silent. Neither should the Christian, enlightened as to coming judgement, be silent. He must not be dumb in view of the danger confronting a guilty world, vv. 7, 8.

The Lord now invites Assyria (RSV) and Egypt to the hills around Samaria to gaze therefrom into the city and see a people who were incapable of doing right, who failed to execute justice, and whose amassed wealth was the result of the ill-gotten gains of robbery and violence. Their behaviour induced spiritual blindness, 'they do not know how to do right', v. 10. Assyria and Egypt had had no special revelation, yet they were called upon to be judge of the people who possessed the truth. Egypt, the scene of Israel's redemption, but not redeemed itself, called upon to be the judge of the redeemed! The shame of it! But they judge Israel because they are the less guilty. Israel sinned against light.

Assyria and Egypt are to listen to the judgement God pronounces on Israel, v. 11. He would use another nation as His scourge, which would be Assyria. That did not mean He approved of the instrument, but He is sovereign and uses whomsoever He will. The message seemed highly unlikely at the time, yet within the lifetime of some then present Assyria devastated Samaria and broke the power of Israel, v. 11. Yet, just as a shepherd saved some part of the animal taken by the predator to verify his story, cf. Exod. 22.12ff, so the Lord would rescue a remnant of Israel. Even in this the scorn of the prophet is heard. The remains of the people of God, the surviving proof of what once existed, consist of a corner of a couch and a part of a bed. What a revelation of their character! Beds, couches, pillows – evidences of sensuality, luxury, idleness – no evidence of spirituality. There was no heart concern for spiritual things. And they claimed to be the people of God!

God calls upon the nations to see the judgement of Israel. The very centre of their religion would be punished. Bethel was the principal sanctuary of the northern kingdom, cf. 1 Kgs. 12.28–33. Amos refers to them as 'the house of Jacob'. He reminds them who they really were, their true position, privileges, obligations. They had inherited the truth received by revelation. Their religious and theological position was so entirely different to that set up by Jeroboam. They had no liberty to invent and innovate; to do so would be to rebel.

The Lord would 'visit the altars at Bethel', indicating quite clearly His rejection of the whole system. The horns of the altar conferred the right of sanctuary upon those who laid hold upon them, cf. 1 Kgs. 1.50, 51; 2.28, but even this refuge would fail Israel in the day of visitation which Amos here foresees. Israel would find no sanctuary. Their material possessions and luxury homes would be destroyed.

Second Discourse, 4.1–13

The wealth of the privileged classes had been wrung from the poor. The men were not alone to blame, the wives were as well, referred to here as 'kine'. Women are the guardians of morals, fashions and standards in society. Where a society is going can be adduced by examining its typical women. Amos notes two things. Firstly here was a way of life that excluded all spiritual dimension – they were like so many head of cattle, content with a purely animal existence, nothing more, v. 1. Secondly, they thrived on the miseries suffered by, and the indignities heaped upon, the defenceless. They cared nothing for the price paid for their pleasures; all they sought was the gratification of their passing whims. They constantly demanded more from their husbands that their desires might be satisfied. To appease them their husbands placed even greater pressure upon the poor, but these women were indifferent to the practices used. So Amos rightly accuses them of the wrongs perpetrated to supply their demands.

God had sworn that retribution would come upon them, v. 2. In swearing by His holiness, God swore by Himself, for He is the supreme, uncreated Justice and Holiness. He warns that 'the days are coming', a phrase especially used of coming evil, though in 9.13 of coming good. It marks the sure and steady approach of the time appointed by God. The days are ever coming. Men put out of their minds what will come. They put far away the evil day. Therefore God so often, in His reminders of judgement, calls them to note these days are ever coming. They would suffer for their evil doing, and they would be dragged from comfort and luxury into slavery.

Their moral laxity went hand in hand with meticulous observance of religious exercises, vv. 4, 5. Indeed, they went beyond the requirement of the law as though they thought this would compensate for their inconsistency of life, and would also automatically guarantee their acceptance by God. They brought the sweet savour offerings daily, and God called upon them in irony to present their tithes every three days. The tithe was required annually. They were diligent. Their offerings were daily, their tithes were paid, they were punctual, indeed so well did they deem themselves to stand with God that there is no mention of sin offering or of trespass offering. They had no sense of guilt. All was done at places of sacred association, Gilgal, cf. Josh. 5.2-9, and Bethel, called by Hosea, 'Bethaven', House of Vanity, cf. Gen. 28.19; 35.7. These places were now associated with idolatry, cf. 1 Kgs. 12.29, 32,33. They presented leaven on God's altar, though this was not allowed, cf. Lev. 2.11. The Lord bids them publish their freewill offerings. Freewill offerings were not obligatory – they were spontaneous, cf. Deut. 23.23. They were supposed to result from devotion of heart to God. They were making such offerings, but they were publishing them abroad. 'This is what you like', says the Lord, cf. Matt. 6:2. The motive was not love to Jehovah, but to appear as lovers of Jehovah to other men. Self gratification was their aim. This rendered the gift worthless to the Lord, cf. Matt. 23.5. The Lord tore away their sham and showed His contempt of their insincerity. He ironically invites them to Gilgal and to Bethel, not to worship, but to transgress. At the very time they were offering sacrifices to God, they were engaging in social malpractices. They were ritualists, content with the externality of things. Let us beware lest our behaviour and conduct do not honour God, or of boasting abroad what we do for God. God has no room for insincerity and unreality.

A series of catastrophes would befall them to arouse them to a sense of their dependence on God, and of the sin that had caused the withdrawal of His benefits from them, vv. 6–11. They were not allowed to go on without warning. 'And I, too, have given you', the Lord says to them. In reply to their worthless gifts God had given them a gift-chastisement. It was a pledge of His love. He cared enough for them so as to chasten them. The pronoun 'I' is worth noting in these verses, vv. 6, 7, 9, 10, 11. The God of the Bible is the Sovereign Ruler of the universe. He works all things according to the counsel of His will, cf. 3.6. Yet God had a loving purpose in what He was doing. 'Yet ye have not returned to me' is said with a sob, not with vindictiveness. There is room left for a human response – to return. His activity was in order to bring them to repentance. He cares for His people so as to chasten them for He will not be satisfied until they come all the way back to Himself. He looks for repentance because there is no other way back to the fellowship which delights Him. But they were oblivious to their need and to His message. There were no genuine fruits of repentance.

Famine, v. 6, was followed by drought, vv. 7, 8. God caused His rain to fall upon one city and not upon another. Clearly it was His work, but they took no notice. Rain was essential in any case, and would be regarded as a gift of God. When rain fell it was a sign of His blessing; when it was withheld it was a sign of His displeasure. They staggered in exhaustion from one city to another to seek water, but they did not return to God. In turn the crops failed, v. 9, cf. Deut. 28.22. Again they should have recognized this as the hand of God, yet they did not turn to God. Pestilence followed, cf. Deut. 28.21, and the sword, v. 10. Young men were killed, and probably their decaying bodies contributed to the effects of the pestilence. Lastly there was earthquake, v. 11. Whole cities must have been overthrown, for he compares it to the overthrow of the cities of the plain. Mercy preserved some of them, plucked like a firebrand out of the fire, but even then they did not return. The nation was obdurately unrepentant.

So there was a final warning, 'Prepare to meet thy God', vv. 12, 13. Because of their utter indifference there remained only one thing more; they must meet Him in judgement whose warnings and acts of discipline they had despised. These were words addressed to them as His covenant people, and so have some relevance to His people today. As

Christians we can be utterly complacent about our position, and yet indifferent to the needs of the people around. We can be careless as to the life we live. There is need to be reminded repeatedly that we all have to stand before the judgement seat of Christ to render account to Him, cf. 2 Cor. 5.10.

The God they are to prepare to meet is the mighty Creator. Before everlasting mountains were, God is, for He made them. Yet He is not Creator only in the past, but also in the present. He forms the wind. He knows our thought more truly than we ourselves. He has disclosed His meditation or plan to man. Much more, He has revealed Himself in Christ, who has made a full revelation of the Father.

Third Discourse, 5.1–6.14

There are three sections to this last discourse 5.1-17; 5.18-27; 6.1-14, each drawing out in different terms the moral grounds of Israel's impending ruin, and ending with a similar outlook of invasion or exile. The first section consists of a lamentation, vv. 1-3, and an explanation, vv. 4-17. The two following sections are 'woes'.

The first three verses are a death song sung by the prophet as chief mourner. Now the predicted judgement of the previous chapter is regarded as a fait accompli. Israel's decease has already occurred. It is time for the final obsequies. He refers to Israel as a virgin maid. She was still an unconquered and independent nation. But he sees her as violated by a savage foe. She would rise no more, not only crushed to the ground, but abandoned. A city may send out 1000 soldiers to defend it, only 100 return; another would send out 100, only 10 would return. Defeat was inevitable. Yet Israel was at the zenith of power and prosperity; how could these people believe that their downfall was imminent?

The only way to avert such an evil was to 'seek the Lord', not at some semi-paganized shrine, but in true contrition of heart. God mercifully offered them a way of escape, vv. 4-17. If they would only seek Him and forsake their idolatry, they would live. Their repentance must be real. This is still a vital ingredient in the preaching of the gospel. There must be the clear call to the sinner to appreciate the evilness of sin, and the forthright challenge to him to forsake his evil ways and turn to the Lord. Their idolatrous centres would not help them, so why turn to them? With what amazement they would listen to Amos's words, 'Do not seek Bethel'. Had not God revealed Himself to Jacob there? cf. Gen. 28.16; 35.11-15. And what of Beersheba? Had not God promised His presence to Abraham there, Gen. 21.22-33, and to Isaac, Gen. 26.23, 24, and to Jacob, Gen. 46.1-4? As for Gilgal, did it not proclaim the inheritance and possession of the promised land according to the will of God, Josh. 4.19; 5.2-12; 9.6; 10.6, 7, 9, 15, 43; 14.6? They listened with horror and disbelief to the prophet's words. But Bethel was no longer the House of God, but a hold of demons, and Gilgal was no longer the place where the reproach was rolled away, but was itself a reproach. The Lord was their only hope. God's judgement was about to break forth on Israel. They would repent and turn to God, or face the consequences of their evil ways.

Justice had been so perverted in the courts that it was bitterness, wormwood to those who suffered, v. 7. Wormwood is often used as a symbol of calamity, cf. Deut. 29.18; Jer. 23.15. Justice was synonymous with bitterness. Right was defeated by might or money. Yet even to men such as these the prophet appealed to seek the Lord.

He described His power, vv. 8, 9. He intended to remind them of the power and majesty of Him whose judgement they provoke, and whose will they defy, the Creator and Ruler of the universe. He created the stars, changed night to day, and vice versa, and raised water from the sea to fall as rain upon the land. He was Jehovah, the covenant God of Israel. He will destroy the fortress of Israel in His judgement. They are heedless to the claims of justice, v. 10; they will not listen to the exposure of wrongdoing, or to the defence of innocence in the gate, the public place of judgement, cf. Deut. 21.19, 20. The one who spoke out against corruption was hated, v. 11. Often those walking sinfully or carelessly, are filled with indignation against any who faithfully rebuke their evil ways.

Their sins were threefold. Firstly, there was the oppression of their neighbours, v. 12. Secondly, there was the taking of bribes. Here is the idea of a ransom which the poor and defenceless were obliged to pay to a tyrannical judge in order to escape a harsh sentence. Thirdly, there was the thwarting of the needy in the gate. Such crimes were strictly forbidden by the law, cf. Exod. 23.1-8. All three were connected with the administration of justice. Those who could have given evidence remained silent, v. 13. Out of their ill-gotten gains they had built things they would never enjoy, v. 11. There was a righteous God in heaven.

The Israelites, as long as their material prosperity continued, imagined the Lord was with them as their patron and defender. Amos replied that the real condition of His being with them is the moral goodness of their lives. He calls upon them to seek good, not evil, and God would yet be gracious to them, v. 14.

Holy living has its negative and positive side, a shunning and a seeking. Holiness is concerned with actions and emotions – hate, evil; love, good; seek good, shun evil. Actions are here placed before emotions. Emotions can be a fickle and false guide. Right must be done because it is right, not because it creates a satisfying feeling. Of course, it is still true that to act lovingly towards a brother or sister in Christ will bring in its train the emotion of Christian love for that one, and that if we give ourselves to obeying, God will graciously add the bonus of prompting in us the corresponding feeling.

They must show the change first in the gate. Justice must be exercised there as evidence of their repentance. God may then be merciful to a remnant of them. The majority would pay the price. Here is the first mention of a remnant, a precious concept which will loom large in Isaiah and later prophets. But why 'the remnant of Joseph'? He was the man whom God was with, cf. Gen. 39.2, 21, 23; 41.38.

Their obstinacy would not go unpunished, vv. 16, 17. God would pass through the land as a destroyer, cf. Exod. 12.12, and judgement would be executed. There would be death and mourning. No longer could they avoid the penalty of their crimes against humanity, or for their social injustices. The Great Judge had taken account.

First Woe, 5.18–27

With astounding self-righteousness they even looked forward to the Day of the Lord. The Day of the Lord is the day in which the Lord manifests Himself in triumph over His foes. The day will be one of vindication and light, they thought. Amos shatters their complacency. It would be for them a day of judgement, of darkness not light, a period of destruction. Escape from one course of judgement would only be to fall prey to another, v. 19. They would avoid one calamity only to fall into a worse. The day will be 'darkness . . . very dark'. The latter phrase is that which is used to denote the gross Egyptian darkness that might be felt, cf. Exod. 10.22, the awful gloom such as fell on Jerusalem at the crucifixion.

But did they not carry out their religious observances? There is no doubt that they went in for religion in a big way. They took their religious duties seriously, the feasts at which attendance by law was obligatory, and the solemn assemblies, v. 21. They entered fully into their religious privileges, bringing burnt offerings, offering whole burnt offerings in which the offerer kept nothing back, meal offerings as well as peace offerings, symbolic of their state as God's people and their fellowship with Him and with each other, v. 22. They offered the best of the fatted beasts. So secure were they that they did not offer sin or trespass offerings. They gave full expression to their religious joys, singing songs to the accompaniment of harps, v. 23. Somehow the liveliness and the thrill of it all comes across. One can almost hear the singing. But God could not. All He heard was noise.

God rejected the celebration of the festivals and their offerings. They brought the sweet savour offerings, but God refused to have any pleasure in them. He rejected them. He would have no fellowship with these worshippers. He closed His ears to their music and singing. How could He accept these things when in heart they were far from Him?

What could they do if these things were unacceptable to God? There must be a revival of justice and right dealings. No rite or ceremonial, however punctiliously performed, is a substitute in God's eyes for moral duties, cf. Isa. 1.16, 17. By justice and righteousness God intends the establishment of the principles and practices of daily living which conform to His word and law.

What was missing in their religious observances? There was no mention of a sin offering. Had they been aware of themselves as sinners, they would have realized that being right with God involved a new way of life. Yet the burnt offering spoke of absolute consecration to God, and the peace offering of fellowship with God and with one another. But it all stopped at the door of the sanctuary; it did not come back into the home, nor into the place of business, cf. 8.4-6.

But what of all the offerings they had made in the wilderness? Their purpose was in order to live a life of obedience and holiness. Their redemption from Egypt required that. They had ceremoniously kept the sacrifices up, but a purely ceremonial religion is not enough. It can never safeguard the truth, nor hold people to the truth. So what is found here is equal to punctiliousness in the religious ceremonies of other gods, v. 26, to which they paid homage, cf. Acts 7.43. The gods of Assyria occupied their hearts long before the troops of Assyria their streets.

Second Woe, 6.1-14

Amos's condemnation now extends, to Judah as well as Israel. To them Zion was impregnable and Samaria unassailable. They were under the protection of Jehovah, and He could not possibly fail them. His covenant was sure. They could relax. They felt the danger threatening the Northern Kingdom was far off, and in any case Samaria could withstand a siege long enough, they thought, to give plenty of time to prepare should the enemy draw near. Their senses were dulled to the dangers which were threatening. They took their ease and were not concerned about obeying the voice of God calling them to repentance, nor did they afflict their souls for the sorrows of their brethren. They were 'at ease in Zion', 'secure in the mountains of Samaria', content in the things which ministered to their carnal appetites, while the laws of God were being broken and the ways of life corrupted because the divine judgement is thought of as distant. That same condition may be seen in many of the professed children of God today, unexercised, unheeding the message for the times, and showing no concern as to walking in the power of the truth.

They were 'the firstfruits of the nations', that is, the choicest and most favoured. Such was Israel as chosen and known of God, 3.2. The reference here is probably to their rulers. The word 'came', v. 1, has the implication that the people came for justice and judgement. These leaders had been raised above their fellow citizens and have to administer justice to them, and yet they are heedless of the interests entrusted to them and live only for themselves, vv. 3ff. The people came to them as rulers and judges. In them they might have looked for examples of uprightness and virtue. What they saw was injustice, pride and wantonness.

They had compared themselves advantageously with surrounding cities, v. 2. Amos puts into their mouths the thoughts which in their pride they were thinking. These were cities destroyed, or about to be destroyed. Were these places, Calneh, Hamath, Gath, more important than Zion or Samaria? Then, says the prophet, do not expect in your wealth and self satisfaction immunity from a worse doom.

They assigned a distant date to the prophet's threats, v. 3, cf. Ezek. 12.27. So they lived to please themselves and would not consider any change in their circumstances. They were secure, they thought. By their very attitude they were hastening the judgement at which they scoffed. They were hastening the coming of 'the seat of violence'. The word 'seat' means judicial seat, cf. Ps. 122.5. They had used violence on others. Violence would overtake them.

They lived in ostentatious luxury, vv. 4–6. Amos rightly condemned their wanton self indulgence which was at the expense of others, and in the presence of other's needs. cf. Phil. 4.5. They ate their gourmet dishes, drank bowlfuls of wine ('drank wine by the waterpotfulls', G. A. SMITH), anointed themselves with the most expensive oils when they should have mourned, cf. 2 Sam. 14.2, and all to the sound of decadent music which they excused as following David. The contrast with David is ironical. They made themselves instruments to please themselves,

David to please the Lord. As David introduced music for divine worship, so these drunkards were inventing instruments to accompany their drunken carousing. The word 'chant' implies they thought more of the sound than of the sense. Music with a spiritual content and application has its place, cf. Eph. 5.19, but debased music is a mark of a nation's decay, and promotes it.

The rich had all they wanted – wealth, ease, luxury, religion, but they did not have the one thing they needed, a heart of pity and compassion. They were not grieved for 'the affliction of Joseph'. They had neither heart for the poverty, nor conscience for the sin of the people. Self indulgence is indifferent to the call of duty or danger. There is ever the possibility of living to please ourselves, rejoicing in our possessions, and forgetting 'the affliction of Joseph'.

What would happen to them? These leaders had attained priority status in Israel – they would retain it – they would be the first to go, v. 7. Their mirth and revelry would end. They would be led away in silence, the first in shame, at the head of the exiles on their way to a foreign land. The judgement was certain – God had sworn by Himself that this would be so, cf. 4.2; 8.7. He had sworn by Himself—it is of the utmost gravity and entirely binding, cf. Heb. 6.13, 17. Notice the Names God gives Himself here: the Lord God, i.e. Yahweh, the divine Name, the God of holiness, redemption and wrath; Lord – the King or Sovereign; God of Hosts – the Omnipotent God. When God swears by Himself He commits the totality of His status as the world's Sovereign Lord, the totality of His nature (the Holy One, the Redeemer, the Judge), and the totality of His effective power as the Omnipotent One.

He abhorred the 'excellency of Jacob'. It was the pride of Jacob He abhorred. The name is of the man who by fair means or foul worked for his own advantage. They prided themselves on making themselves what they were, and denied thereby the supremacy of God. The phrase is used again in 8.7, but as a description of God Himself, but they had ceased to acknowledge that which they had received from Him, and their excellence became pride in themselves and their achievements. He abhorred their pride. Pride is an abomination to God. God detests pride at any time, but never more strongly than when He finds it among His own people. He has gone out of His way to eliminate the possibility of it by making the weak and helpless the recipients of His blessing, cf. 1 Cor. 1.27–29. Their palaces were hateful to Him because they had been founded on oppression and robbery. They also trusted in their strongholds and considered themselves invulnerable. Their confidence was completely misplaced – it should have been in God. He was their Rock and their Fortress. If He did not protect them, their strongholds would have been to no avail. They would be delivered up.

Many of them would die, many by plague, vv. 9, 10. There would be so many that the normal process of burial would be given up for cremation, which was permissible only in the most exceptional circumstances, cf. Lev. 20.14; 21.9. In carrying out the work of removing the bodies of the dead the Name of the Lord was not to be mentioned, because they feared the further infliction of judgement. None would escape the judgement, neither rich nor poor, v. 11.

The senselessness of the conduct of Israel is indicated by a couplet of questions in verse 12 to which the answer is in the negative. That horses should climb up steep cliffs, or oxen plough in the rocky gorge were absurd propositions. Israel had taken a course equally as absurd and wrong from which nothing would be gained. It was absurd to seek gain from oppression and injustice to which God had linked woe and loss, both temporal and eternal. Men know that God cannot be mocked in the natural world, yet they believe that He can be defied with impunity in the spiritual sphere.

They boasted in their victories and prosperity. What were they? A thing of nothing. They boasted in their own strength and ascribed their victories to themselves, and forfeited them. 'By our own strength', they said, and not 'by the help of God'. They failed to realize that their power must come from God. We need to remember the Lord's words, 'without me ye can do nothing'. In Him alone is the secret of spiritual success. God was meanwhile raising up a nation against them which would spare no part of the land, v. 14.

(4) Visions of the Judgement of Israel, 7.1–9.10

Punishment was announced in chapter 6; now some details are filled in by a series of visions. These visions were an authentication of the prophet's message. Revelation on God's part became visions on the prophet's part.

The Vision of Locusts, 7.1–3

Locusts were regarded as an instrument of God's curse, cf. Deut. 28.38, so the people recognized the hand of the Lord was against them. The God who formed the mountains, 4.13, still works and forms the locust. He has never stopped working, cf. John 5.17. The time was that of the latter growth which came after the latter rain, when the grass after being mown, began to grow again. This latter growth was after the tribute levied by the king, 'the king's mowings', had been paid. If there was no aftergrowth because of the locusts, there would be no supply for the winter. Just when there seemed to be no possibility of survival Amos prayed for them, and here, and in the second vision, the Lord rejects the thought of total destruction among His people. It was the Lord, the Sovereign Jehovah, who affirmed this, v. 6. There is the certainty of absolute guarantee to what He proposes to do. They will not be totally destroyed because the Lord Himself says so. No earthly calamity can threaten the continuance of the people of God. After all, it was God who formed the locust with all the delicate art of a potter. 'Do you see the trouble coming?' Amos is saying. 'Look beyond it and see who has planned and fashioned it, who controls and limits it. It is God, the Sovereign and Gracious, who has pledged that no temporary calamity can destroy His people'.

The divine patience did not come into operation immediately, however. It necessitated prayer on the prophet's part. He had to obtain it, cf. Gen. 18.23–33; Exod. 32.9–14. Note the intensity in the petition, and it is for Israel, not the prophet's own Judah. God is just, but His justice is wonderfully open to entreaty. God loves to be entreated. He delights to answer when He hears the cry of those who bear His people in their heart, cf. 1 Tim. 2.1–4; 1 Sam. 12.23. God has put us in this world to seek men's salvation, not to take pleasure over their destruction. The message of judgement must be stated, but there must also be a fervent and compassionate prayer for mercy in our hearts.

But what does it mean that God 'repents'? It does not mean that God changes His mind, nor regrets any actions taken or proposed, cf. 1 Sam. 15.29. It cannot include any sense of sin, error or wrongdoing on the part of God. God always knows well what He is going to do. There is no uncertainty or caprice with God. Here anthropomorphic terms are being used that we might be certain that God's anger is real, and that He is not indifferent to wrong.

The Vision of Consuming Fire, 7.4–6

In this vision not only the remaining pasture, but the deepest springs of moisture are scorched up in blaze. This time the Lord bids them enter into judgement with Him. He will try their cases with fire, cf. Isa. 66.16. This was the divine fire, the instrument of divine wrath. Just as in Exodus 3.2, it needed no fuel to feed it, so here there is no substance which can quench it. It 'would have eaten up the land', RV, i.e. the portion or allocation. It must surely refer to the particular land the Lord allocated to His people. It would have resulted in utter destruction. The prophet intercedes again, and his prayer is answered. It is by prayer that God's will is wrought on earth. It is as if the Lord wanted that prayer to be made, for otherwise why would He have allowed Amos into the secret of what He was doing? cf. vv. 1, 4. Prayer is a means by which the Lord of all brings His determined purposes to pass.

Amos adopts the divine estimation of the situation. 'How can Israel stand; he is so small?' They did not think so themselves. Prayer starts by seeing things and people as God sees them, focusing their needs as estimated in Heaven. Then prayer looks up to the divine mercy. The judgement was halted by divine decree – 'This shall not be', v. 6.

The Vision of the Plumbline, 7.7–9

The wall was a symbol of Israel. It had been made by a plumbline, perpendicular and straight. God had made it upright. He had watched over it to keep it as He had made it. Now He stood over it, fixed in His purpose, to destroy it. The wall was out of true. He had marked its inequalities and irregularities. To set a measuring line, or a line with weights attached, to any building, means to devote it to destruction, cf. 2 Kgs. 21.13; Isa. 34.11. God is personally provoked by sin, and eventually His patience is exhausted. A day will come when God's patience will run out.

God has provided the standard for their conduct. God had demanded that in the whole of their daily life they should reflect His likeness, cf. Lev. 19.2. Leviticus 19 is remarkable for the repetition of 'I am the Lord'. What He enjoins there of His people must be done because it is a reflection of His character. Because He is their Redeemer the law laid down the proper pattern of life for them to follow, cf. Deut. 7.8–11. And so it is still. God has not left His people in ignorance of the life which pleases Him. For us the word of God is a plumbline. Unerringly it tests every soul, showing each departure from its standard. Israel had departed from the standard set to such an extent that the wall must be levelled to the ground.

Note that here the Lord calls the prophet by name, as a familiar friend, known and approved by Him, cf. Exod. 33.12, 17; 2 Tim. 2.19. He is asked what he sees, v. 8. As Amos looked he realized all the irregularities the plumbline revealed. There was no intercession. Doom was determined. God refers to Israel as 'my people'. Those who are brought near God cannot avoid being tested and judged. God will not 'pass by' them anymore. He will not spare them.

The first to fail the test were the shrines, v. 9. The second was the house of Jeroboam. Note what is said of Jeroboam I in 2 Kings 14.24: The sin of Jeroboam, the son of Nebat, was basically the sin of disobedience to the law of God. His kingdom was given him on moral conditions, cf. 1 Kgs. 11.38. But Jeroboam did not fulfil them – he set up the golden calves.

Amaziah's Interjection, 7.10–17

There is no service of God without opposition, persecution and trial, cf. 1 Pet. 4.12. Amaziah did not recognize God's voice in the prophet's words. To Amaziah Amos was merely a political agitator and was guilty of treason against the king. Note the scene – a priest facing the servant of the Lord. The charge, 'He speaks against Caesar', cf. John 19.12; Jer. 37.13; 38.4; Acts 16.20, 21. He had 'conspired', yet God was his only fellow conspirator. Amaziah attributes the words to Amos alone, 'thus Amos saith', v. 11. Again, his words are made to mean what in fact he never said, cf. Matt. 5.11. Amos had not said that Jeroboam would die by the sword – it was his house that was so threatened. A lie mixed with truth is the most deadly form of falsehood, the truth serving to gain admittance for the lie. 'Since this much is certainly true, why should not the rest be so?' Furthermore there was a suppression of the truth. The denunciation because of the oppression of the poor which was the ground of the threat, was omitted; so, too, was the call for repentance and the promise based on it, 'Seek ye the Lord and live'. He omits also the prophet's intercession for the people. He selects the one prophecy which would give a more political character to the whole. Suppression of the truth is a yet subtler form of falsehood.

The priest questions Amos's motives in serving God. True, he addresses Amos as 'seer', normally a title of honour, but it is here used contemptuously as ridiculing Amos's claims. He tempts Amos to act out of self interest, 'Go, flee', that is, for your own sake, or a very unpleasant fate will befall you. Then he tempts Amos to seek success for its own sake, 'to Judah', that is to say, his message will have greater acceptance there, so he should speak the message where it will be heard, rather than where it needs to be heard. Finally he tells Amos to 'eat bread there'. 'Go there and live on your profession as a prophet'. The insinuation is that Amos prophesied for the sake of a living.

Amaziah was not beyond 'pulling rank', cf. Acts 5.28, 29. Note his reference to Bethel. 'Chapel' is 'sanctuary'. The Hebrew word is normally applied to God's sanctuary, cf. Exod. 25.8; Lev. 19.30. One man could not so appropriate the sanctuary, v. 13. In God's sanctuary God was enthroned. God had ordained it for Himself. His Presence had sanctified it. A high priest at Jerusalem would not have used these words, 'it is the king's'. He knew that the temple was the sanctuary of God, and would not have called it 'the king's sanctuary'. The sanctuary at Bethel, however, had no other sanction than what it had from the king.

So Amos was told to depart. The awful peril of imploring God's messenger to depart is often referred to in scripture. Men blinded by prejudice besought the Lord to depart from them, cf. Luke 10.10–12; Mark 5.17.

In response Amos gives the explanation of his call. As a genuine servant of the Lord he was above financial considerations, and the threats did not affect him. His was the authority of commission, 'Go', and of revelation, 'the Lord said . . . prophesy'. His authority was not self-generated. An authoritative hand from outside had gripped him and he became what he was not before, and what he could never have made himself. Neither was his authority given by man. In the Bible nowhere do we read of one man empowering another to speak the word of God. Amos entered upon his ministry by the direct call of God, cf. Gal. 1.1. God alone gives the gift and accredits the servant. With Amos it was not a case of turning prophet to earn a living; it was a case of leaving his living to act as a prophet. The fire of God was burning in his soul, and, as with Paul later, it was a case of 'Woe is me if I speak not'. Because he was called of God his message was of divine authority. If God calls there is no need for fear. The One who calls is the One who equips and empowers. This is what holds the man of God firm in the time of trial and opposition; he is where he is by divine appointment.

Then comes the prophet's declaration of what would happen. He is faithful to the word of God. The first word concerned Amaziah and his family. Amaziah rejected the word of the Lord, and the Lord rejected him. In attempting to silence Amos, Amaziah had tried to silence God. For that he was divested of office, and everything he valued was taken from him. It is a serious thing to challenge the Almighty. The second word told of Israel's impending captivity.

The Vision of the Basket of Summer Fruit, 8.1–14

The last vision had declared that the approaching judgement was certain; this, that it was final and close at hand. It was harvest time and Israel is ripe for judgement. God would not pass them by. Harvest time was one of feasting and happiness, but the songs which filled the palace would be changed to the wailing of mourners. The bodies of the dead would be too numerous for burial. The dead would be everywhere, and so they would have none of the usual respect paid to them. The bereaved in their sorrow would cry 'Hush', in acknowledgement that nothing could be said in the presence of the One God who had inflicted the blow. Yet God still refers to them as 'my people'. This is the language of love and pity. 'My people' still, though they refuse to be Mine.

The prophet now states his indictment of the traders who had exploited the poor. Human misery meant nothing to them. They swallowed up the needy in their covetousness, making the poor of the land to fail, v. 4. Their religious observances were a sheer mockery, v. 5. The Sabbath was threatened by the same worldliness and love of money which trampled on the helpless. The interests of the Sabbath are the interests of the poor; the enemies of the Sabbath are the enemies of the poor. All illustrates the Lord's saying, 'The Sabbath was made for man'. They could scarcely wait for the religious observances to end so that they could proceed with the ruthless pursuit of their own interests. Holy days meant nothing to them. They were simply a hindrance to their occupation with what mattered far more to them. They are not without their counterparts today who regard time spent on sacred activities as a nuisance, and an appalling waste of time which might be better spent on the pursuit of normal business. The holy days were a duty not a delight. Outwardly they observed them, but they longed for the close of the day to come so that they might buy and sell and get gain.

Their measures, weights and balances were fraudulent. The balance was the very emblem of fairness and justice, and it was perverted to be the means of the most sordid gain. They loved gain more than honesty. The use of a perfect and just measure was a condition of their remaining in the land promised to their fathers, cf. Deut. 25.13-15; Lev. 19.35, 36. They, however, gave short measure and defrauded the customers. They used different weights for buying and selling, always to their own advantage. They sold chaff as wheat to make more money, v. 6.

Punishment was inevitable. God swore by 'the excellency of Jacob'. He bound Himself by an oath never to forget any of their deeds. They must be called to account for them. He swore by Himself, 'the excellency of Jacob'. God must cease to be God if He did not do what He swore to do; punish the oppressors and defrauders of the poor. The judgement would come 'as a flood', v. 8. It would be complete. An earthquake was promised. It was no mere natural happening; it was the hand of God at work to punish the guilty inhabitants of Israel.

There would be an eclipse of the sun, v. 9. Again it was God's hand, as again at Calvary. There would be mourning, v. 10, cf. Ps. 137.1. Feast times would become times of sorrow rather than joy. The sorrow would be as great as that experienced on the death of an only son. An only son would have carried on the family name. Nothing ever escapes the eye of God. He may allow men to continue unchecked for a long time, but the day of reckoning will eventually come. There would be a famine, a spiritual famine of the word of God. There would be no revelation from heaven. In the general distress there would be an eagerness to hear the word of God which had been scorned and rejected. Men will search everywhere throughout the land to find a prophet who will disclose it to them, but in vain. If there was no divine message, it implies that either God has disowned His people, or was not prepared to intervene on their behalf. They would search the land for something to satisfy the hunger and thirst of their soul and find nothing. Even the young men and women would be exhausted as a result of their fruitless search. There would be no renewal of strength for those who had not waited upon the Lord, cf. Isa. 40.30, 31. There would be destruction, v. 14. Judgement was pronounced on those who worshipped the Lord in an idolatrous fashion, or in a way He had not ordained. God had commanded that all appeals by oath should be made to Himself, who alone governs the world, to whom alone His creatures owe obedience, who alone reigns, cf. Deut. 6.13; 10.20; Josh. 23.7. It was a direct substitution of the creature for the Creator in ascribing to it the attributes of God.

The Vision of the Altar at Bethel, 9.1–10

Disobedience would result in worldwide dispersion. It had been promised; it was now fulfilled, cf. Deut. 28.63–68. It starts with a vision of the Lord standing by the altar, Jeroboam's altar at Bethel. The title of the Lord here is significant - not Jehovah, the God of the covenant, but Adonai, the Sovereign. He stands by the altar filled with their foolish sacrifices, the God they had insulted, and they felt secure in the place of their religious devotions and observances. All is shattered by the command to smite. The resultant collapse of the building would cause the death of many of the worshippers, cf. Judg. 16.29, 30, and those who escaped would perish subsequently by the sword. No-one would escape. There would be no hiding place from the judgement of God, vv. 2–4, cf. Ps. 139.7–12. In the psalm the thought of God's ubiquity was rich comfort to the loyal psalmist; here it spells relentless doom for the ungodly. Height and depth are alike open to the omnipresent God. They would pay dearly for their evil ways.

God was able to carry out what He was promising to do. As proof of this a revelation of His power is given, vv. 5, 6. Furthermore, it was Jehovah, the Self-Existent One who comprehends all things, it is He who will achieve all this.

They had acted like the heathen nations who had no relationship with the Lord. God would treat them as such, v. 7. God, by bringing them up out of Egypt, had pledged His truth to them to be their God, to protect and preserve them. This would be as long as they retained God as their God, and kept His laws. By casting Him off as their Lord and God, they cast themselves off and out of God's protection. By estranging themselves from God, they became as strangers in His sight. His act in bringing them up from Egypt had lost its meaning for them. It became no more than any other event in His providence as when He brought up the Philistines from Caphtor, for example. They had boasted in being an elect nation, but election was of no value to those who were idolatrous in heart and practice. As degenerate, they were no more to God than these despised Cushites. Let them not take refuge in the fact that He had brought them up out of Egypt. He had also directed the movements of other nations. God was making it clear that He was not the private and exclusive property of Israel. He was concerned with other nations of the world as well, cf. Rom. 3.29. The same divine government operates over all the earth.

Yet God would preserve a remnant, vv. 8-10. His covenants would therefore be fulfilled. His promises to the fathers, and His word as to the Coming Seed, must not fail. So He excepts a remnant. God's eyes are against the sinful kingdom, and He will destroy it from off the face of the earth, save only if the kingdom be that of His chosen people; it will not be destroyed by Him utterly. Only the sinners in it would perish, those who say, 'The evil shall neither overtake nor hinder us', v. 10.

He will shake Israel. The nation must go into exile; it must be shaken to and fro among the nations, as in a sieve. The whole world is, as it were, one vast sieve in the hands of God in which Israel is shaken from one end to the other. No sound grain of corn would fall to the ground and be lost. The trash would be lost. Such were confident no evil would overtake them. They would be the very ones who would be destroyed. There are those who believe they are immune from trouble because they belong to Christ. God is more concerned with life and conduct than with pious profession and confident claims.

Epilogue. Restoration, 9.11–15

God is going to work yet again in the nation of Israel. Note the words, 'I will raise', 'I will build', v. 11; 'I will bring', v. 14; 'I will plant', v. 15.

There will be the restoration of the Davidic house, v. 11. Israel will once more be under one king as in the days of David. God had made a covenant with David, cf. 2 Sam. 7.12–16; 1 Chron. 17.11–14; 22.9, 10. David's line would continue for ever, and his kingdom would be for ever. That did not imply that there would be an unbroken succession of kings of David's line, cf. Ps. 98.38–45, but fulfilment of the promise required that a descendant of the royal house should sit on the throne, cf. Jer. 33.17–21. In the light of the impending invasion and captivity that must have seemed a remote hope. 'In that day' indicated some future event, and 'days of old' indicated that it would be in the distant future.

James used this scripture in the Council of Jerusalem, cf. Acts 15.16, 17. We learn from the passage in the Acts that during this age the Gentiles are visited to gather out from among them a people for His Name, that is, the church. When this is completed the Lord returns, and as a result of His return the restoration of the tabernacle of David takes place. The kingdom will be restored to His people, Israel, and the Lord Jesus will be enthroned as the King upon the throne of David. Other nations will be involved in the blessings of His reign.

Note the phrase, 'I will build it as in days of old'. It clearly has to do with a promise of the past, and is to do with a nation and its land. So there yet remains a glorious future for Israel, Amos avers, despite the judgement he has predicted.

The kingdom will be restored to the proportions of the days of David and beyond, v. 12. It may be asked why is Edom singled out here. Edom always showed hostility to the people of God, cf. Num. 20.14; Amos 1.11. The overthrow of Edom therefore speaks of a real and complete end of opposition. But it also speaks of the power and the presence of the new David, for alone of the kings David had conquered and held Edom, cf. 2 Sam. 8.14. Thus when Edom falls, all worldly opposition is finally ended, and the second and greater David will certainly have arrived. But here it is 'the remnant of Edom', and also 'the heathen who are called by my Name'. Gentiles will be blessed.

There will be a restoration to the land, vv. 13–15. The natural and obvious meaning of the promise in verse 15 is that the people of Israel shall yet be returned to their own land. So fertile will it be that the ploughman will overtake the reaper in his preparing the soil for the next harvest. The hills, normally barren, will flow with wine. There will be peace and prosperity.

Amos started his book with 'The words of Amos', 1.1, and he ends it with 'saith the Lord thy God'. It is God who commits Himself to raise up the King in His Kingdom, v. 11, to restore the fortunes of His people, v. 14, and plant them in their inheritance, v. 15. God will plant them— none will disturb them.

CHAPTER FOUR

THE PROPHECY OF
OBADIAH

by KEN RUDGE

The Historical Backcloth

EVERY INSPIRED WRITING has its own historical and human context. It is this that gives it colour, depth and individuality.

Obadiah's small but vivid prophecy describes for us one of the occasions when Jerusalem was sacked and overrun by powerful enemies. It was at such a time that blood-related neighbours might be expected to respond with help and protection. Describing Israel's condition as 'the day of their destruction, distress and calamity' Obadiah scathingly condemns Edom, Israel's blood-brother, for appalling apathy and eventual unbridled revenge, vv. 11–14. Edom was not the main aggressor and we have nothing within the book to pinpoint the particular historical event referred to. Most would place it earlier than the final Babylonian invasions and possibly the events described in 2 Chronicles 21.

Edom had a history of evil intent and revengeful reprisal against Israel so that Obadiah is not alone in pronouncing the divine condemnation of this nation, Jer. 49.7–22; Joel 3.19; Ezek. 35.5.

The significance of the prophecy does not lie in knowing the specific events indicated but rather in the amazing searchlight the revelations bring to the 'end times' when an established Israel will take her place among the nations in fulfilment of the divine purposes for her blessing.

The book clearly warns any would-be aggressor to Israel of divine retribution and provides delightful encouragement to faith in the fulfilment of the promises of God.

The Spiritual Framework

There are three spiritual 'truths' that the reader does well to hold in mind while considering the detail of the prophecy. These 'truths' unite and mould the whole into a message that is greater than its immediate implications. They offer healthy precepts for a life of faith in every age.

Firstly, Obadiah is the Prophecy of Answered Prayer. At a later date the captives in Babylon sit down beside the rivers to weep and mourn over the destruction of Jerusalem, Ps. 137. Their captors require some 'songs of Zion' but their inability to sing on account of their circumstances calls forth a sombre prayer for divine judgement upon both Edom and Babylon. Obadiah provides the answer of God to their prayers in relation to Edom, even before they implored Him to move on their behalf. The prophecy reveals that Edom, for the precise sins of which the complain, Ps. 137.7, has already been assigned to divine wrath. 'Before they shall call . . . I will answer them', Isa. 65.24. So we have an encouragement to faithful, fervent prayer both in adversity and prosperity, Ps. 102.2.

Secondly, Obadiah is the Prophecy of a Divine Principle. This is the principle stated in verse 15, 'As thou has done, it shall be done unto thee' and 'thy reward shall return upon thine own head'. The apostle Paul restates it in more familiar words in Galatians 6.7, 8 and again in 2 Corinthians 9.6, 7. The principle is that 'what you sow you also reap'. This is a part of God's judicial dealings with all men. There has never been a time when He hasn't operated it. Under law Israel was called upon to enforce it in its negative sense as a just retribution, Exod. 21.24.

Obadiah uses the word 'for' in verse 10 to draw attention to the divine response conditioned by Edom's behaviour in word and deed to Jacob, his brother. Edom need not think, even for a moment, that all has not been seen and will be evenly balanced out by the 'Judge of all the earth'. The central section hinges upon this single principle.

Paul's use of the idea clearly indicates its positive blessing as well as its negative effect. The force of the divine part: 'God loveth', 'God is able to make', 'God is not mocked', serves to remind us that the desire of our God is always to bless as a response to the sowing of good.

Thirdly, Obadiah is the Prophecy of Spiritual Conflict. The constant referral by the Lord to the nations of Edom and Israel by their ancestral fathers' names, directs our attention to the embittered struggle between them that began in the womb of Rebekah, Gen. 25.22-23. To the perplexed mother, the Lord revealed the truth that two nations and two manners of people, in their as yet unborn fathers, were already struggling against each other in her womb.

The record of their subsequent lives unfolds the drama of how the stronger and the elder, Edom, makes spiritual decisions that give the weaker and the younger, Jacob, the ultimate place of blessing in God's purposes, confirming the divine election of which he was the subject.

It is this prophecy that crystallizes the moral and spiritual issues of the struggle, and declares the final destruction of the House of Edom and exaltation of the House of Jacob in fulfilment of the promises of God.

This then typifies the conflict that has been at work from the beginning of time. It commenced with Cain and Abel and will consummate with Christ and Satan, Rev. 19.11-19; 20.7-9. We are part of the struggle between light and darkness in this our day and can be comforted that in whatever loss we may suffer, or in whatever sacrifice we may make, the end is sure. We fight a defeated foe and the glory of the Lord shall yet shine from shore to shore and the earth be full of His knowledge, Isa. 1.9; Hab. 2.14.

The prophecy can be easily divided into the following sections:−

Section 1 − The Destruction of Edom, vv. 1–15

(a) vv. 1-4 The **Declaration** of the Destruction − from the Lord.

(b) vv. 5-9 The **Accomplishment** of the Destruction − complete, utter.

(c) vv. 10-15 The **Reasons** for the Destruction − retribution, immediate and ultimate.

Section 2 − The Deliverance of Israel, vv. 16–21

(a) vv. 16-18 The **Certainty** of the deliverance − 'shall'.

(b) vv. 19-21 the **Extent** of the Deliverance − 'shall possess'.

Section 1, vv. 1–15 − The Destruction of Edom

(a) Verses 1-4 The **Declaration** of the Destruction

Obadiah has no doubt as to the source of his declarations. He is but as his name means, 'the servant of the Lord'. The nations are to be an instrument of retribution against Edom, v. 1, but it is to be clearly understood that it is the Lord who is acting in and through them to accomplish His own ends, vv. 2, 4, 'I have', 'I will bring'.

The security of the mountainous and inaccessible region occupied by Edom and unassailed by invading armies, had made the nation immeasurably proud. Pride had marked Esau in his independence of God and man and so characterized his offspring in their rock fortresses, vv. 3, 4.

Pride has so often led the way to sin and destruction – Lucifer, Isa. 14.12-15; Eve, Gen. 3.6; Ananias and Sapphira, Acts 5.1-2. It still lurks within every human heart and can be the motive that robs and destroys all that is spiritual.

There was to be no 'hiding place' from the Lord, v. 4, and we all await a day of revelation when nothing can be hid. We need to live now in the light of that day soon to be.

(b) Verses 5-9 The **Accomplishment** of the Destruction

The descriptions that follow set out in startling terms the thorough character of Edom's judgement. The two initial parables warn us of its severity. Both thieves and grapegatherers would have left Edom something after they had been, but the Lord would leave nothing, v. 5.

No secret thing would remain hidden, v. 6, and no confederate or ally would be found, despite past alliances or covenants, v. 7. No wisdom vested in men of understanding would avoid or turn the onslaught, v. 8, and no army, however brave, would be able to stand before the divine wrath, v. 9. Edom, alone and without support or strength, would be utterly removed, v. 9.

The centuries of history tell the story of the rise and fall of Edom so that today she is no more as a distinct nation. Her utter extinction may well yet await the judgement of the living nations in a day to come. One thing we learn of God in this is solemn enough – He is slow to wrath, but when He does come to it then it is swift and complete.

(c) Verses 10-15 The **Reasons** for the Destruction

King David established his kingdom under the hand of God, enlarging its borders and subduing enemies. In the course of this he 'put garrisons in Edom' and all they of Edom 'became David's servants', 2 Sam. 8.14. Edom became a smouldering fire. When the kingdom began to crumble Edom was amongst the first to revolt and pursue a course of revenge, 2 Chron. 21.8. The character and form of this revenge is now recounted by the Lord as the just cause for His awesome pronouncement against Edom.

We must note the slow but certain manner in which Edom became personally involved in taking revenge. It began with 'standing on the other side', v. 11 – a matter of wilful indifference, which was in fact passive involvement. It soon became 'rejoicing over', v. 12; and then 'speaking proudly', v. 12; and then 'entering into the gate', v. 13. Ultimately Edom was 'laying hands on their substance', v. 13, and 'cutting off those that did escape', 'delivering up those that did remain', v. 14. The tie of brotherhood, now consumed by a blazing hatred that only sought the ruin and distress of those it should have shielded and supported. The divine remonstration is a constant 'thou shouldest not', again and again.

The human heart is a tragic thing when deprived of pity and care. Even the stance of indifference to the circumstances and needs of others, whether saints or sinners, can leave us open to the condemnation of 'thou wast as one of them'. Divine compassion should be the eyes through which we view the world.

'For' is the word that introduces the second reason, v. 15. A Day of Wrath was near for all the nations, not only an Edom. Thus the prophetic beam sweeps down the ages, passing over the Valley of Grace and our present dispensation, to spotlight the end of the ages.

These verses take us to when Gentile dominion will be no more. The image of Daniel 2, which represents Gentile kingdoms, is smitten in the feet and falls. Its place is taken by God's little stone which becomes a great mountain and fills the whole earth, Dan. 2.44-45.

Section 2, vv. 16–21. The Deliverance of Israel

(a) The **Certainty** of the Deliverance, vv. 16–18

The characteristic word of this section is 'shall'. There is no doubt as to the fact that it will happen. It is from the Book of the Revelation that we learn how it will come to pass. The Divine Deliverer will descend with His armies from heaven and overcome the Gentile nations and their leadership even as they surround and seek to eradicate the faithful remnant of Israel, Rev. 19.19-21. Obadiah sees it as the just reward for every act of Gentile aggression against God's chosen people, v. 16.

There will be deliverance for 'Zion' – the highest part of Jerusalem and the ultimate goal of pilgrimage. There, true holiness is established and maintained at last. The House of 'Jacob', the man that held the birthright and the blessing, comes into its promised possessions.

But for 'Esau', the dispossessed man, he and all his will be devoured, until no more, by the house of 'Joseph' – the rejected but ultimately exalted man, v. 18. It is the awaited day of regeneration for Israel.

None can deny what the Lord has spoken, v. 18. Let us strengthen our own hearts in His unbreakable word.

(b) The **Extent** of the Deliverance, vv. 19–21

These verses describe the geographical extent of the possession – southwards, westwards, eastwards and northwards. Here is a glimpse into Millennial days. Israel becomes the head of the nations and the instrument of rule for the reign of Christ. Obadiah's closing vision is of justice carried out righteously and the worldwide dominion of the Lord bringing blessing for men. The Kingdom is the Lord's.

Obadiah's prophecy marks for us the fulfilment of the promise of 'Mahanaim', Gen. 32.1–2. Prior to Jacob's natural fear of his brother Esau with his four hundred armed men, God assured him of the 'heavenly' host which was ready to defend and protect him. Jacob failed to hold on to the vision but the promise remained and, in Obadiah's words, finds an ultimate fulfilment.

CHAPTER FIVE

THE PROPHECY OF

JONAH

by MALCOLM HORLOCK

5

Introduction

CHRONOLOGICALLY, JONAH MAY WELL have been the very first of the 12 Minor Prophets. Apart from the book of Jonah, the only other place in the Old Testament where the names 'Jonah' and 'Amittai' occur is 2 Kings 14.25. It is more than likely therefore that the same person is in view there. We are able therefore to date Jonah and his ministry to the reigns of Joash and Jeroboam II, kings of Israel.

The book of Jonah is distinguished from the other Minor Prophets in that it comprises an historical narrative and not a prophetical message. Our Lord's references to the key events exclude the possibility that the book represents some form of parable or allegory. If Jesus' resurrection is accepted as an historical event, then so too must be Jonah's abode in the great fish, Matt. 12.40. Again, it is absurd to suppose that Jesus warned His hearers that imaginary characters, who were said to have repented at the imaginary preaching of some imaginary prophet, would actually rise in the day of judgement to bear witness against them, v. 41.

At its simplest, the book can be divided as follows:

Chapter 1 – Jonah's **disobedience** to God's word.

Chapter 2 – Jonah's **deliverance** from God's chastisement (see 'thou' and 'thy', v. 3).

Chapter 3 – Jonah's **declaration** of God's judgement.

Chapter 4 – Jonah's **displeasure** at God's mercy.

Taking account more accurately of the book's structure, we have Jonah's six encounters:

   (i) His first encounter with the word of the Lord, 1.1–3. 'Rise, go, cry', v. 2 – destination Tarshish, v. 3.

 (ii) His first encounter with **the heathen**, 1.4–16. 'That we perish not', v. 6. The men on the ship who feared the Lord, v. 16.

(iii) His first encounter with **the Lord Himself**, 1.17 – 2.10. He 'prayed unto the Lord', 2.1. Jonah's thanksgiving.

(iv) His second encounter with the **word of the Lord**, 3.1–3. 'Rise, go, cry', v. 2 – destination Nineveh, v. 3.

 (v) His second encounter with **the heathen**, 3.4–10. 'That we perish not', v. 9. The men of Nineveh who believed God, v. 5.

(vi) His second encounter with **the Lord Himself**, 4.1–11. He 'prayed unto the Lord', 4.2. Jonah's complaint.

Jonah and the Word of the Lord, 1.1–3

The book opens with the Lord's commission to Jonah to go and cry against Nineveh, the metropolis of Assyria. As far as is known, Jonah's previous ministry had been restricted to his own nation but now, in effect, God said to him, 'Depart: for I will send thee far hence unto the Gentiles', Acts 22.21.

Chapter 1 tells of several 'great' things; the great wind, v. 4; the great tempest, vv. 4, 12; and the great fear, vv. 10, 16. Here Nineveh is described as a 'great' city, v. 2 (cf. 3.2; 4.11). It was great in every way – in its size, population, wealth and power. But it was also great in its sins, conspicuously those of violence, deceit, immorality and witchcraft, Nah. 3.1–4.

God informed Jonah, 'their evil (the Hebrew word implying evil-doing to others) has come up before my face', v. 2 lit. As earlier in the cases of the antediluvian world, Gen. 6.5–6, the Amorites of Canaan, 15.16, and the city of Sodom, 18.20–21, the sins of the Ninevites cried out to God for His direct intervention in judgement.

It was Jonah's business to announce Nineveh's doom. But Jonah had other ideas! In response to God's, 'Arise, go to Nineveh' (which was situated north east of Israel), he 'rose up to flee unto Tarshish' (at the western extremity of the Mediterranean). David had once sighed, 'Oh that I had wings, like a dove! for then would I fly away', Ps. 55.6. Well, this 'dove' (for this is the meaning of the name 'Jonah') would spread his wings and fly away from his allotted task and mission.

This could have been no light decision for somebody like Jonah, who was characteristically God's 'servant', 2 Kgs. 14.25; cf. Amos 3.8. Indeed, the many unmistakable references to earlier Old Testament passages in Jonah's prayer of chapter 2 demonstrate how much he treasured God's word in his heart. For such a man deliberately to have disobeyed God's command must have been a very painful thing, even before he began to suffer the chastening of the Lord.

The 'presence of the Lord' from which Jonah fled was undoubtedly God's special and localised presence among His people and in His land, see Gen. 4.16; Jer. 23.39; and especially 2 Kgs. 13.23 (written concerning the very time that Jonah lived).

A prophet who acknowledged the Lord as 'the God of heaven, which hath made the sea and the dry land', v. 9, would not have been so naive as to believe that he could elude God's omnipresence. His prayer of chapter 2 proves him to have been well versed in the psalms of David. He could hardly have been ignorant therefore of David's assurance that

God's 'presence' was inescapable – even at the 'uttermost parts of the sea', Ps. 139.7–10. We conclude then that it was from the Holy Land, where God had placed His Name and glory, that Jonah fled.

Initially, all seemed to go well for the fugitive prophet. He arrived safely at Joppa, where, it so happens, some 800 years later we meet another famous preacher with a marked reluctance to carry God's message to the Gentiles, Acts 10.8–43. Certainly providence seemed to smile on Jonah's plans, for at Joppa he found a ship going to his intended destination. We have to learn that circumstances by themselves are no safe guide to the will of God for us. For, if circumstances alone are a believer's yardstick, Moses should have held on to his position as son of Pharaoh's daughter, Heb. 11.24, David should have slain the Lord's anointed, 1 Sam. 24 and 26, and Jonah was right in heading for Tarshish.

Jonah and the Heathen Mariners, 1.4–16

Jonah soon discovered that he was to pay a higher price for his disobedience than the fare to Tarshish, v. 3. For, in His mercy towards Jonah, God intervened and 'hedged up his way with thorns', Hos. 2.6. And so the 'but Jonah' of verse 3 soon became the 'but the Lord' of verse 4.

Gathering the wind in His fists, Prov. 30.4, the Lord 'hurled' ('cast forth' as in verses 5, 12, 15; cf. 1 Sam. 18.11) it into the sea. The resultant tempest drove the heathen 'mariners' (a word derived from that for 'salt'; cf. our 'old salts') to both prayer and urgent action. Satan once observed, 'all that a man hath will he give for his life', Job. 2.4, and, in the face of extreme danger, these seamen soon jettisoned their cargo.

For a third time Jonah went 'down', vv. 3, 5 (cf. 2.6), this time below deck to the bottom of the ship. (The word translated 'ship' at the end of verse 4 indicates 'that which is covered with boards', namely, a decked vessel).

While terror reigned on deck, Jonah, doubtless weary and exhausted after his journey, slept soundly, v. 5 (the Hebrew word signifying a particularly deep sleep; cf. Gen. 15.12 and 1 Sam. 26.12). Neither the noise of the storm nor any stirring of conscience served to keep this prophet awake. We contrast Another who slept through a great tempest and who too was rudely awoken, Mark 4.38; Jonah's presence in the ship was the cause of his companions' danger but Jesus' presence in the boat was the guarantee of His companions' safety!

Having fled from his mission to rebuke a heathen city, Jonah found himself rebuked by a heathen sea-captain, v. 6. 'Why are you snoring?' is the Septuagint rendering of the shipmaster's question. Perhaps, as the Jewish writer Philo suggested, it was Jonah's loud snores which drew the captain's attention to him! It is sad when our inconsistent behaviour earns us a rebuke from the world; cf. Gen. 12.18–20. Contrast, how, many centuries later, the apostle Paul stood on board a ship which was caught in a tempest on the self-same sea and, in the power of both clear conscience and consistent conduct, rebuked those with him, including the master of the ship, Acts 27.11, 21.

'Call upon thy God', was the summons of the sea-captain but Jonah knew that, in his present spiritual condition, there was no point at all in his praying, Ps. 66.18; Prov. 28.9; 1 John 3.22.

The casting of lots by the crew of the ship was understandable. This method of establishing the identity of the person sought was not infrequent in Old Testament days; cf. 1 Sam. 14.42; Prov. 16.11. Yet the men would not rely on the indication of the lot alone and sought confirmation from Jonah himself, firing at him a salvo of questions about his character, calling and country, v. 8.

Though Jonah's sense of the **greatness** of His God caused him to reverently fear Him, v. 9, sadly his very appreciation of the **goodness** of his God was the direct cause of his rebellion and flight, 4.2.

Why had he fled from the presence of the Lord? This was the heathen crew's perfectly reasonable question, v. 10. It is a question which we ask too. We later learn that his reason for running away lay in his expectation, based upon God's known character, that the Lord would use his preaching to spare Nineveh, 4.2.

We can rule out therefore any suggestion that Jonah was intimidated by the magnitude of the task set him. That was certainly not his concern and we respect him for it. After all, Nineveh was the most renowned city on earth, the very citadel of heathen glory and worldly pride.

It is equally clear that (contrary to the opinion of the Jewish historian Josephus) Jonah did not flee out of regard for his own safety. Yet Assyria was in fact renowned for its violence, the only nation of antiquity in the Near East which gloried in cruelty. For its part, its capital Nineveh later earned itself the epithet, 'the city of blood', Nah. 3.1

No – Jonah's fear lay in an altogether different direction. Remarkably, he feared what most preachers earnestly covet; namely, success. He could not bear the thought that his message would yield a harvest of faith and repentance and that, in turn, God would Himself 'repent' of Nineveh's declared destruction.

There is no evidence, however, that Jonah was worried that, as a consequence of Nineveh's deliverance, (i) his own reputation as a prophet should suffer (cf. Deut. 18.21–22), (ii) the prophetic office in general should be discredited, or (iii) the God of Israel should be charged with being fickle or irresolute. The explanation must be sought elsewhere.

Jonah was a true patriot (cf. 'my country', 4.2) and we could well understand his reluctance to carry the message of God to a Gentile city. Nevertheless, given his concern for the wellbeing of the heathen mariners, 1.12, it seems hardly likely that this alone accounts for Jonah's attitude. We must distinguish then between the prophet's general view of the Gentile world and his attitude to the occupants of Nineveh.

Doubtless, his antipathy towards Nineveh stemmed from the city's status as capital of Assyria. Israel had already suffered badly at the hand of Assyria and, though the empire was then relatively weak, it still represented a major threat to Israel's future prosperity and blessing. It seems highly likely, therefore, that Jonah's reason for fleeing lay in his love for those of his own nation rather than in hatred for those of other nations. He had previously foretold that God was to save Israel by the hand of Jereboam II, 2 Kgs. 14.25; he had no ambition to be the one by whose hand God was to save the capital of Assyria!

Earlier the mariners had asked **who** Jonah was, v. 8, and **why** he had fled, v. 10. Now they enquired **what** they should do to him, v. 11. Told to cast him overboard, they nobly made every effort to avoid doing so, v. 13. Note that every other instance of the word translated 'rowed' refers to violently breaking through a wall or enclosure. Here it suggests the forcing of the ship through great walls of water. We remember too that this was a large sea-going vessel, a far cry from the small fishing boat of Mark 6.48. Finally convinced that they had no alternative but to abandon Jonah to the sea, they showed themselves as determined to avoid sin as to avoid danger, v. 14, and gave every evidence of true conversion, v. 16. Their vague 'fear' of verse 10 had been transformed into a reverential awe which had the Lord as its object; cf. Jonah's testimony in verse 9.

Jonah and the Lord Himself, 1.17–2.10

The God who made the sea, 1.9, had 'appointed' (not 'prepared' in the sense of specially created; cf. the same word in 4.6, 7, 8 and Dan. 1.5) a 'great fish' to save Jonah from a watery grave, v. 17. We cannot be sure which sea monster God used but it is appropriate that a chapter which commenced with a reference to a man who would not open his mouth at God's command should conclude with a reference to a marine creature which would!

Possibly we are meant to see in Jonah's horrific experience a mirror-image of the history of his nation. God's 'servant' Israel also failed in her mission as God's witness to the nations, Isa. 43.10; Gen. 12.3. As a result of disobedience she too has been swallowed up and carried away; cf. Deut. 4.27. Miraculously preserved, the nation shall yet emerge and be recommissioned by the Lord to fulfil His original purpose for her.

We learn several important lessons from Jonah's prayer:

(i) He prayed 'out of the fish's belly'. What a great privilege is ours that we can pray to God everywhere, 1 Tim. 2.8; cf. Ps. 57 title and Neh. 2.4. Great stress is laid on prayer in the book of Jonah, every chapter providing at least one example, 1.5, 6, 14; 2.1-9; 3.8; 4.2 etc.

(ii) Adverse circumstances sharpen our prayer lives. On board the ship Jonah had been exhorted to pray his God, 1.6; in the stomach of the fish he needed no exhortation, 2.1.

(iii) Backsliding does not sever the believer's relationship with the Lord. The mariners can cry only to 'the Lord' but Jonah can still pray to '**his** God'.

(iv) Jonah's prayer was saturated with the word of God. Embedded in it we discover no less than 7 separate echoes from the book of Psalms; viz Ps. 5.7; 18.6; 31.22; 42.7; 120.1; 142.3; 143.4. Unable now, for obvious reasons, to consult the sacred scriptures directly, Jonah is able to call upon a memory stored with God's truth.

(v) Jonah was able to relate his knowledge of scripture to his own experience and to employ it intelligently when praying – in effect taking arrows from God's own quiver to aim heavenwards.

It seems clear that Jonah's prayer took the form of thanksgiving rather than intercession. He was looking back on his timely rescue – upon God's unmistakable answer to an earlier prayer when cast into the sea, buffeted by its waves and sinking into its depths; note especially the recurring past tense, 'I cried . . . he heard', v. 2, 'yet hast thou brought up my life from corruption', v. 6, 'my prayer came in unto thee', v. 7. Jonah was not praying for salvation from the great fish but praising God for saving him by means of the great fish. Truly, God had intervened to transport him from 'the belly of sheol', v. 2, to the 'belly of the fish', v. 1; although it should be noted that 'belly' translates two different Hebrew words.

Jonah also looked beyond all second causes and recognized that ultimately his earlier plight had been the result of God's chastisement; compare 'thou hast cast me into the deep', v. 3, with '**they** . . . cast him forth into the sea', 1.15.

Jonah had already re-consecrated himself to God's service. He now affirmed his determination to 'pay' that which he had promised, closing his prayer with reference to the same two expressions of gratitude (sacrifice and vow) which had marked the delivered mariners in 1.16.

The chapter closes with the record of Jonah being regurgitated and vomited onto dry land. He had been incarcerated 'in the belly of the fish three days and three nights', 1.17. We know, on the authority of our Lord, that this experience of Jonah corresponded to His own experience of burial and resurrection, Matt. 12.40.

This represents just one of the many parallels between them: (i) both were from lower Galilee, Jonah coming from Gath-hepher, just three miles north-east of Nazareth; (ii) both were prepared to give their lives as a ransom for many, Jonah 1.12; Mark 10.45; (iii) both were delivered from 'sheol' (the abode of disembodied spirits) and 'corruption' (the pit; ie the grave), Jonah 2.2, 6; Acts 2.27, 31; (iv) both were buried for '3 days and 3 nights'. The significance of this expression is provided by the first century *Jerusalem Talmud*, 'A day and a night constitute a full-day, and part of a full-day counts as a whole full-day', quoted in *Kittel* vol.II page 950. The scripture claims then that both Jonah and our Lord spent one whole day and part of two other days in their respective 'graves'; and (v) in both cases, God's salvation-bringing message was preached to the Gentiles only after their 'resurrection' experiences, Jonah 3.4; Eph. 2.17 (ct. Matt. 10.5–6; 15.24).

Jonah and the Word of the Lord, 3.1–3

Although God had graciously spared Jonah's life, the prophet had no right to expect that God would ever condescend to employ him again in His service. Yet he soon discovered that, such was the mercy of his God, he was not only pardoned but fully restored to his office as God's servant. In New Testament days both Peter and John Mark were similarly to prove the wonder of God's complete forgiveness.

It seems that Jonah 'marched under sealed orders' and was given the details of his message only when he actually arrived at Nineveh, 3.2. (Note that 'preach' is the same word as 'cry' in 1.2.) Previously he 'rose up to flee', 1.3; this time he 'arose and went', 3.3; cf. Matt. 21.28–29. At this point he could well have identified his experience with yet another quotation from the Psalms, 'Before I was afflicted I went astray: but now have I kept thy word', 119.67.

Jonah and the Heathen City, 3.4–10

We note that Jonah is not mentioned personally at all after verse 4: the conversion of Nineveh was altogether a divine work. Jonah simply discharged his responsibility as God's spokesman and faithfully proclaimed His message.

The results were astonishing; indeed they were nothing short of miraculous. Far from being ridiculed (cf. Gen. 19.14), regarded as a public nuisance and arrested, Jonah was recognized by the inhabitants of Nineveh as God's ambassador and his proclamation was received 'not as the word of men, but . . . the word of God', v. 5; 1 Thess. 2.13.

Jonah may not have been sent to preach repentance to the Ninevites but he certainly preached the Ninevites to repentance! The tide of conviction, humiliation and repentance rose higher and higher until it reached even to the royal court. Having produced fruit in every district and suburb of the city, Jonah's word 'touched even to the king', v. 6 lit. The king's subsequent self-abasement is all the more striking in the light of the pomp and magnificence normally associated with 'the great king' of Assyria, 2 Kgs. 18.19, 28.

Nineveh's repentance was prompted by a combination of faith, v. 5, and fear, v. 9. The reality and depth of its contrition were evidenced by prayer and fasting (often associated together in both Testaments, 2 Sam. 12.16; Ezra 8.23; Dan. 9.3; Acts 13.3; 14.23) and 'fruits meet for repentance', Matt. 3.8. It is hardly surprising that, in Jewish tradition, the book of Jonah forms part of the ritual of the Day of Atonement; see Lev. 16.29, 31 and 23.27, 32. What do we know of repentance from sin?

With the 'decree' (the technical word for edicts issued by Assyrian and Babylonian kings) of verse 8 can be compared a letter from an unnamed Assyrian monarch to the governor of Gozan, 'Decree of the king. You and all the people, your land, your meadows will mourn and pray for three days before the god Adad and repent . . . that there may be rest'.

No doubt many factors accounted for Nineveh's serious response to Jonah's declaration of imminent destruction. We observe, for instance, that at the time Jonah preached Assyria was passing through a period of extreme weakness. The kingdom was suffering from a succession of feeble rulers, from internal strife and disintegration, from severe plagues and famines, and from formidable and menacing powers in the north.

Both militarily and politically Assyria was in a very rickety state, with many of Nineveh's rival states (including Asshur) having revolted; indeed, it is possible that it was the precarious political situation which accounts for the reference to the 'king of Nineveh', 3.6, rather than the normal 'king of Assyria' (occurring over 90 times in the Old Testament). The period proved, in fact, to be the beginning of the end for the then-ruling dynasty of the Assyrian Empire; within a matter of years it had been toppled and replaced by Tiglath-pileser III (the 'Pul' of 2 Kings 15.19). In such circumstances, the occupants of Nineveh could not afford to laugh too quickly at Jonah's prophecy of sudden doom.

Far more important, however, is the statement of our Lord that Jonah was himself 'a sign' to the men of Nineveh, and that he was such in respect of his experience in the great fish, Luke 11.30; Matt. 12.40. Like Jonah, the Lord was Himself to appear alive again after three days. Although the book itself does not record the fact, the Lord (the best Commentator of all!) thereby clearly taught that the men of Nineveh were informed of Jonah's plight and deliverance – compare 1.9-10, where something else which had been said was not recorded at the time.

The Lord's own experience of death, burial and resurrection served to accredit and confirm the truth of His claims, John 2.19; Rom. 1.3-4. In the same way, Jesus taught, Jonah's remarkable experience in the fish provided the men of Nineveh with supporting evidence for the truth of his message. In his experience the Ninevites saw an unmistakable demonstration of both the 'goodness and the severity of God'. Our Lord made it clear that this 'sign' played no small part in bringing Nineveh to its knees before God. Jonah's experience provided the basis for Nineveh's repentance and faith – just as the Lord's death and resurrection was to provide the same for later generations.

The implications of this are enormous. It goes without saying that, if the prophet had not been swallowed and later disgorged by the fish, he would not have been a 'sign' to anyone of anything; in which case, it seems clear, Nineveh would not have repented at all. And yet Jonah enjoyed the hospitality of the fish only as a result of his own disobedience. It follows, therefore, that (as part of His sovereign purpose) the Lord had over-ruled Jonah's very waywardness to bring about the repentance and thereby the deliverance of Nineveh. As in the case of Joseph's brothers' hatred, God had brought good out of evil, Gen. 45.5-8; 50.20.

Herein lies the main twist to the story. At the very beginning Jonah had suspected that God intended to use him as the means of sparing Nineveh from its well-deserved destruction, 4.2. What he never imagined in his wildest dreams was exactly how God was to bring this about. He had been outwitted, completely out-manoeuvred by the God

whose gracious purpose he had attempted to frustrate. Small wonder he
was so angry, 4.1.

Finally in this section we note the expression 'God repented', 3.10.
This is just one of the twenty occasions in the Old Testament where the
Lord is said to have repented; for example see Gen. 6.6 and 1 Sam.
15.11. Yet we know that God and His purpose are unchangeable and
therefore He does not and cannot 'repent', Num. 23.19; Isa. 46.10; Mal.
3.6; Heb. 6.17-18. How are we to reconcile these two propositions?

First, we note that there cannot be any real contradiction between
them because they can both be employed in the same passage without
any sense of incongruity; see 1 Sam. 15.29, 35.

Second, we consider the principle which lies behind God's 'repentance', Jer. 18.7-10. Each time God responded to a change in the character of those with whom He was dealing. Are we to charge the sun with
being fickle because it both hardens clay and melts ice? We know that
the sun itself remains constant; the reason for its diverse effects lies
entirely in the nature of that upon which it shines. And so it is with the
Unchangeable God. In the case of Nineveh, for example, the wicked and
violent occupants (who were the declared objects of His anger) had, in
one sense, ceased to exist; they had been radically transformed into
contrite, God-fearing people. It was because God's character and righteousness could not change that His plans (as perceived by men) for
Nineveh had to.

Jonah and the Lord Himself, 4.1-11

Jonah became aware (by divine revelation?) that the repentance of Nineveh had prevailed with God and that Israel's most dangerous potential
enemy was to be spared. But the fact that God had 'repented of the **evil**'
which He had said that He would do to the Ninevites, 3.10, was '**evil**' to
Jonah, 4.1 lit. The prophet was filled with anger, 4.1, because God had
turned away from His anger, 3.9. Jonah's chagrin and displeasure over
Nineveh's salvation stands in marked contrast with his earlier joy and
thanksgiving over his own, 1.17 - 2.10.

Though now roused to anger by Nineveh's deliverance, Jonah had
suspected all along that this had been God's design. His complaint to
God reveals his inner feelings at the very outset. Whereas the king and
nobles of Nineveh had been uncertain about God's likely response to
their repentance ('Who can know ... ', 3.9 lit), Jonah asserts with
confidence, 'I **knew** ... ', 4.2.

Jonah shared the understanding of God's character common to all sections of the Old Testament – historical, Exod. 34.6, poetical, Ps. 103.8-9; 145.8, and prophetical, Joel 2.13. It was this, his knowledge of the character of God, which had led him to interpret his original commission as a divinely-appointed means to Nineveh's salvation. Hence his Tarshish-bound flight. Alas that a man should know so much about the character of God and be so little affected by it! Does my life reflect my knowledge of God?

Bitterly disappointed that the advertised fireworks were now unlikely to materialize, Jonah prayed in effect, 'If Nineveh must live then let me die'. The man who, when in the depths of the Mediterranean sea, had pleaded for his life to be spared now begged to have that very life taken from him, vv. 2, 3. Some 100 years previously another of Israel's prophets had prayed to die – because he deemed himself to be a **failure**, 1 Kgs. 19.4. By way of contrast Jonah's peevish outburst sprang from his astonishing **success**.

When questioned by the Lord about the propriety of his anger, the prophet simply turned his back on Him (for a second time!) and stormed off in high dudgeon, v. 5. It seems, however, that Jonah decided to stay around until the end of the 40 days period on the off-chance that God would change His mind again.

The east side of Nineveh was skirted by hills and it was doubtless on one of these that Jonah found himself some suitable vantage point from which he could see what would become of the city; ct. Gen. 19.27, 28. There, under his makeshift shelter, he sat – a pathetic, sullen, solitary figure. Though by meaning of name Jonah was 'a dove', he was perched like some great vulture awaiting hungrily the death of its prey.

In heaven angels rejoiced over many sinners repenting, Luke 15.10, but on earth God's servant could only fume and frown. How out of touch he was with the feelings of God and how very different his emotions from those of One so much greater than he who, around 800 years later, looked over another great city – which was irreversibly doomed to destruction, Luke 19.41-44.

Right to the end the Lord proved Himself exceedingly gracious and patient with His prophet. Far from punishing his petulance or discarding him now that he had completed his mission, He showed tremendous consideration and care for him.

Clearly there was no point in the Lord attempting to argue or reason with His prophet. This would have done more harm than good. But the all-wise God knew how best to handle His servant and He set about creating a situation which would help Jonah to understand (if not actually to share) His feelings for Nineveh.

First, God caused a large-leafed spreading plant to supplement the rough booth which Jonah had constructed for his own benefit. The same God who had earlier 'prepared' a fish to deliver Jonah from the terrors of the ocean beneath, now 'prepared' a plant to deliver him from the broiling sun in the sky above. Though still 'exceedingly' displeased on account of the salvation of Nineveh, v. 1, Jonah was 'exceedingly' glad on account of the gourd and the shade which it afforded him, v. 6.

But, alas for Jonah, his welcome shelter proved to be shortlived: God caused the plant to wither as quickly as it had grown, v. 7. Jonah was devastated – his gourd, his lovely gourd, was gone. And then, to add to Jonah's discomfort, God set in motion, like the blast of a furnace, the burning and blistering hot wind of the desert. In addition, the sun's unbroken rays beat down on the prophet's defenceless head. Now it was Jonah's turn to wither! All this proved too much for the poor prophet and in strikingly paradoxical terms he 'begged for his life that he might die', v. 8 lit. And, when God raised with Jonah the question whether he was justified in being so angry on account of the gourd, he well-nigh exploded, v. 9.

The Lord's response to Jonah's outburst provides not only the conclusion but the climax of the book. 'You pitied the plant', He pointed out, 'which cost you nothing (and was indeed of little value) and yet you dare to find fault with Me because I have had pity on a city with an extensive population of human souls (of infinitely greater value than any number of plants) – not to speak of its many cattle. You maintain that you do well to be angry; I maintain that I do well to be merciful'.

With great wisdom and skill, God had redirected Jonah's fierce anger from the **sparing** of something (the city of Nineveh, v.1) to the **destruction** of something (the gourd, v. 9). Jonah had been greatly distressed over the loss of the plant – and yet he had not created it, v. 10. Could he not now appreciate something of God's feelings for the city of Nineveh? The Assyrian people were not only a 'rod' and 'staff' in His hand to be used as an instrument of His anger, Isa. 10.5–15; they were objects of His pity and care and had a place in their faithful Creator's heart.

Here the book ends very abruptly; we are provided with no record of Jonah's response to God's argument. To his credit the prophet is content to pass off the scene disgraced and silenced that we might feel the more forcibly the power of the divine reasoning. 'Is he the God of the Jews only? Is he not also of the Gentiles?', Rom. 3.29.

CHAPTER SIX

THE PROPHECY OF MICAH

by ARTHUR SHEARMAN

The Book of Micah

Introduction

MICAH OF MORESHETH, or Moresheth-Gath, was one of the eighth century BC prophets. He prophesied later than Amos, but was a contemporary of Isaiah and Hosea. Yet he shared very much the burden of Amos for loyalty and justice. The times of his ministry covered the reigns of Jotham, Ahaz and Hezekiah of Judah. Thus he saw the closing decade of Samaria and the beginnings of the final decline of Judah. It was therefore in times of the saddest days of the nation's history that he brought the word of God to the people.

Moresheth-Gath was a town about 25 miles from Jerusalem, and not very far from Gath, near the Philistine border. It has been described as a town that was fortified, and defended the western approaches of Jerusalem; it was an administrative centre, often visited by military and court officials from Jerusalem. Little is said about the character of Micah. He is not a statesman-prophet like Isaiah, nor a herdsman like Amos. Neither was linked to the priesthood as Hosea was said to have been. He was a man with a message from the Lord for his day and generation. He listened and spoke. His message was relevant.

The overall burden of his prophecy was twofold; he demanded loyalty to God and justice for the poor and downtrodden of the people. He saw mainly four groups of powerful persons and directed his message to them.

1. Political leaders, princes, elders etc., who were like 'wolves – tearing their victims' – the poor, common people.

2. Judicial authorities, judges and elders who used their office for

their own ends and enrichment and did not defend the rights of the needy.

3. Religious leaders, priests and prophets who were profane in their worship and false in their prophecies. There was no integrity or power in their words.

4. Economic powers, the rich landowners and merchants who deceived, stole and cheated to deprive the poor of their basic rights and dignity. Thus the word from the Lord was one of judgement, expressing the anger of a righteous God and issuing predictions of certain judgement. Yet Micah gave witness to a God who would not break faith with His chosen nation but would pardon, bless and restore those who repented.

Outline

1. Approaching Judgement, Chapter 1.
2. Answering Retribution and Restoration, Chapter 2.
3. Authorities Condemned, Chapter 3.
4. Anticipations of Glory, Chapter 4–5.
5. Approved Religion, Chapter 6.
6. Affirmation of Divine Promise and Blessing, Chapter 7.

Chapter 1

Outline

verse 1, Introduction.
verses 2–4, Nature and God's Intervention.
verses 5–7, Samaria and God's anger.
verses 8–16, Judah's incurable wound.

Exposition

Verse 1. The introduction to the prophecy is very brief. The most important fact of it is contained in the declaration of the word of the Lord. Not much is known of the speaker, but his intention was to bring to the nation a word relevant to their need and for their times. We shall find that this message penetrated into the sins of the present, it was a forth-telling of God's mind at that time. We shall also notice that it has elements of foretelling of future events, unfolding the purpose of God for days to come. These two elements stamp this book as giving to us the essence of true prophecy. See general introduction for details of times and places etc.

Verses 2–4. The words of these verses represent a dramatic call from the Lord to creation, to witness against the nation in its condition of departure from God. Notice, 'against you', making clear the displeasure of the Lord with His people. He views them from the vantage point of His holy temple. The prophets of old were often confronted with the burning holiness of the presence of the Lord. Compare the experience of Isaiah as he saw the Lord 'high and lifted up', the consciousness that he had of the burning holiness of the Lord who was to call and commission him, Isa. 6.1–7, cf. Hab. 2.20. From the highest levels of purity the sins and impurity of the nation are observed and judged.

Yet this is no passive exercise on the part of the Lord. Notice that He comes forth, He will come down, He will tread on the high places of the earth. The very elements of creation will melt with the fire of His fury. In the unfolding of His message, Micah will not only tell of what the Lord thinks and feels about the sinfulness of His people, but he will speak in very definite terms of the actions that will be taken to deal with these evils. The thought of mountains melting and elements being disturbed is often expressed in scripture, cf. Judg. 5.5; Ps. 97. 4–5.

Verses 5–7. Most of the prophecy of Micah is directed towards Judah, the Southern Kingdom. But he could have witnessed the closing decade of the life of the Northern Kingdom of Samaria and some of his utterances apply to their conditions. The sins of the house of Israel could cover the nation as a whole. Verse 5 makes clear that the sins that brought such anger from the Lord were common to both Samaria and Judah. In spite of so many godly kings, Judah eventually developed the trends of evil that cursed Samaria, and about 150 years afterwards shared the fate of exile with her. Behind these threats of judgement we remember that Assyria was in the ascendance. Notice the severity of the judgements pronounced against Samaria. God says 'I will'; He has His instrument that He will use in His sovereignty to achieve His purpose. Who will make them an heap? How will all the graven images be beaten to pieces, be burned with fire and be laid desolate? The sins of idolatry and profanity demanded judgement, and God will use a godless nation such as Assyria to destroy them, cf. 2 Kgs. 17.1-23. These are solemn words in the context of God's ability to judge.

Verses 8-16. The prophet wails and howls because of what he sees in the nation. He turns to Judah, and finds a condition of incurable sickness. What he is saying is that the evils of the people are so deeply ingrained in the nation, that no healing process is enough to meet the need. We shall notice that the sins that were exposed by the prophet covered every aspect of national life, religious, social and domestic. All relationships were soiled by sin, but in particular the nation's relationship with God, cf. 6.6-8. Yet we shall see that the God who condemned such evils, was a God who in mercy was ready to pardon, cf. 7.18. Even a nation ripe for judgement could find pardon in repentance.

Verses 10-13 give details of some of those cities that surrounded Jerusalem. They were witnesses to the life of the nation, and at different times exercised their influence on it. As Micah felt the shame of his nation's sin, it would seem that he did not want it spread abroad. 'Declare ye it not at Gath, weep ye not at all'. These words are similar to those uttered by David as Jonathan and Saul fell on the field of battle, 2 Sam. 1.16-21. True patriotism is devastated at the thought of others, some of them enemies, knowing of the fall of those favoured of God. There were those who waited for good, but evil came down, v. 12. There were nations whose sins influenced the nation and brought shame to it, v. 13. Yet for the godless to hear of the evils of a people who claimed to be set apart in holy relationship with God, not only dishonours them, but brings disgrace to the Name of the God who calls them. 'Declare ye it not in Gath'. The remainder of the chapter leads into a call to the people to lament their condition. The kings of Israel and the glory of Israel are deceived and brought down to Adullum' (see NIV). One translation of verse 16, gives, 'make thyself bald and shave thee for thy darlings'. The city is addressed as a mother told to go into mourning for the loss of her children. Shaving the head was common as a token of mourning. Captivity was near, retribution for evil. They should be humbled and lament.

Comments

We can learn three practical points from this chapter. Firstly, that accumulated sin in the life and experience of the Lord's people eventually lessens the consciousness of the seriousness of sin, and inevitably leads to departure and its consequences. Note the letter to the church at Laodicea, Rev. 3.14-22. Secondly, it is a sad day for the people of God when the world outside becomes aware of the sins that are practised by them. It should be the greatest care of all God's people, to see that His Name is not dishonoured among the ungodly by gossip concerning other Christians. Finally, we learn that God is sovereign in all His ways and dealings with those He loves. He may use the ungodly to chastise and punish His chosen ones, even as He did with Israel and Judah, banishing them to exile. But eventually He will punish those whom He uses to chastise them. In wrath He remembers mercy, cf. Hosea 11.5-9.

Chapter 2

Outline

verses 1-6, Condemnation of Oppression.
verses 7-11, Response to the Prophetic Word.
verses 12-13, Return of the Remnant of Israel.

The chapter as a whole gives an answer of the Lord to the attitude of the people, especially those who are in power. The answer is given to the cruel oppression of the poor of the land. But there is also a word of promise that indicates the purpose of God to spare a remnant of the nation to enjoy the promised blessings of restoration.

Exposition

Verses 1-6 have a clear message in them. There runs through the prophets of the eighth century, a constant stream of condemnation in regard to those who were exploiting the poor. This poverty was very often the outcome of the greed of landowners who robbed them of their inheritance. The days of Judah under Uzziah had been prosperous and the rich had grown wealthy in land, with abundance of cattle. Their standard of living was luxurious and they employed many as servants.

It is evident from these verses that much of their wealth was gained through oppression. The picture in verse 1 is vivid. They planned their evil on their beds and then at morning-light practised it. Power to operate in this way was in their hands. Through covetousness and violence they defrauded men of their inheritance. This was contrary to God's plan for the continuance of the inheritance of His people in the land. The land was the Lord's and He bequeathed it to families as a sacred possession. 'The land was to be protected and cared for, so that it could be handed down as a sacred trust from generation to generation', ALFARO. So landgrabbing was a serious evil, cf. Isa. 5.8-9; Prov. 23.10, 11; 1 Kgs. 21, Naboth's vineyard.

'Therefore' – the Lord has something to say. He will devise evil against the oppressors. Notice how the times are described as evil. What will the Lord do to them? There will be no escape from disaster. Their illegally gained possessions will be taken away by treachery. Their place and their names will be removed from the congregation of the Lord.

Notice the answer of the oppressors in verse 6. They do not want to hear the word of condemnation. They will not face their shameful actions. They want the voice of the prophet silenced. 'Do not keep harping on such things', they say. This attitude towards the Lord's messengers was not uncommon in such times as Micah's. Amos was told not to prophesy, 5.10; 7.10-13. Isaiah had a similar experience, 30.9-10. The message is clear, that justice belongs to the Lord and He will not overlook the cause of the poor, cf. Jas. 5.1-6.

Verses 7-11 reveal reactions from the Lord, answering the protests of those condemned, 'O thou that are named the house of Jacob'. The Lord reasons with them as those who are His. Were the fruits of their evil practices to be reckoned to Him? If they reaped barrenness because of their dishonesty and lack of integrity, was it His doing? He could challenge them as to the effect of His word if they walked uprightly. It could only bring them prosperity and good. All the weight of evidence concerning the value of God's word was that obedience brought with it blessing, Deut. 6.17-18; 7.12-16.

These oppressors had become enemies of the people. They disturbed the peace of those who desired security. They turned women and children out of their pleasant homes. One translation puts it, 'from their babes ye take away my glory forever', v. 8. The dreadful situation is strongly condemned by Micah as he brings to them the word of the Lord. Thus it is that because of their pollution of the land they would suffer 'sore destruction'. Their retribution would be painful. Yet it would seem, from verse 11, that if some lying prophet came along, speaking falsehood while promising material satisfaction, a word to satisfy the senses, they would be glad to accept him as the prophet of the people. Instances of this reaction of the people to prophetic messages were not unknown in Israel's history. Forsaking the true, they were open to listen to the false, to those who spoke the words they wanted to hear, cf. Isa. 41.28-29; 1 Kgs. 22.12-13, 22-23.

Verses 12-13 give us a shaft of light on a very dark condition of life in the nation. The prophet lifts up his eyes and sees the prospect of ultimate blessing for the remnant of Israel. Out of a nation of whom God said that her wound was incurable, there would surely be a regathering, a remnant preserved for blessing. This is to be an act of shepherding, they will be put together as the flock in the midst of the fold. This would remind us of the opening words of Psalm 80, 'Give ear, O Shepherd of Israel, thou that leadest Joseph like a flock'. These are lovely thoughts. The chapter ends with a promise of hope for future days, and the Lord is seen at the head, going before His people. As we look at the chapter, we see the folly of corrupt men whose actions through cruelty and selfishness could only destroy the inheritance of the land. But in the caring kindness of the God of Israel, we see purposes that would at all costs work for its preservation.

Comments

There are two vital factors in God's dealings with His people that come out of this rather sombre chapter. The first is that those who walk uprightly can enjoy the benefit of the values of the word of God. The tragedy with Israel at this time, and with us very often, is that we switch off rather than apply the truth to ourselves. The word is for our good, notice especially 2 Tim. 3.15-17. Given by inspiration of God, God-breathed, there is sufficiency in its contents to edify, exercise and equip for all situations, those who obey it. Paul went on to tell Timothy of days that would come when similar conditions to those in Israel, would exist. They would not endure sound doctrine, 2 Tim. 4.2-4.

The second factor to notice is the deep love and care God had, even for a people so wayward and rebellious. The shepherd-care implied in the re-gathering of the remnant of Israel, encourages us to trust the God whose longsuffering kindness bears with our weakness and failure. The 'I wills' of the rebellion of His people, are more than matched by the 'I wills' of divine grace and forgiveness. He is a God that is ready to pardon, cf. Isa. 55.6-7.

Chapter 3

Outline

verses 1–8, Denunciation of Princes and Prophets.
verses 9.12, Doom of Zion foretold.

Exposition

The chapter intensifies what has already been said of the sins of oppression and rejection of the word of the Lord. It also confirms the inevitable doom of the nation.

Verses 1–8. When a nation's leaders are astray, there is very little hope for the well-being of the people. To the heads of Jacob, and the princes of the house of Israel, it seems that Micah speaks with personal fervour. 'And I said, Hear I pray you'. There is something of a sense of hurt in the question he asks, 'Is it not for you to know judgement?' He expected better of them, they should have known the meaning of integrity and justice. Instead they hated good and loved evil. Their behaviour-patterns betrayed a complete lack of responsibility in leading the nation.

Note the violence of their oppression of the poor. Eating their flesh and flaying or tearing their skin; each of these actions shows their complete disregard for the good of the poor. They were behaving like wild beasts devouring their prey, cf. Amos 8.4–6. This suggests oppression of unbelievable savagery. The implication of verse 4 is that God hears the cry of the poor and the downtrodden, but will not hear the cry of these oppressors; He will hide His face from them.

The Lord has also a word for those prophets, spiritual leaders of the people, who were prophesying falsely and causing them to err. For those who gave them to eat, they preached peace, but for those who would not pay they declared war against them. This was a terrible state of affairs. The exercise of this sacred office was turned into a mercenary occupation, where if people paid the right price they were given the word to please them. Note how the Lord Jesus described such people in His day. 'Beware of false prophets, which come to you in sheep's clothing, but inwardly they are ravening wolves', Matt. 7.15.

The reward for their wicked betrayal of the people is terrible indeed. Night would descend upon them and there would be no vision. All would be dark, the light of revelation would be lost. Shame and confusion would cover them and there would be no answer from God. How sad for the people who looked to them for a word from the Lord.

Spiritual darkness would be the result, and this actually was the condition that Micah saw. It is interesting to compare this situation with the days later on in the history of Judah, when Jeremiah prophesied, cf. Jer. 23.16–32. Here the prophets were making false assertions in the Name of the Lord. They were foretelling peace when there was no hope of peace. They were resisting the authentic word of the Lord through Jeremiah. The Lord was against them. All Jeremiah could say was, 'He that hath my word, let him speak my word faithfully. What is the chaff to the wheat? saith the Lord'.

Micah looked at the character of these men and their messages, and then he took stock of himself. In verse 8, he says something very significant about the ministry. 'I am full of power by the spirit of the Lord, and of judgement and of might'. In this consciousness and through this spirit he could declare that which God wanted the people to hear. He could declare unto Jacob and Israel the realities of their sins. There was therefore authority and authenticity in the messages that the prophet brought to the nation. Resist it they may, but evade it they could not. It tells us that all the way through the history of the prophets who spoke in the name of the Lord, the Holy Spirit that came upon them was the agent of revelation and effectiveness, Zech. 4.6–10.

Verses 9–12. The word comes again to the heads and the princes of the nation. They are the ones who also abhor judgement and pervert all equity. They should have been the guardians of truth and justice. Under them the people should have felt secure. Instead a charge of the most serious character is brought against them. They built up Zion with blood, or bloods, and Jerusalem with iniquity. It suggests that the innocent were suffering, even being put to death. We think again of the case of Naboth in 1 Kings 21. In Hosea 4.2, the same indictments are levelled against them. Killing and stealing, they break out and blood toucheth blood, cf. Isa. 1.15; Ezek. 22.27.

The whole attitude of these leaders was steeped in materialism and selfish gain. It is almost beyond imagination that such could be setting themselves forth as guides of the people. But the eye of the Lord was upon the poor who suffered. He knew the situation. Yet even worse was the accusation against them that they reckoned themselves beyond condemnation. 'Is not the Lord among us? none evil can come upon us'. Over all their evil practices, they spread a veneer of outward conformity to religion. They leant upon the Lord. The Lord Jesus saw something similar, when casting the money-changers out of the temple. He accused the money-changers of making His Father's house a den of thieves, Matt. 21.12–13.

Notice how the judgement of Zion and Jerusalem is described. It would be for their sake, because of them, that the places would be destroyed. A terrible responsibility rested upon them. They should have led the nation into blessing and prosperity. Their standards of justice and judgement should have laid the foundation for security and peace. Instead, because of them, doom would come and judgement would fall. Serious consideration, indeed!

Comments

Those who are the guides of the Lord's people, and those who are responsible for bringing His word to them hold a position of weight and responsibility. Against the background of the verses considered, we can compare the words of Paul to the Ephesian elders in Acts 20. In verse 28 he says, 'Take heed to yourselves and to all the flock over which the Holy Ghost has made you overseers, to feed the flock of God which he has purchased with his own blood'. These words tell us of the preciousness of God's people to Himself and the purpose for which the Holy Spirit had appointed them overseers and guides. In the light of those who would devour and destroy the flock, how great was their trust. It is worthy of note that Paul, as he spoke of his commitment to the ministry, could say that his hands were clean, that he was pure from the blood of all men. Happy are all those who bear the burden of leadership, who can say the same thing!

Chapter 4

Outline

verses 1–7, Prosperity and Peace in Mount Zion.
verses 8–10, Doom of Exile and Promise of Restoration.
verses 11–13, Triumph of the Nation.

Exposition

Verses 1–7 These opening verses give an example of true predictive prophecy. They look on to that period of time which is termed 'the last days'. The emphatic nature of this statement, is set against the close of chapter 3, where the destruction of Zion and Jerusalem is foretold. 'But in the last days', looks on to a marked period of time, in the end of time, when these events now envisaged will take place. It is to be noticed that this expression is used in different connections. Jacob used it as he spoke of his sons just before his death, Gen. 49.1. Balaam spoke to Balak of 'what this people shall do to thy people in the latter days', Num. 24.14. As Daniel interpreted the dream to Nebuchadnezzar he spoke of what shall be in the latter days, Dan. 2.28. Notice also the New Testament references to this time, e.g. 1 Tim. 4.1; 2 Tim. 3.1; Heb. 1.1. It is clear that the conditions or events mentioned in this connection are not all the same. The context has to be studied to gain the meaning.

In these verses it is clear that the events and conditions spoken of have not been fulfilled. Never has the nation of Israel known the blessings mentioned here. Therefore we must relate them to a time that is yet to be when the nation will be the centre of the earth and blessings will flow from it, and people will come in to Zion as the place of blessing. Notice the *place*. 'The mountain of the Lord, and to the house of the God of Jacob', v. 2. Here is the place of elevation, exalted above the hills, v. 1. It is interesting to read the Psalms that have the place of Jerusalem in mind. It was the beloved city to God's people, but it was also the place where God would delight to dwell, see Ps. 48; 87.1–3; 132.13–15, etc. A study of the various contexts is worthwhile.

The *purpose* of the Lord for this time is clear. As people find their way to the mountain of the Lord, they will find guidance and understanding of His ways as He teaches His way through His word. Thus they will walk in His ways. Notice verse 4 in this connection. The people of Israel separate themselves from those who walk by other gods. They will walk in the Name of the Lord their God for ever. How often this separateness was disregarded in their history. In this time to come, Israel will be only for her God.

These will be times of *prosperity* and *peace*, conditions of perfection. There will be no more wars or strife between peoples. Weapons of war will become instruments of peace and production, cf. Isa. 2.1–5. The weak, 'her that halteth', will be gathered, and will be made a strong nation. The Lord will reign over them in Zion for ever. The prophet in these verses gathers together inspiration and hope for a nation that is going to be exiled, and during the centuries scattered and persecuted.

When will these days be? Space does not allow us to expand, but there is no doubt that they look on to Millennial days, when Satan will be bound and the Lord Jesus Christ will reign in righteousness for 1000 years, cf. Rev. 20 1–8. The restoration of the nation of Israel to the land, and the reign of Christ over the earth will be for universal peace and blessing. This is the hope of Israel.

Verses 8–10. The tone of these verses is a contrast to the vision of glory in the previous word. The assurance is given that the kingdom shall come to the 'daughter of Jerusalem'. The phrase 'the first kingdom' could be a look back, to the glory of the days of Solomon and the united kingdom. But the affirmation is given that the establishment of the nation at Jerusalem is sure. Yet at present, the prophet recognizes the state of confusion in the present conditions. 'No king in thee? is thy counsellor perished?' The sins of the nation caused pain, like to the pains of child-birth. But that which would result was the tragic conditions of exile in Babylon. Whatever degree of glory the future held, the present was bleak and painful. Verse 10 is an interesting word of contrast: the exile of Babylon with all its sadness, yet the delivering hand of the Lord with all its gladness. Israel would be redeemed from the hand of all its enemies. Surely a word yet to be fulfilled.

Verses 11–13. 'Now also many nations are gathered against thee'. In the days of Ahaz there was the unholy alliance of Samaria with Syria against Judah and Jerusalem, Isa. 7.1–2. And in the days of Hezekiah, Sennacherib came up against defenced cities of Judah, Isa. 36.1ff. Yet Micah sees their opposition as the result of ignorance of the counsel of the Lord. It was a blindness that would end in their destruction. This is an encouraging insight into the absolute certainty of the Lord's purpose concerning His chosen people. His thoughts and plans are for their good, cf. Jer. 29.11–14. Prophecy indicates that there will be a climax of battle against the 'beloved city' as Satan gathers the forces together in the final conflict. The blindness of satanic forces to the true position is evident. Jerusalem will be invincible. Fire from heaven will devour them and Satan, the deceiver, will be cast into the Lake of Fire, Rev. 20.7–10.

The chapter ends in a call to Zion to arise. The Lord will empower them to 'beat in pieces' many people. There will be strength enough to thresh as in the days of harvest. The mixing of metaphors here is to be noted; the gain realized is to be consecrated to the Lord. We notice that He is called here the Lord of the whole earth. His sovereignty and power in possession must be recognized.

Comments

In many ways this is the most interesting of all the chapters of Micah. The outstanding feature of it is the deep assurance that it gives of God's love for, and eventual establishment of, Jerusalem as the centre of the earth when Christ comes to reign. We call to mind Messianic Psalms such as Psalm 2: the clash of heathen forces, the noise of pagan rage. All is antagonism directed against the Lord and against His Anointed.

Behind it all we see satanic hatred and rebellion, not primarily against the city but against the glorious Person enthroned in it. Over this chapter we can write those words of declaration, 'Yet have I set my king upon my holy hill of Zion', Ps. 2.6. When He is finally enthroned there, the earth will know perfection and peace. In an opposite way, the chapter highlights the ignorance of those who seek to undermine the purposes of God. That these can never fail is hidden from the enemies of the Lord. It is good for us today to move with our God, who works all things according to the purpose of the counsel of His own will, Eph. 1.11. Paul's prayer is relevant as he prayed for the Ephesians, 'The eyes of your understanding being enlightened; that ye may know what is the hope of his calling,' 1.18. We, like those of old, need men who have understanding to know the times. The Christ who will come for us, will be the Christ who will reign.

Chapter 5

Outline

verses 1-6, Out of Bethlehem, yet from Eternity.
verses 7-9, The Emergence and Might of the Remnant.
verses 10-15, Chastisement and Purification of the Nation.

Exposition

Verses 1-6. The focus of the earlier verses of chapter 4 was upon the ultimate times of Israel's history. Now we look at verses which are a definite prophecy of the birth of the Messiah, the Lord Jesus. That this is so, is confirmed by the way in which the scribes in Herod's palace in Jerusalem immediately referred to the prophecy when the Magi arrived from the East, Matt. 2.6. It is worthy of note that there was no hesitation in their answer to the king, and also there was no doubt in Herod's mind as to whom they referred. He immediately planned in his schemes for ways to destroy Him. How valuable is Messianic prophecy! To any who study the ways of God in history it is essential to grasp that the sufferings of Christ and the glory that should follow are central to the on-going revelation of God's purposes.

We can note also that Isaiah, partly a contemporary of Micah, gives three prophecies at least, related to the birth of Christ, Isa. 7.10-14; the sign of the virgin's son, Isa. 7.14; the Immanuel prophecy; and Isa. 9.6-7, the prophecy of the Child that was to be born and the Son given, cf. Matt.1.23; Luke 1.26-27.

It does seem that verse 1 of the chapter follows on from chapter 4. The words concerning Bethlehem begin a new vision in the prophet's words. We consider the smallness of the town, 'little among the thousands of Judah'. We think of the greatness of Him who would come out of this unimportant town, 'to be ruler of Israel'. But then the sheer miracle of it unfolds, 'whose goings forth have been from of old, from everlasting'. It is difficult to put into words the mystery of the incarnation. Yet these thoughts help us in appreciating the fact of it; God manifest in the flesh. In terms of prophetic truth, this reveals the accuracy of scripture; that some 700 years before Christ, the very place that He should be born was foretold.

We consider the other facts that are in the context of this word. Verse 3 suggests that Israel would be given up until 'she which travaileth has brought forth'. When Christ came, 'He came unto his own'. The shepherd character of Christ's rule is the subject of verse 4. Wonderful His strength, and His greatness unto the ends of the earth. He would also be the source of peace to a troubled nation. The Assyrian would be defeated, the nation delivered. Looking at verses 5–6, they perhaps indicate the defeat of Sennacherib under Hezekiah, as the Lord intervened on behalf of His people. It is interesting to notice the association of peace with this prophecy. 'And this man shall be the peace', v. 5. Isaiah could speak of Him as the Prince of Peace, 9.6. At His birth the angels celebrated peace on earth, Luke 2.14. Through the cross He made peace between Jew and Gentile, making 'one new man', Eph. 2.14–17. And when He reigns the world will know peace as never before.

Verses 7–9. These three verses concern the remnant of Jacob, that part of the nation preserved through the troubles. They are viewed as being in the midst of the people and exerting their influence there. Two different similes are used. 'As a dew from the Lord', they fall quietly on the grass, and as showers that fall regardless of man. And also as a lion among the beasts, just the opposite, being violent and destructive. So the assurance is given that all their enemies will be cut off. We are again reminded that God will take up a part of His people, even after the years of dispersion and destruction.

Verses 10–15. We are brought face to face with declarations of God, as He utters His 'I wills' of chastisement of His people. 'In that day' tells us of a specific time when these activities will take place. Notice the far-reaching extent of these judgements. The strength of the nation will be destroyed. Cities will be cut off. All the signs of their sinfulness, the witchcraft and evil practices, the idolatry and false worship, every manifestation of departure and evil, all will be removed as God executes His vengeance. There is no doubt that these actions of judgement took place when Nebuchadnezzar came from Babylon and destroyed Jerusalem and plundered, and absolutely devastated, the cities of Judah. But this execution of God's anger took place at other times, most notably when Jerusalem was destroyed in A.D.70, and the nation was finally scattered.

Comments

We can enjoy the prophecy of verses 2-3 in appreciation of the wonder of the person of the Lord Jesus Christ. His humanity was so real and yet His deity without question. Perhaps there are not many Old Testament scriptures that distinctly teach the pre-existence of the Son. We know Proverbs 8.22-31 indicates that Christ, as the personification of wisdom, was there before time began. The theophanies, the appearances of the Angel of the Lord, also portray the same, see Gen.18.1-3 and Judg.13 as examples. But here in Micah the thought of everlastingness is positively stated. The 'goings forth' of the One out of Bethlehem were from eternal days. In these days when so much is questioned concerning the inspiration of the bible and the deity of Christ, this assertion is vitally important.

Chapter 6

Outline

verses 1-5, Controversy of the Lord with His people.
verses 6-8, Character of True Religion.
verses 9-16, Condemnation of the Wickedness in Israel.

Exposition

Chapters 6 and 7 join together to highlight matters which bring to a climax the burden of the prophet. The tragic sin of the nation is detailed, and condemned. The character of the religion that should have been manifest in the life of the people is described. Yet the book ends with the compassion and love of God being clearly declared.

Verses 1-5. 'Hear ye now what the Lord says', v. 1. In the face of all that the people are doing, God must be heard to speak. This must be the main thrust of all prophetic ministry, that God's voice is heard. It is a sad fact, that when God's people are out of the way, they have little inclination to hear His voice. Sin not only blinds the eyes, but closes the ears. God speaks with contention as He wants to call attention to the evils of the day. He calls to the mountains to listen to the controversy He has with Israel. There is a pathos about the words of verse 2, 'He will plead with Israel'.

We notice how God reasons with the nation. He asks them to spell out what He has done to deserve the treatment they are giving Him. We feel the hurt in the words, 'O my people'. He has not given them up in spite of their persistent rebellion. He calls upon them to state their case. It is interesting how this approach is often seen in God's dealing with the nation, cf. Isa.1.18. God reasons, although He had the right to destroy.

The Lord calls to mind the history of His blessings on His people. They were redeemed out of Egypt and given leaders to go before them. The events relating to Balak and Balaam give evidence that God turned curse into blessing, that they might know His righteousness. The salvation history of Israel was a valid vantage point from which God could plead His cause. God's abundant will to bless, exposed the wretchedness of Israel's will to sin. We do well to note this.

Verses 6–8. These verses could be described as presenting the very heart of the message of Micah. They have moral implications far beyond his times, and present a challenge to the hypocrisy of his day. The questions asked probe deeply into the hollow sham of those who hid their wrongdoing behind the outward rituals of a dead religion. How should they approach the Lord? What should they bring? It is noticeable that Micah speaks in the first person, challenging them to state their convictions. He identified himself with the requirements that they should understand and fulfil. What is the attitude of the Lord to animal sacrifices, to the rituals of the ceremonial law? We may well ask this in the light of the words of verse 7. Some would teach that the ceremonies of the old economy and the importance of sacrifice were beginning to wane. This is certainly not true. Here we have a matter of moral rectitude. What good were these outward expressions of atonement for sin, if the inward stains and the outward behaviour patterns were wilfully wrong? God desired more than this, cf. Ps. 51.16.17; Isa. 1.11–15. The blood of sacrifice could never answer for hands and lives that were cursed with the innocent blood of the oppressed. No way could God accept them or be pleased with them. 'He hath shewed thee, O man, what is good'. Here are three vital statements which express that which will bring pleasure to the Lord. In *action*, do justly; in *attitude*, love mercy; *in association*, walk humbly with thy God. Thus the requirements of God go straight to the heart of the nation's sin, cf. Deut. 10.12–13. It is interesting to compare the words of the Lord Jesus to the scribes and Pharisees of His day as He exposed their hypocrisy. They paid attention to the small matters of tithing, mint and anise, but left the weightier matters of the law undone. These, such as judgement, mercy and faith, they should have attended to as well as the others, Matt. 23.23. These words tell us that actions, attitudes and associations have to be right before we can worship God acceptably. To Saul, Samuel had to put priority on obedience rather than on sacrifices, 1 Sam. 15.22-23. How essential to learn the lesson of walking humbly with our God.

Verses 9-16. The voice of the Lord calls to the city. In these verses there is a condemnation of the nation's wickedness in categorical terms. One translation gives, 'to fear your name is wisdom'. The call is to take heed to the rod and the appointer of it. Verses 10-12 explore the nature of the wickedness found. They are decribed as treasures in the house of the wicked. These described the dishonesty and deception practised. There is violence and lying, and how can God count them pure? There is something penetrating about these words, which come from a God who knows all.

The Lord says what He is going to do about such wickedness. Sickness and desolation would come as the Lord smote them. Eating without satisfaction would follow; there would be no deliverance and no security. There would be much effort to produce but no harvests at the end of their labour. Evil would rob the people of all that the land held for them. The word of God spoken in earliest days of the nation's history would be fulfilled, cf. Deut. 28.15; 38-40.

We may well ask where the rot set in, that such evils should be there to expose? Verse 16 reveals that in the days of Omri and Ahab of Samaria, evils were introduced into the life of the nation that did spiritual damage which was never eradicated. Jezebel the wicked queen, and the idolatries and immoralities of the house of Baal, left a spiritual cancer at the heart of the people's life that eventually could only end in disastrous judgement. Judah eventually partook of the nature of these sins and shared Samaria's fate.

Comments

We notice three points of value in these verses. Firstly it is to be noticed that when God would reason with His own about their sin, He calls for remembrance of His earlier blessings. To those who would backslide, the remembrance of former mercies can act as a stimulus to repentance. Think of the prodigal and his thoughts on the Father's house, Luke 15.17-20, cf. Deut. 8.1-6.

Secondly, we learn that a humble walk of sincerity and truth most befits those who would worship and serve Him. We call to mind the woman at the well and her conversation with the Saviour. She was concerned with the outward trappings of worship. Jesus had to speak to her of a Father who seeks worshippers who worship Him in spirit and truth, John 4.19–24. No outward form of religious ceremony can cover a condition of heart that is not pleasing to God. Think on Romans 12.1–2!

Lastly, we can learn a solemn lesson concerning the effects that a period of weakness can have upon the generations of the people of God. We consider the words concerning Jeroboam of Israel as the man who made Israel to sin. Perhaps we need to consider these things in the light of present day trends in assembly life, and the legacy we are leaving behind for future generations, should Christ not have come in the meantime. Notice the advice to Timothy from Paul, 2 Tim. 2.1.–2.

Chapter 7

Outline

verses 1–7, Lament for Lack of Loyalty.
verses 8–10, Challenge to the Enemy.
verses 11–13, Walls Rebuilt and Decree Removed.
verses 14–17, Prayer of Hope.
verses 18–20, Climax of Confidence.

Exposition

This final chapter is the most full and the most varied in thought of all in the prophecy. Notice it begins with 'Woe is me'; the prophet identifies with sadness, with the evils of the nations. But it ends with a glad assertion of the faithfulness of God, 'Thou wilt perform the truth to Jacob', v. 20. What a difference the picture displays, when we look from ourselves to the God who is ours. We need to bear this in mind as we end our consideration of the book.

Verses 1–7. The prophet is in despair. He is expressing unfulfilled desires, longings that have not been realized. He longs for fruit but there is no cluster to eat. All is barren. In terms of the condition of the nation, there is a complete absence of goodness and righteousness in the land. The atmosphere is conditioned by violence and mistrust.

In verses 3 – 4 the corruption and dishonesty are described in vivid terms. Bribery and mischief are rife. The best of them is as a briar, prickly and dangerous to deal with. Note that the characters who are guilty, are those who should be the leaders and guides of the nation. Such conditions can mean only one thing. The days of judgement will visit them. They will be plunged into perplexity.

Thus the prophet declares the extent of the cancer eating away at the heart of the nation. No friend can be trusted. The enemies are found right at the heart of the family life of the people. There is no integrity, no loyalty, even where they should most be found. It is interesting that Jesus alludes to these verses in Matthew. 10.36. We can reflect, that when a nation gives up its loyalty to God, every measure of lesser loyalty suffers. Therefore the prophet turns from his lament and he looks to his God, a lovely shaft of light in the dark conditions he experienced. His God is the God of 'my salvation'. The righteous can triumph however dark the day may be. Micah was sure he had the ear of his God. The implications of this passage demand careful thought, cf. Hab. 3 17-19.

Verses 8-10. These verses are written in the first person, and it seems as if the prophet speaks as the nation. The voice of challenge sounds out. We notice that the conditions of defeat and disaster are not irrevocable. The enemy will not have it all his own way. There will be recovery after fall, light after darkness. The spirit in which it is stated is one of humble confession and submission to the God against whom the sin has been committed. These words express hope in the justice of God. It will be light and righteousness that will be seen. There is a sense of defiance towards the enemy that questioned, 'Where is the Lord thy God?' As the prophet stands with, and for, the nation in its tragic condition, he throws down the challenge to the enemy who he knows will, eventually, be overthrown. The God of Israel is the God of the nation's recovery.

Verses 11-13. 'In that day'. This phrase is often repeated in the prophetic books. It marks times when God will do certain things, and when certain events will take place. It can refer to a time near at hand such as the return from exile, or it can look right on to the ultimate of God's dealings with His people, cf. Jer. 39.15-18; Zech. 12-14. It is good to study the contexts of the prophetic words with this phrase in mind. Here in these verses we read of the time when the walls of Jerusalem would be rebuilt and the decree of judgement far removed. Gentile nations would come into the city from far away. This is the vision for the city already expressed in 4.2, and looks on to the great day of Israel's earthly restoration. Yet the desolation of the city, as Micah spoke these words, was evidence that God must punish His people for their doings. The exile in Babylon was definitely a time experienced by them for the evils of their ways. Surely this is a sad reflection on the nature of sin and its effects in human experience.

Verses 14–17. These verses have been described as a prayer expressing the hope that God still cared about His own and would intervene for their recovery. 'Feed thy people ... the flock of thine heritage'. The margin has 'rule', as also the RV translation, cf. 5.4. The shepherd relationship of Jehovah with His covenant people was something very precious to the nation. He was the Shepherd of Israel, Ps. 80.1. It was a Messianic concept, cf. Isa. 40.11. In their loneliness away from God, under the despotic rule of the kings of Babylon, longings were created as they looked back to the history of God's care in days of old. Verse 15 suggests this, as the days of the exodus are remembered, when marvellous things were done by God. Once the gracious care of the Lord has been tasted, backsliding souls are often left with an 'aching void' within cf. Luke 15.17.

The hopes of recovery are clearly implied in verses 16–17. Nations would witness the dramatic intervention of the God of Israel. We see the wonderful precision of God's dealings, when after the 70 years were completed, Cyrus, whom God referred to as His servant, was stirred to proclaim the release of the nation from captivity, 2 Chr. 36.22–23. Micah looks on to this, and speaks of the astonishment of the surrounding nations, when a nation so weak and defeated would rise again to recovery. This would be the cause of fear and dread, so dramatic will be the change. We can only try to imagine what the ultimate restoration of Israel will mean when, fully gathered into the land, they exercise sway under the rule of the Lord Jesus as their Messiah-King.

Verses 17–20. Micah's name means, 'Who is a God like thee?'. How significant, that this final, confident word of the prophet should begin with these very words. It is turned into an exclamation of wonder. There are dark words of judgement and condemnation, spoken so often out of a sense of horror and shame, that a nation so privileged could sin so grievously. Surely this cried out for justice to be done and judgement executed. But Micah looked up to a God who could 'pardon iniquity' and 'pass by' transgression. A God who would not keep His anger against them always. Wonderful expression, because He delights in mercy! So compassion will be displayed, deep evidence of a loving heart, and all their sins will be cast into the depths of the sea. The intensity of these words, and their far reaching meaning, is staggering. We need to read them thoughtfully and carefully.

In these words we have the tension between God's love and His hatred of sin, between mercy and judgement. We dare not underestimate the seriousness of sin, nor misread the claims of God's holiness. We are bound to read these words in the light of Calvary, an event which at this time was yet future, but the central place in all God's dealings with human sin and the provision for pardon and forgiveness. The depth of meaning in the ways of God lies in His sovereignty, cf. Exod. 33.19. As God revealed His character to Moses in the light of His people's failure He said, 'I will proclaim the name of the Lord before thee; and I will be gracious to whom I will be gracious, and will show mercy to whom I will show mercy'.

The final verse of the book is a cry of triumph in the face of adversity. It proclaims the faithfulness of God. He will perform, and He will act in the light of His truth and His mercy. The oath of God, 'sworn to our fathers from days of old', gives hope to the prophet in the darkest of days. It is good to realize that here for the nation was the anchor of hope in the immutability of a God who cannot lie, cf. Luke 1.54–55; Heb. 6.13–20.

Comments

Did Micah ever see the effects of his ministry on the people to whom he spoke? We never hear of him again. We know that judgement fell on the nation to whom he prophesied, and that the people paid the penalty of their sin. But far beyond Micah's day the word had its fulfilment. In the birth of Christ and in the ultimate blessing of the nation in the land, the full meaning of the message has some of its relevance. But more than this. In the message of the prophets are enshrined the imperishable values of the doctrines of the covenant people, and in these doctrines and commands is revealed the character of the God of Israel. How important, then, that the word should be given, even though rebellion and disobedience were the reactions shown by the people.

To Isaiah God said, 'So shall my word be that goeth forth out of my mouth: it shall not return unto me void, but it shall accomplish that which I please, and it shall prosper in the thing whereto I sent it', 55.11. Micah has long passed from the scene of time. But the word lives on. 'Who is a God like thee?' – this the meaning of his name. We in our generation, as he in his, are left to explore the wonder of this question as we study God's sovereign acts in the movements of His people.

THE PROPHECY OF
NAHUM

by CYRIL G. CANN

Preface

THE PROPHECY OF NAHUM is a powerful statement of the certainty of
God's judgement upon the nation of Assyria and its capital, Nineveh. It
describes in eloquent language the manner of Nineveh's overthrow and
the joy of the people of God, the Southern Kingdom of Judah, in consequence of this.

Much has been written about the text of the prophecy. Some have
seen it as fragmentary remains of a larger document, have detected
elements of an alphabetic psalm in 1.2–10 and have suggested that
1.11–2.2 is an insertion by a later editor. Such criticisms cast doubt upon
the integrity of the book and its message. Its origin, in human terms, is
of little consequence. The Holy Spirit in His wisdom has been pleased to
preserve the book to us in its current form as part of that which relates to
and illustrates the eternal truth of God. It reads as an entity and is
accepted as such. In literary terms the book in its original form is in
poetic style and Nahum is given a high place amongst ancient Hebrew
prophet-poets.

The proud, arrogant and successful (in human terms) Assyrian nation
was fundamentally corrupt. It perpetrated a brutally dominant regime
and its values and associated conduct brought it into conflict with principles of holiness which characterize the God of Israel and Judah. Nineveh was warned and Jehovah waited in quiet patience whilst the city
revealed its true character. Judgement then was swift and total. The
One in whom Judah trusted is in control of all nations. Moral principles
associated with His rule operate amongst all peoples and will never be
set aside.

It is not possible to remove a Messianic association from a reading of the book. Some of the assertions go beyond the immediate situation involving Judah, 'Though I have afflicted thee, I will afflict thee no more', 1.12; 'Behold upon the mountains the feet of him that bringeth good tidings, that publisheth peace!' 1.15. These statements can only be completely fulfilled in a millennial context although elements of fulfilment may be seen in the period following the destruction of Nineveh. In their completion they look forward to a day when the nation will be united and will be seen to be God's chosen people. They will then bear testimony throughout the whole world to His universal and just rule.

The book of Nahum is directly relevant to the present time. The same God is still in control amongst the nations and is working out His purposes even in our day. Our confidence in this is unshakeable because it is underpinned by Christ's supreme victory upon the cross over the powers of evil. We rejoice that there He dealt with sin in its principle and root, defeated Satan and conquered death. None can challenge His purposes nor His rule!

Introduction

Nahum

Little is known about Nahum. Like so many of the Old Testament prophets, he is a man hidden behind the message God gave him to proclaim and over which he was so deeply exercised. The message is powerful and vivid and was probably first presented verbally to the people; later it was written down in the power and inspiration of the Holy Spirit to form part of holy scripture. Nahum means 'Comforter' and this he was to the people of God in a dark and difficult day.

Little is known about Elkosh where Nahum lived. If it is to be identified with Capernaum (which means 'Village of Nahum') in Galilee then Nahum could well have been a descendant of the Israelites who remained in the north or who returned there following the overthrow of the Northern Kingdom by the Assyrians as recorded in 2 Kings 18. The prophecy relates to Assyria but was addressed to the Southern Kingdom of Judah; it must be assumed that Nahum spent some time in Judah and might even have visited Nineveh.

Date of the Prophecy

There is evidence in the book of the period within which the prophecy was written. The fall of Nineveh is viewed as a future event, 1.14 and it is generally accepted that the city fell in 607 or 606 BC. In chapter 3 verse 8 the prophet speaks of the capture and destruction of No-Amon as having taken place. No-Amon is Thebes which was the capital of Upper Egypt which fell under an attack from Ashurbanipal, King of Assyria, in 663 BC. The writing of the prophecy is, therefore, placed between 663 and 606 BC. There is no agreement on a precise date within these parameters but it is generally taken to be towards the end of the period, probably between 610 and 607 BC.

Theme of the Prophecy

The theme of the prophecy is the certainty of the judgement of God upon the nation of Assyria and upon its capital city Nineveh in particular. The nation was wicked and arrogant in its wickedness and opposition to the things of God. It constantly troubled the people of God. Jonah, some 150 years before, had been used by God to warn Nineveh of the consequences of their sin and the city had repented. Subsequent generations returned to their wicked, ungodly ways and became the recipients of divine judgement.

God is patient and the judgement was delayed. This gave opportunity for repentance but also allowed the evil of the nation to be fully revealed; in this way the judgement was established on the basis of righteousness and justice. When divine judgement fell upon the city it was total and unmitigated. So complete was the devastation of Nineveh that it is recorded that Alexander the Great marched his troops over the ground and was not even aware that the proud city had once flourished there!

Historical Context

Assyria was the dominating world power. They were an ancient people known even in Moses' day, Gen.2.14. The Assyrian nation does not appear in Jewish history until about 770 BC when Menaham was king of the Northern Kingdom. It is recorded in 2 Kings 15.19-20 that he (Menaham) paid tribute of a thousand talents of silver to Pul, the king of Assyria. The Assyrian nation was the rod used by God to punish the ten tribes of the Northern Kingdom because of their sin and unfaithfulness. The Northern Kingdom was defeated and removed by Assyria as recorded in 2 Kings 17.6. 2 Kings chapter 18 indicates that the Southern Kingdom of Judah was also troubled by the Assyrians.

Assyria was a cruel nation which dominated and oppressed weaker kingdoms demanding homage and tribute. Its religion consisted in the worship of a range of minor deities under the head of Asshur who was the deified patriarch of the nation, Gen.10.22. Conquest of a country by the Assyrians resulted in the establishment in that country of the 'Laws of Asshur' and 'Altars to the Great Gods' which were in opposition to the teaching and practice of Judaism. Herodotus, the Jewish historian, records that the Assyrians were 'Lords of Asia' for 520 years. By 668 BC when Asshurbanipal acceded to the throne, the Assyrian army had been so successful that no serious enemy remained.

The fall of Nineveh was predicted by Isaiah, 10.5-19, as well as Nahum. The Medes in alliance with the Babylonians besieged Nineveh but it remained impregnable until the hand of God intervened. It was devastated before the enemy entered!

Outline of the Book

This is based upon the chapter division of the King James Version of the Bible.

Chapter 1. Principles of God's Judgement.
Chapter 2. Extent and Description of God's Judgement.
Chapter 3. Reasons which Justify God's Judgement.

Chapter 1.
Principles of God's Judgement

Verse 1

The prophecy of Nahum contains a rich and profound presentation of the character of God. He is presented as Jehovah – the One who governs His people and is concerned about their relationship with the nations which surround them. Each Gentile nation presents some aspect of the worldly scene: the Assyrian nation and the city of Nineveh represent the haughty glory of this world. Nineveh appeared impregnable with walls 100 feet high and wide enough for chariots to drive upon. It had a perimeter of some 60 miles and was adorned by 1200 towers; it boasted that no power on earth could overcome it.

The expression 'burden of Nineveh' refers to the pressing, severe judgement which would (and did) fall upon the city. It is an expression used often by Isaiah: 'burden of Babylon', Isa. 13.1, 'burden of Moab', Isa. 15.1, 'burden of Egypt', Isa. 19.1 and relates to the certainty and the extent of the judgement. 'The vision of Nahum the Elkoshite' indicates the source and the vehicle of the message: the source was Jehovah because the vision was from Him and Nahum of Elkosh was the vehicle for its delivery.

There has been much discussion about the location of Elkosh. W. KELLY assumes its location in Galilee and notes that Jonah, who took an earlier warning to Nineveh also came from Galilee (the town of Gath-hepher). Galilee bordered on Assyria and this would have produced awareness and sensitivity to the relationship between that nation and the people of God. It would also have equipped and prepared both prophets for the solemn task they were later to be given. Such sensitivity and exercise relative to the ungodly is still a requirement of each believer in our day.

Verses 2–6

These verses outline in vivid language the character and awesome power of the One who judges. Nothing can withstand the anger and vengeance of Jehovah; not even the mountains, the seas, the storm nor the whirlwind which are the seats of power upon the earth. It is important to understand that the judgement is not vindictive.

Vindictive judgement is hasty and capricious. We have here a principle which is in harmony with the character of Jehovah, 'He will not at all acquit the wicked', 1.3. Because it is principle, the judgement can wait unchanging and unchangeable so that the mercy of Jehovah, which is also principle, may operate. Jehovah's judgement never falls without warning and opportunity for repentance; His judgement is associated with patience! 'Jehovah is slow to anger', 1.3.

Anger is a totally appropriate emotion to associate with a Holy God. The Lord Jesus Christ who came from heaven and 'declared' the Father upon the earth, John 1.18, demonstrated holy anger in His abhorrence of that which was evil. In Mark 3.5 it is recorded that 'he ... looked round about on them (the Pharisees) with anger'. Holy anger was part of the moral glory that shone forth from the Saviour when here on earth. As believers we are too often angry in a manner which reflects our jealousies and disappointments but holy anger, against the things which displease and dishonour the Lord, places the believer upon high moral ground.

Verses 7–15

The subject is still the judgement of Jehovah. There is unlimited judgement upon the Assyrian nation and its capital city, Nineveh, and some indication of the manner in which it was to be overthrown. As already mentioned, it was impregnable to attack from the most powerful army and only fell under the hand of God: the river Tigris overflowed its normal course and swept away the foundations of large parts of the city. In despair it was burned by its inhabitants before the Babylonian armies entered. 'With an over-running flood he will make an utter end of the place thereof', 1.8.

In contrast to this Jehovah has made provision for His own. We read 'The Lord is good, a strong-hold in the day of trouble; and he knoweth them that trust in him', 1.7. But this is not to assume that the principle of judgement is set aside for His own; it operates, but to a different end – to the end that His people might be purged and chastened to walk more carefully and faithfully in His revealed ways. To the God of holiness, sin in His own people is as displeasing as it was in the wicked nation of Assyria, and in both it must be dealt with so that His holiness might be vindicated. In the latter case it was unmitigated, total judgement without mercy because the period of patience had expired; in the former it was for the purpose of chastening and was measured. Verses 12 and 13 apply to Judah, 'Though I have afflicted thee, I will afflict thee no more. For now will I break his yoke from off thee, and will burst thy bonds in sunder'. But the words to Assyria are much more strident, 'Jehovah hath given a command concerning thee, that no more of thy name be sown. Out of the house of thy gods will I cut off the graven image and the molten image: I will make thy grave, for thou art vile', v. 14.

Verse 15 is, in one sense, prophetic of what would happen following the destruction of Nineveh. It is possible to imagine the way in which the bearer of the news would be perceived and received. The words are, however, more powerful than this. In a millennial day, when the power which Assyria only typified will be defeated, God's earthly people will declare true peace and be bearers of this good news to the whole earth.

Chapter 2
Extent and Description of God's Judgement

Verses 1 and 2

These verses commence a vivid description of the process of Nineveh's destruction which is the very heart of Nahum's prophecy. Jehovah's supreme power is revealed. He is sovereign and orders the greatest of nations and world powers according to His eternal purposes and none can resist His mighty strength. The metaphor of a 'hammer' is used in verse 1 to depict this power which opposed Assyria, 'He that dasheth in pieces!' Despite all their military might – munitions, city guards, well trained soldiers and strong fortifications – they would be devastatingly defeated.

Verse 2 refers to an earlier rôle God gave to the Assyrian nation. The metaphor 'axe' is used in Isaiah 10.5 when the Northern Kingdom of Israel is defeated and removed because of their unrepented sin. It is significant that the One who would remove Assyria summarily from the scene was the One who had taken them up and used them in a particular way to further His purposes. Jehovah is sovereign and all is subservient to His ultimate eternal purpose. It is a principle which operates today. It may not always be possible to perceive this because we only have a limited perspective but we must always assume it is there and will work to His ultimate good which, in turn, is best for His people.

The reference to the vine in verse 2 relates to a matter already considered in verses 12 and 13 of chapter 1 – the different ways in which God deals with sin in those who trust Him and those who oppose Him. In Isaiah 5.7 we read, 'For the vineyard of the Lord of Hosts is the house of Israel, and the men of Judah his pleasant plant'. Israel (and later Judah) were judged with a view to their subsequent return. Jehovah is the One who exalts and lays low according to righteousness. Sin is a threat to His holy nature and cannot be set aside under any circumstances; it must be dealt with in all situations.

Verses 3–10

The assault, capture and sacking of Nineveh is vividly described in these verses. Even though we are not able to benefit from the power of the original text, the words are terrible and solemn and are spoken with great awe; there is, however, running throughout, a clear thread of exultation.

The attacking forces are fearsome, vv. 3–4, but it is the strong hand of Jehovah which breaches the defences. The river Tigris, in unique flood, overflows its banks and washes away the foundations of parts of the city wall and other buildings including the royal palace, v. 6. The most secret parts of the palace are exposed, and the queen who normally led a life of seclusion was dragged into the streets to the great distress of her attendants, v. 7.

Poignantly, the proud city which was thought to be impregnable, and which for centuries was undisturbed by any foe, is likened to a pool of water which is draining away. The cry, 'Stand!', goes unheeded and defender and inhabitant flee the city, v.8. The ultimate humiliation is the open plundering of the city. The hoard of gold and silver was the basis of the boast and vain glory of the city, but now, 'She is empty, void and waste', v. 10. The picture is not of honourable defeat but of total devastation and humiliation.

Verses 11–13

The picture of the lordly lion in his den, vv. 11–12, is appropriately applied to the city of Nineveh. The lion is a creature that causes fear, dominates other beasts and only cares for its own. Assyria had long behaved in this manner towards the surrounding nations. But now the question is asked in exultation, 'Where is the dwelling of the lion?' The question is rhetorical because the answer is self-evident – Nineveh is no more!

The One who confronted proud Assyria with its impregnable capital Nineveh and predicted its humiliating defeat is now shown to be the Lord of hosts (Jehovah of Tsebahoth – Lord of Warrior Hosts!), v.13. This is the last name of God to be revealed in the Old Testament and its main usage is late in the Old Testament. God revealed Himself to His people in a manner appropriate to the situation in which they found themselves. The name Lord of hosts appears in scripture when all appears to be lost and there is none other to whom the people of God can turn. The use in Nahum is in harmony with this: the Lord of Hosts was the only One who could protect them from the threat of the proud lion of Assyria. His subsequent decree is equally sure, 'the voice of thy messengers shall no more be heard'.

Chapter 3.
Reasons for God's Judgement

Verses 1–3

The description of the attack upon Nineveh is continued in these verses but the perspective is different. Having established the principles upon which Jehovah acts, and having described most eloquently the judgement which was meted out, Nahum is now able to explain the reasons for the judgement. In verse 1 the evil principles under which the nation and city operated are indicated: violence and deceit. Assyria had preyed upon nations for centuries and her hands were covered with blood. Verses 2 and 3 contain the most vivid descriptions of the battle in the whole book. The reason for her violent end was the violence which she practised. The nations, including Judah, must know that the evil doer cannot set aside moral principles and pursue selfish, evil ways with impunity. The accounting day will come to all.

Verses 4–7

Assyria's conduct was also immoral. Her relationship with the nations around her was that of a harlot; her strategy to involve them in her religion and idolatry involved seduction as well as violence. The harlotry is associated with sorcery or witchcraft which indicates that the source was Satan and the associated powers of evil. These are completely opposed to the things of God and give priority to attack upon those who attempt to follow in His ways. Jezebel is accused of similar conduct and association in 2 Kings 9.22. The word of Jehu to Joram was, 'What peace, so long as the whoredoms of thy mother Jezebel and her witchcrafts are so many?' Jezebel more than any other was morally corrupt and opposed to the things of God and was judged accordingly.

Whilst the immoral and amoral character of Assyria persisted and developed, Jehovah was patient. When the time of judgement arrived she was shown to be an empty shell; she was not only devastated physically but she disappeared from the scene as a world power. It is significant that she is not included amongst the world powers represented by the image in Daniel 2 even though her ascendancy over other nations lasted for more than 500 years!

The immoral character of the nation and her capital Nineveh was the reason for her humiliation and exposure to the nations in verses 6 and 7; she was exposed for what she really was.

Verses 8–16

The imagery presented in these verses shows to us the city as it was in God's sight. The pictures are those of the city of Thebes, ripe figs on the fig tree and the fire which ate away like a cankerworm.

Thebes, vv.8–10, was the grand capital of Upper Egypt. It was reputed to have a hundred gates and boasted it was impregnable; its overthrow was, however, predicted by Jeremiah, 46.25, and Ezekiel, 30.14–16. The significance of the reference is that Assyria was the weapon used by God to overthrow Thebes. The Assyrians knew the power of Jehovah and how the greatest could be laid low, but they still went their own haughty, violent way. Jehovah hated their violence.

The picture of Nineveh and its inhabitants as ripe figs on the fig tree, vv. 11–12, is completely apart from other associations of the fig tree in scripture with the nation of Israel. The inhabitants of Nineveh were arrogant and proud and boasted in their strength. They were to be shaken by the power of Jehovah and then would fall like first-ripe figs and be consumed. They had no strength against Jehovah.

The fire and the cankerworm, vv. 13–15, relate to that which works from within. When Nineveh was defeated the king saw that his escape was impossible and set fire himself to the palace and the city. It was like the cankerworm which destroys from within. Nineveh was morally corrupt and this corruption is most vividly pictured here.

These pictures clearly present reasons for the judgement of Nineveh. Jehovah hated their violence, arrogance and moral corruption and they were judged accordingly.

Verses 17–19

The conclusion to Nahum's prophecy contained in these verses is conclusive and solemn. Haughty Nineveh, proud capital of Assyria is desolate. The power which for centuries cruelly dominated the eastern world is stilled. Proud princes and captains are not even remembered, 'their place is not known!' v. 17. The leaders of the city sleep and its nobles are brought down to the dust; the people are scattered. Jehovah's holiness is vindicated and finally only His voice is heard, 'There is no healing of thy bruise, thy wound is grievous; all that hear the report of thee shall clap the hands over thee; for upon whom hath not thy wickedness passed continually?', 3.19.

Conclusion

Nahum's prophecy is different from that of other prophets in that it did not condemn the people of God with powerful reminders of their sin. Rather it focused upon the nation which caused distress and opposed Judah. That is not to say that Judah was without fault and that its sin would not be dealt with. This is shown in that Assyria was not only the object of judgement but was also the instrument of God's judgement upon the Northern Kingdom.

We have seen in our brief consideration of Nahum's prophecy that it was concerned with underlying moral principles as well as the more obvious revelations of sinful conduct. There is a moral principle which operates among the nations even though they oppose the ways of God with impunity and appear to go their own way. The principle emanates from the Almighty God who is sovereign amongst the nations and who can, therefore, wait in patience knowing that judgement will and must operate upon the basis of righteousness. His people must understand that, however grim and hopeless the outlook, His righteousness will always overcome evil. This has been a source of great encouragement down through the ages to the people of God, and should yet be to us today.

It has been said that 'holiness' is the characteristic word for God in the Old Testament and 'love' in the New Testament. This is not true! The God of holiness and righteousness is always the God of love, mercy and grace, and has been from eternity: His moral character and glory do not change. The One who cried on the cross, 'My God, my God, why didst thou forsake me!', Ps. 22.1, is also the subject of John 3.16, 'For God so loved the world that he gave his only begotten son'.

Judah was not without fault but their attention is directed through the witness of Nahum to the defeat of impregnable Nineveh as evidence of the mercy and grace of God towards them that they might be encouraged to trust Him and walk in His ways. They did not appreciate the context and importance of this, and continued in their sin and were judged in that they went into captivity in Babylon.

The important point is that the holy God always operates within a context of love; and His love always operates on the basis of righteousness. This is beautifully illustrated by the incident contained in John 21 involving Peter. He and his companions had decided to forsake all they had been associated with relative to the Lord Jesus Christ. Peter says, v. 2, 'I go a fishing!', and his companions reply, 'We also go with thee!' After toiling all night and knowing the misery of failure, cold and hunger the Lord Jesus hails them from the shore and provides success, warmth and food. In this way He prepared the context in love for that powerful challenge He was to make to Peter and which was to transform Peter's life, 'Simon, son of Jonas, lovest thou me more than these?', v. 15. As the people of God we must pursue righteousness in all our personal, family and assembly relationships and this, in the current dispensation, must be done on the basis of the truth revealed in God's word. But let us never forget this important principle which Nahum's writing has brought before us: righteousness and truth must always be held and pursued within a context of love.

Finally, let us note the principle of mercy operating even toward the nation of Assyria whose haughty, worldly glory and greatness was built upon corrupt foundations and crumbled so spectacularly, as we have considered. In Isaiah 19 we read of the restoration of Egypt and Assyria (not Nineveh!) in the millennial kingdom and their being made subject to the reunited nation of Israel.

Our consideration is well summarized in the words of the apostle Paul:

'Behold the goodness and severity of God', Rom. 11.22.

We would wish to respond:

'O the depth of the riches both of the wisdom and knowledge of God! How unsearchable are his judgements, and his ways past finding out!', Rom. 11.33.

CHAPTER EIGHT

THE PROPHECY OF
HABAKKUK

by HOWARD BARNES

An Overview

THE PARTICULAR VALUE OF THE BOOK OF Habakkuk is not the *amount* of prophetic information given to us – more can be read in the contemporary prophecies of Jeremiah and Zephaniah – but for the way in which we see the prophet coming to terms with his message. The prophecy follows the personal pain of Habakkuk at the degenerate state of society around him: God uses the man with his own burden to transmit the burden of prophecy. God, in taking on the man, has to take on his problems and answer them. This He does, and we read the story of the remarkable change in Habakkuk's attitude, going from trouble to trusting, and questioning to quiet rest.

Habakkuk had asked, 'How long?' and God replied, 'I am working a work in your days' – God was already at work; God is always at work, He never slumbers nor sleeps, cf. Ps. 121.4, but is in immediate control. No doubt if challenged Habakkuk would have given the orthodox answer that God is always in control, but for the moment he is overwhelmed by the prevailing conditions around him which seemed to be going on unchecked for ever. He had been crying out to God about them for some time now, and no answer had come; no salvation had appeared. Further, in Habakkuk's eyes it was God's apparent passivity that was 'causing him to look upon perverseness', RV, and he asked 'Why dost thou shew my iniquity?'.

'Behold ye among the nations' (RV) is God's reply. Habakkuk had been looking in the wrong direction! So preoccupied had he been with the state of Judah that he could not think that God's remedy lay elsewhere. When God did tell him His plans, he was bewildered; not only had God seemed to be doing nothing about the wickedness in Judah,

He was actually going to use a nation that was more wicked than they! He eventually gives up his own thoughts and decides to wait for God's complete answer and then give his considered opinion. 'Be still' is often God's word to us. God's answer came, but it put first things first. Whatever he thought, Habakkuk's primary task was to 'Write the vision and make it plain upon tables'. The work of this prophet was to see to it that the message was clearly written. Only then could he come to terms with it himself.

God was going to use the Chaldeans, who without doubt were a hostile and violent nation. But firstly Habakkuk was to learn that, in their turn, they too would be judged; they too would be overwhelmed. This is always God's way of judgement. Secondly, Habakkuk would be assured of the preservation of the righteous – those who lived by faith.

Habakkuk then had a vision of God in all His power and majesty, as shown during a reliving of Israel's earlier history. The experience had a remarkable effect on him. He is transformed from a questioning and worried man to one who not only had come to terms with the possible difficulties that lay in the future for him – when the Chaldeans came and almost everything could be lost – but one who can claim, 'The Lord God is my strength', and say, 'Yet I will rejoice in the Lord, I will joy in the God of my salvation'. No longer is he saying, 'Thou wilt not save'.

Historical and biographical notes

The deportation of Israel – the Northern Kingdom – had occurred almost a century before, and seemed to have been long forgotten by the now careless Southern Kingdom of Judah. The true prophets' warnings were being ignored, false prophets were giving an optimistic picture, and reforms – even when led by kings like Josiah – were superficial. Habakkuk, along with Jeremiah and Zephaniah are used to deliver a final warning.

The Chaldeans were a warlike, aggressive people who lived in southern Babylonia near the Persian Gulf, on the lower Tigris and Euphrates. The people of Babylon – who had been brought into the Assyrian empire by force – could not forget their magnificent history, when they had blossomed while Assyria was merely in its infancy. They were constantly rebelling and sometimes won independence, but it was usually lost again. At a moment of particular weakness in the Assyrian empire, they saw an opportunity of again seizing power in the old capital city of Babylon. In 625 BC Nabopolasser, a Chaldean, seized the throne of Babylon as soon as Assurbanipal had ceased to be king of Assyria. Numerous conflicts then took place between Assyria and Babylon, but in 612 BC in alliance with Cyaxares the king of the Medes – whose daughter was married to Nabopolasser's son Nebuchadnezzar – and the Scythians, the Babylonians attacked and overcame Nineveh the capital city of Assyria and devastated it, Nahum 3.1–3. Cyaxares eventually ruled the old Assyrian empire to the north and northwest and the Chaldeans/Babylonians controlled the rest.

It was quite natural at the same time for Egypt also to try to gain advantage from the weakening of Assyrian power. Palestine and Syria had once belonged to Egypt by right of conquest. When Necho II succeeded his father, he set about the reconquest of Syria and Palestine which then belonged to Assyria. Josiah, king of Judah, vainly opposed him at Meggido and was killed. Necho reached Carchemish on the northern Euphrates in 605 BC and was confronted by Nebuchadnezzar at the head of his father's armies. Necho was utterly defeated in one of the greatest battles in all history and was pursued to the Egyptian borders, Jer. 46.2. However, news arrived of Nebuchadnezzar's father's death and he returned at once to Babylon, otherwise no doubt he would have then invaded Egypt. Now Palestine and Syria were held by the Chaldeans. Later even Egypt became a conquered land and the Chaldean armies eventually over-ran much of the then known world. Nebuchadnezzar then concentrated on making Babylon city the most splendid metropolis of antiquity, so fulfilling his father's desire to rebuild and beautify the city, Dan. 4.30. In the city the Chaldeans excelled at the art of astrology together with other forms of the occult. They founded the science of astronomy, and managed to measure the length of the year to within thirty minutes of the now accepted value!

The eventual and sudden fall of the Chaldean empire took place in 538 BC, Dan. 5.30. 'That so small a land as Chaldea should produce a conquering race of sufficient power to overcome and rule the world of the time is one of the marvels of history', UNGER. In twenty years from rising from obscurity, the Chaldeans and their Babylonian empire almost ruled the world. However, less than 100 years later it had all gone, and the Medo-Persian empire held sway.

It is impossible to arrive with any certainty at a precise date for Habakkuk's prophecy. The only reliable evidence is internal, and even using this, estimates have varied from the reign of Manasseh through to that of Jehoiakim. However, it seems most likely to have been during the latter years of Josiah's reign or during the reign of Jehoiakim, with the latter being most probable, coinciding with the sudden rise of the Neo-Babylonian Empire.

Jehoiakim means 'Jehovah raises up', which is ironic because Pharaoh Necho put him on the throne after he defeated Josiah and deposed his eldest son Jehoahaz. Jehoiakim then 'did that which was evil in the sight of the Lord, according to all that his fathers had done', 2 Kgs. 23.37. Jeremiah prophesied that Jehoiakim would be 'buried with the burial of an ass', and 'cast forth beyond the gates of Jerusalem' as food for the vultures, Jer. 22.19. In the days of Josiah, the word of God was discovered and acted upon; but in Jehoiakim's day it was destroyed and ignored, Jer. 36.21-32. The attitude of the king was reflected in that of the people.

As to any external evidence about Habakkuk himself, we have only apocryphal accounts which are themselves conflicting. From reading his prophecy however, we find that he seems officially qualified to compose for and take part in the liturgical singing in the temple, and therefore would have belonged to one of the Levitical families who were charged with the maintenance of the temple music by king David, and therefore Habakkuk would have been of the same tribe as Jeremiah and Ezekiel. Habakkuk would then have been a regular singer of Psalms and it shows clearly in his use of numerous phrases from the Psalms in his prophecy. He also quotes extensively from other scriptures. He is a man of the scriptures to begin with, but when he has been through the experience described in his prophecy, he becomes a man of the God of the scriptures, which is a far deeper thing.

An outline of the book

The book has obvious divisions, being delineated by who is speaking at the time; alternatively Habakkuk and Jehovah:

a. 1.1–4   The prophet's twofold complaint – Judah's sin and God's silence.

b. 1.5–11   God's reply – the Chaldean invasion.

c. 1.12–2.1 The prophet's third complaint – Chaldean cruelty and God's silence.

d. 2.2–20   God's response – Israel's salvation and woes to the Chaldeans.

e. 3.1–19   The prophet's prayer – a request, a theophany and a cry of faith.

Chapter 1 give us the *problem*, chapter 2 the *prophecy* and chapter 3 the *prayer* of Habakkuk. Some verses of the book stand out particularly, for instance, 'The just shall live by his faith, 2.4'; 'the earth shall be filled with the knowledge of the glory of the Lord, as the waters cover the sea', 2.14; and 'Yet I will rejoice in the Lord, I will joy in the God of my salvation', 3.18. The book is easily read at one reading; special note should be taken of the very poetic and dramatic language employed that has always been the admiration of Hebrew scholars.

In the same way that Habakkuk quotes extensively from other Old Testament writers, he himself is often quoted in the New Testament, i.e. 1.5 in Acts 13.40, 41; 2.3, 4 in Hebrews 10.37, 38 and 2.4 in Romans 1.17 and Galatians 3.11.

A detailed study of the book

A: 1.1–4 The prophet's twofold complaint

Habakkuk's *burden*, v. 1, was something he *saw*: this reminds us of the ancient title of prophets as seers, 1 Sam. 9.9, furthermore, the verb 'to see' in this verse is usually reserved for seeing visions or seeing God, e.g. Lam. 2.14. The word 'burden' was an expression readily understood as a divine revelation, a prophecy, but obviously no light thing; it was serious and weighty. There were burdens of Nineveh, Moab, Damascus, Egypt, and 'of the Lord' in various prophecies.

'O Lord how long' is a well-used cry by the psalmists, for instance 6.3, 13.1, 35.17, and 94.3. The last two of these quotations particularly echo Habakkuk's words, 'O Lord, how long wilt thou look on?', and 'O Lord how long shall the wicked triumph?'. The prophets rarely question God as to His actions or apparent inactivity, but the psalmists frequently did – Habakkuk is more like the latter. In 2 Samuel 22.3 David speaks of God saving from violence. It is now as if Habakkuk wants the God of David to be his God – a Saviour God. However, after Habakkuk's many prayers, God seems to be doing nothing.

The expressions in verses 2 to 4 – showing the deep despair of Habakkuk – come in pairs: 'iniquity and grievance'; 'spoiling and violence'; 'strife and contention'. These expressions occur numerous times in the Old Testament, often however translated differently. For instance, we find 'strife and contention' translated as, 'iniquity and perverseness', Num. 23.21; 'iniquity and wickedness', Job 4.8; 'affliction and trouble', Job 5.6; 'mischief and vanity', Job 15.35, Ps. 10.7; 7.14; and Isa. 59.4, 'mischief and sorrow', Ps. 55.10, and 'labour and sorrow', Ps. 90.10. Likewise the words 'spoiling and violence' often occur together, Jer. 6.7, 20.8, Ezek. 45.9 and are translated otherwise as: 'wasting and violence', Isa 60.18 and 'robbery and violence', Amos 3.10. Then the word pair 'strife and contention' also appear together Prov. 17.14; Jer. 15.10 and are otherwise translated as 'strife and strife', Prov. 15.18, and 'strife and contentious', Prov. 26.21. Hence, what upset Habakkuk had been seen too many times among the children of Israel already. Finally, we see that often the expression 'law and judgement' are connected, for instance: Deut. 17.11; Isa. 42.4, and Ps. 89.30. One of the first things to suffer in a godless society is justice. Men of any station should be able to resort to it to address their complaint against all and sundry, however powerful they might be. However, threats and coercion, and intimidation and bribes were being used to deny people their legal rights, and what legal decisions were made were perverted, v. 4.

Habakkuk was particularly concerned with these social evils around him. God too was concerned, and soon said so, 'Run to and fro in Jerusalem, and see now and know, and seek in the broad places thereof, if ye can find a man, if there be any that execute judgement, that seek the truth; and I will pardon', Jer. 5.1.

At the same time the other prophets were prophesying about the concomitant spiritual evils – for instance Jeremiah, e.g. 2.28 and Zephaniah, e.g. 1.5. The people of Judah were challenged by God as to their new gods – 'But where are thy gods that thou hast made thee? let them arise, if they can save thee in the time of thy trouble: for according to the number of thy cities are thy gods, O Judah', Jer. 2.28. Those who should have upheld spiritual values were failing, 'her prophets are light and treacherous persons: her priests have polluted the sanctuary, they have done violence to the law', Zeph. 3.4. Whether we think of Judah's spiritual or her moral sins, both had the same root – no concern for God or His word. Thus the Lord was able to say, 'Is this house, which is called by my name, become a den of robbers in your eyes? Behold, even I have seen it, saith the Lord', Jer. 7.11.

God was constantly warning His people, 'Since the day that your fathers came forth out of the land of Egypt unto this day I have even sent unto you all my servants the prophets, daily rising up early and sending them', Jer. 7.25, and now they are to hear the worst.

B: 1.5–11 God's reply

Habakkuk is told to, 'Behold . . . regard', or 'look . . . see' among the surrounding nations, because so far he had been looking in the wrong direction. Whatever thoughts he had in his mind as to how God was going to save were misdirected. God was already working, but Habakkuk was so involved with the problem of the conditions around him, he could not look further to see the solution – God's answer was among the nations (the heathen). God was raising up a people to use for His purpose, and their king would rule over the first God-ordained Gentile empire, Dan. 2.37, 38.

Actually verse 5 is addressed to all the people, not just Habakkuk, i.e. not *thou* and *thee*, but *ye* and *you*. Habakkuk eventually believed, but the people never did, and it was too late. This verse was later quoted in Acts 13.41, where Paul similarly warns the Jews of impending judgement.

Verse 6 shows us that the prophecy is very specific, not just *Babylonians* but *Chaldeans*, who although a minority in Babylon, were the current driving force, responsible for the upsurge of strength and conquering power in the Babylonian nation.

Other prophecies also gave God's consistent message concerning the Babylonians in general and the Chaldeans in particular, 'I will give all Judah into the hand of the king of Babylon, and he shall carry them captive into Babylon', Jer. 20.4. 'I will give thee into the hand of . . . Nebuchadnezzar king of Babylon, and into the hand of the Chaldeans', Jer. 22.25. Also the nature of the invasion is always said to be the same, 'violence and spoil is heard in her; before me continually is grief and wounds', Jer. 6.7; 'Thus saith the Lord, Behold, a people cometh from the north country, and a great nation shall be raised from the sides of the earth. They shall lay hold on bow and spear; they are cruel, and have no mercy; their voice roareth like the sea; and they ride upon horses', Jer. 6.22-23 and, 'Lo, I will bring a nation upon you from afar . . . it is a mighty nation, it is an ancient nation, a nation whose language thou knowest not', Jer. 5.15.

The detailed description that is given by God in verses 6-11 shows that He knew exactly what He was doing, for He knew every detail of this nation. There was no mistake on His part, for He knew their behaviour in conquest, how devastating were their attacks!

Habakkuk's contemporary, Zephaniah, was saying of Judah that 'her princes within her are roaring lions; her judges are evening wolves', 3.3. This compares with the Chaldeans, who are described as 'more agile than the evening wolves', Hab. 1.8, JND. The princes who behave like lions will be faced with horses 'swifter than leopards', who 'fly as eagles'. The king and princes who scorn God's messengers will themselves be scorned by Nebuchadnezzar and his army; they would be objects of derision not honour, and kings would be a laughing-stock. How true this became, for the Chaldeans showed mercy to neither kings nor princes and now God matches the sin with the following judgement, 'And the Lord God of their fathers sent to them by his messengers, rising up betimes, and sending; because he had compassion on his people, and on his dwelling place: But they mocked the messengers of God and despised his words, and misused his prophets, until the wrath of the Lord arose against his people, till there was no remedy. Therefore he brought upon them the king of the Chaldees . . . he gave them all into his hand', 2 Chr. 36.15-17; see also 2 Kgs. 25.

Jeremiah also tells us in detail about the swiftness of the horses of the Destroyer of the Gentiles, 'Behold, he shall come up as clouds, and his chariots shall be as a whirlwind: his horses are swifter than eagles', 4.13.

From verses 10 and 11 the rendering should be in the singular and refer to *he, his* and *him*, not *they* etc, and could well refer to Nebuchadnezzar, the prototype Chaldean who led the Babylonian army and as we have seen showed scant consideration for any members of royal families. Also in verse 12, Jehovah is said to have ordained 'him' for judgement; and 'thou . . . hast appointed him for correction', JND. So powerful would he be that eventually 'this his power is become his god', v. 11, JND.

C: 1.12–2.1 The prophet's third complaint

Habakkuk had worked out according to his own logic what he thought God should do, based on what he knew of God. But he had still to learn the truth of what God had said through Isaiah, 'My thoughts are not your thoughts', Isa. 55.8.

He asks God – 'Art thou not from everlasting, O Lord my God, mine Holy One?', v. 12. Habakkuk was trying to equate God's eternal nature with His actions now. 'O Lord my God' is a phrase common in the Psalms, being found about 10 times, while the title 'Holy One' addressed to God is the favourite expression of Isaiah who uses it nearly 30 times. On the basis of who and what God is, Habakkuk is assured that the nation would not die. This was true indeed, for God was going to say, 'Nevertheless in those days saith the Lord, I will not make a full end with you', Jer. 5.18. Habakkuk had now come to terms with the fact that God would indeed use the Chaldeans for the correction and judgement of his people, but he still had great problems with God's choice.

So then, Judah, although they would survive, were to be judged and corrected by Jehovah, and how Judah needed correction! 'In vain have I smitten your children; they received no correction: your own sword hath devoured your prophets, like a destroying lion', Jer. 2.30; 'They have refused to receive correction: they have made their faces harder than a rock', Jer. 5.3; 'She obeyed not the voice; she received not correction; she trusted not in the Lord', Zeph. 3.2. Judah had no right now to say 'Wherefore doeth the Lord our God all these things unto us?', Jer. 5.19.

The 'mighty God' of verse 12 of the AV should be translated as, 'O Rock'; the AV giving the interpretation of the figure used. Viewing Jehovah as the Rock is a well-used picture in the Old Testament scriptures, for instance in the Psalms alone it occurs dozens of times (sometimes translated in the AV as strength or might, as here). The picture of the Rock is perhaps that of the place of safety and last resort. For instance, when recourse to all human help had failed for David in the wilderness, there were always the rocks to give protection.

Habakkuk's problem was how could God use a nation that was even worse than Judah? He was to learn that God is sovereign, and takes up whomsoever He will, Dan. 2.38, but balanced by this He will still punish those evil nations, even though He uses their actions to serve His purpose.

From verses 14 to 17 we learn that the Chaldeans would eventually trawl through the nations, taking them as simply as a fisherman takes fish. The leaders of nations were powerless to organize any effective defence. Would such activity go on unchecked, would they 'not spare continually to slay the nations?', v. 17. Habakkuk is soon to have his questions answered.

Habakkuk was sure that God would continue speaking to him, 2.1, hence he goes to the watchtower, the place of vision and separation, where he would not be disturbed. Habakkuk would stand there, attentive and waiting for further revelation, cf. Isa. 21.8, 11. He knew that his heart was not yet fully in tune with God's intentions, and that God would have to correct him. The correction (or reproof) was necessary, but also beneficial. God's reproof should always be seen as for our benefit. About fifteen times in Proverbs, the advantage of accepting reproof is stressed, e.g. 3.11, 10.17, 12.1, 13.18, etc. 'If any of you lacks wisdom, let him ask of God', says James 1.5. Habakkuk was in the right place at the right time, and soon he would be in the right condition of mind also.

D: 2.2–20 God's response

Habakkuk found the truth the Psalmist had experienced, 'I called upon the Lord in distress: the Lord answered me, and set me in a large place', Ps. 118.5. God gave the vision, but it was the prophet's responsibility to write it in such a way that it could be plainly read in public, on wooden boards set up where they could be seen (this being a helpful suggestion for those who set up texts in public). Those who read the prophecy and were so-minded could quickly pass on the word to others.

The word for vision in verse 3 is first found in 1 Samuel 3.1 – 'no open vision'. The expression 'appointed time' is usually used of solemn feasts etc., when God appointed a time when His people would meet Him. But it is also a prophetic word, see particularly Dan. 8.19; 11.27, 29, 35; 12.7, where it is translated 'time', 'times' and 'appointed time'. God has times when He will intervene in history. He tells His servants when they are about to happen. Daniel also was told of the blessedness of those who waited patiently for such appointed times, which although not occurring immediately, will not be behind God's time, Dan. 12.12. In Hebrews 10.37 this verse is quoted, but the word *it* is changed to *he*. The Hebrews would know this quotation from the Septuagint version of the Old Testament where it is translated 'he that shall come will come, and will not tarry'.

The Chaldean's soul and that of the unbowed inhabitant of Judah 'which is lifted up is not upright in him', but for those like Habakkuk 'the just shall live by his faith', v. 4. This is always God's way from Abraham onwards, Gen 15.6. This verse became central in New Testament teaching, Rom. 1.17; Gal. 3.11; Heb. 10.38 – 'In Romans JUST is the emphatic word; in Galatians FAITH; in Hebrews LIVE', (Dr PIERSON quoted by HODGKIN in '*Christ in all the Scriptures*'). It is used in the New Testament as a 'decisive factor in evangelical argument', J. SIDLOW BAXTER.

The Chaldean's weakness for wine, his insatiable appetite for military conquest and his idolatry are the reasons for his eventual downfall, see Dan. 5, for he will become the subject of divine judgement as indicated by the five woes:

'Woe to him that increaseth that which is not his', 2.6
'Woe to him that getteth iniquitous gain to his house', 2.9
'Woe to him that buildeth a town with blood', 2.12
'Woe to him that giveth his neighbour drink', 2.15
'Woe to him that saith to the wood, Awake!', 2.19

'God had used Babylon as His banner to punish the nations, and He was about to break the hammer itself in pieces, Jer. 50.23', (HODGKIN in '*Christ in All the Scriptures*').

Three nations were a source of trouble to Israel – Edom, Assyria, and Babylon. Obadiah gives the fate of Edom, Nahum tells of the end of Assyria and Habakkuk here gives us a vivid picture of the demise of Babylon in verse 7, when the woes come to fruition.

Amazingly, in the middle of the pronouncement of the woes, we have the sublime statement that 'the earth shall be filled with the knowledge of the glory of the Lord', v. 14. The demise of the *final* world empire would usher this in, and here in the midst of the foretelling of the demise of the *first*, we are told about it! The difference between this verse and the similar one, 'for the earth shall be full of the knowledge of the Lord, as the waters cover the sea', as foretold by Isaiah, 11.9, is that the knowledge of the *existence* of the LORD will be universal at one point, as for instance at the end of the great tribulation, but then – as foreshadowed on the mountain of transfiguration – in the Millennium, it is the *glory* of the Lord that will be universally known.

At the end of the woe pronouncements we have the statement that the Lord is in His holy temple, so all the earth is commanded to keep silence before Him. The irony is that He speaks and all else must remain silent, whereas the Chaldeans call on their idols to speak, and they remain silent because they are dumb stone. Zephaniah similarly says, 'Hold thy peace at the presence of the Lord God', 1.7.

E: 3.1–19 The prophet's prayer

This chapter is in the form of a psalm. It suggests, along with the reference to a stringed instrument, that Habakkuk was a Levitical temple singer, and thus very familiar with the psalms which formed their repertoire. Like this one, six psalms in the psalter have 'A prayer' as a title (17, 86, 90, 102, 142 and 143), so Habakkuk was following a well-established tradition. The musical instructions are also given, cf. Ps. 7.1.

Like this psalm, 22 psalms of David begin with the cry, 'O Lord'. Throughout his translation of this prophet, J. N. DARBY consistently drops the vocative 'O!', and also in most of the Psalms' references also. Thus Habakkuk is addressing 'Jehovah' personally. Only on one occasion in the 16 or so times the deity's name is used here is He called anything but Jehovah. This reminds us that all Habakkuk's dealings with God were on the basis of His covenant name to the nation.

In thinking about Habakkuk's expressed fear in verse 2, we note that people in the scriptures expressed fear for many reasons. Adam was afraid and had every reason to be so when he realized what he had done and the consequences it would bring, Gen 3.10. For other reasons Jacob, Gen. 31.31; Moses, Deut. 9.19; Job, Job 3.25; and Daniel, Dan. 8.17 all admitted to fear. God of course is a God to be feared for what He is, note Deut. 10.17 where 'terrible (AV)' means 'fearful'. On the other hand, for men who fear God, He tells them not to be afraid; men such as Abraham, Gen 15.1; Moses, Deut. 3.2; Joshua, Josh. 8.1, 10.8, 11.6; and Gideon, Judg. 6.23. God should be feared by all, Gen 42.18; Exod. 18.21; Job 1.9; Ps. 66.16; Luke 23.40; Acts 13.16; 1 Pet. 2.17; Rev. 14.7. Those who fear God, need fear nothing and no one else.

Habakkuk prays that God will work in the midst of the years, that is, as quickly as possible, when God had said that His work would eventually come. Now Habakkuk is more in tune with God who had said, 'I work a work', 1.5, JND, and asks 'in wrath remember mercy'.

From verse 3 through to verse 15, we have a very striking account of Habakkuk's vision of the God of Israel in His triumphal march with His people, bringing them out of Egypt; going via Sinai and the southern parts into Canaan; through the day of the sun standing still in the days of Joshua, into Canaan and fighting with His people. To be specific we note that Teman is the grandson of Esau whose other name was Edom. It was at Edom that, having refused the Israelites safe passage, the Edomites were afraid when they passed by at the side of the country, and as noted later in the song of Deborah, 'Lord, when thou wentest out of Seir, when thou marchedst out of the field of Edom, the earth trembled, and the heavens dropped . . . the mountains melted before the Lord, even that Sinai from before the Lord God of Israel', Judg. 5.4, 5.

At Sinai, Exod. 16, the glory of the Lord was seen for the first time ever on earth. There was indeed the hiding of His power, even Moses could not look on His face, only on His back parts. Sinai became like a volcano. Then we move on in picture to the way that the fear of the Lord went before the nation to the inhabitants of Canaan. In the day of Joshua the statement is literally true – the sun stood still, Josh. 10.13. The nations were threshed, v. 12, as the picturesque language says – Israel could not be stopped when God was on their side.

In verse 16 we have Habakkuk's reaction to the vision: it is very dramatic, his whole body reacted; his belly, lips, bones and his inside generally. His desire is that he might rest in the day of trouble, when God was coming in the same way as before, though now not with the children of Israel, but against them. He will invade with His troops, the Chaldeans. Will Habakkuk find rest in this day of trouble? In the following verses we find that he is given rest. He pictures all the worst consequences of the impending invasion, particularly the plundering of the crops to feed the army whose only supplies were what they could steal. He knows he will survive, but more than that, although every source of food is cut off, 'Yet I will rejoice in the Lord, I will joy in the God of my salvation'. Paul says similarly, in Romans 5.3, 'we glory in tribulations also'.

The one who had lost all strength in himself had found that the Lord was his strength, cf. Phil. 4.13. He would give him the experience of David in 2 Samuel 22.34 and Psalm 18.33, that 'He maketh my feet like hinds' feet: and setteth me upon my high places', God could give him security in difficult circumstances. The hinds' natural habitat was among the precarious rocks, but God had so endowed them with sure-footed balance that they could move about there safely. Habakkuk like David before him had found that God so ordered his steps that he never lost his footing, however dangerous the circumstances, see Ps. 73.2.

In the middle of the vision, v. 13, we have a Selah – 'a call to pause and be silent that the soul may listen to the divine illuding' – HODGKIN, or as E. W. ROGERS used to translate it – 'stop and think about that!' It is only found here outside the Psalms.

Verses 17 to the end show us the thorough-going transformation in Habakkuk; he fully acknowledges the great material difficulties that would pertain when the Chaldeans come, when their armies, like all invaders of their day, will take all the available food, 'And they shall eat up thine harvest, and thy bread, which thy sons and thy daughters should eat: they shall eat up thy flocks and thine herds: they shall eat up thy vines and thy fig trees', Jer. 5.17 and 'there shall be no grapes on the vine, nor figs on the fig tree, and the leaf shall fade', Jer. 8.13. However, Habakkuk will then say, 'Yet will I rejoice in the God of my salvation', v. 18. His prayer to find 'rest in the day of trouble', v. 16, will be fully answered.

The book finishes with instructions on how he accompanied himself when he sang this psalm, and how he suggested the chief singer in the temple should so do, also.

Conclusion

What a change Habakkuk has undergone, what a new attitude to God, what trust and what an experience that led him to that position! His transformation shows us the power of faith. Becoming too preoccupied with our circumstances can rob us of our joy in believing. However, we can learn along with Habakkuk that God can be trusted; He is already at work, and no matter how strange the means He chooses to use, His glory will eventually come through.

What does a prophecy written about 2600 years ago have to tell us today? What had changed Habakkuk from the one who asked 'How long?' and 'Why?' to the man of peace and trust? Surely the vision of Jehovah described in chapter 3 that had left him trembling and strengthless. He found 'rest for the day of trouble' in God the Almighty One. He learned the fear and faith of God all over again. He had learned again the truth of the God who in wrath could remember mercy.

With the advantage of hindsight, we can see the plan of God. He would use the Chaldeans for the correction and punishment of Judah. He would then allow Babylon to rise to the zenith of its power, and within it raise up His people like Daniel and his friends. At that time He would inaugurate a series of world powers with the Chaldean Nebuchadnezzar as the first and greatest, the head of gold, Dan. 2.38. Then, when His purpose is fulfilled, He will bring about the prophecy of Habakkuk, that the Chaldeans would themselves be overthrown; 'in that night was Belshazzar slain', Dan. 5.30. God then brought in the Medo-Persian empire and a ruler who was sympathetic to the Jews. The remnant would be allowed to return, and eventually under Ezra and Nehemiah they would rebuild the temple and the walls, and reinstate the old way of worship. Certainly the statement that 'they were for correction' is then fully vindicated, and the nation did not die, but survived, though chastened and cleansed of idolatry.

In our generation we have seen the collapse of an empire: the Soviet empire which began in the lifetime of many living today and grew to be feared and dreaded. It was acknowledged as an 'evil empire', and had enormous influence and power. Now it is gone, and the once powerful eastern block is reduced to a series of poor countries, reliant on the generosity of western nations for survival. How interesting that it is like the Babylonian empire, which at one point was so powerful that it seemed nothing could stop it. However, within a lifetime it too had collapsed. Babylon was the first world empire sanctioned by God, with scripture acknowledging the fact. After Babylon, other empires came in their turn, and today we are seeing the pre-movements necessary for the re-establishment of the fourth, the Roman empire. This too will eventually come to nothing, but then it will not be God working behind the scenes, but the Lord Jesus Christ will personally come and destroy it.

Habakkuk's thoughts of God have been well described, 'the God who controlled the destinies of men and peoples was Himself governed by discernable principles of morality and righteousness. In the thought of Habakkuk, the concept of the justice of God formed the central issue in any attempt to comprehend history from a religious point of view. Spiritual rectitude is an absolute necessity for both individuals and nations; that wealth is at best a treacherous foundation for a secure life; that evil is bound to fail ultimately even though it may experience a temporary triumph at the expense of good', R. K. HARRISON, 'Introduction to the Old Testament'.

Are we still surprised by God's choices? Would we believe certain things, even 'if it had been told' us? When John Major opened his first cabinet meeting as Prime Minister of the United Kingdom, his first words were: 'Well, who would have thought it?' And who would?; the youngest prime minister this century, with no university degree, and a father who had been a trapeze artist. He had been turned down as a bus conductor for being too tall, he was out of work, a general labourer for a year until getting a job as an insurance clerk. God takes up whomsoever He will.

In our lifetime we have heard publicly such statements as, 'God will never allow man to get to the moon', and 'God will not let the United Kingdom join the Common Market'. If we have taken in the truth of the book of Habakkuk, we realize that such statements cannot and should not be made. God is sovereign, and will use who and what He will, irrespective of what we think of them, Dan 4.17. It is for us to come to terms with His will, and to better trust the God of our salvation.

CHAPTER NINE

THE PROPHECY OF ZEPHANIAH

by DAVID NEWELL

Introduction to Zephaniah

THE **SETTING** OF ZEPHANIAH'S PROPHECY is stated in the opening verse: it concerns Judah during the reign of Josiah. At the age of sixteen, King Josiah 'began to seek after the God of David his father', 2 Chr. 34.3, and, as a result, led the nation into a period of spiritual revival, 2 Chr. 34.3–33. Yet that revival was neither deep nor lasting, for Zephaniah had to remind his hearers that divine judgement was inevitable. Momentary ripples of repentance and occasional seasons of spiritual renewal cannot check the downhill slide of this sinful world towards judgement.

The **SUBJECT** of the book could hardly be plainer: Zephaniah is the great herald of 'the day of the Lord'. 'Day' appears 20 times in all, and is governed by the first occurrence in 1.7, 'the day of the Lord is at hand'. As with so much Old Testament prophecy this has both a short term and a long term significance, for the day of the Lord describes any intervention by Jehovah in judgement. Zephaniah looks ahead to the Chaldean capture and devastation of Assyria, Zeph. 2.13, in 612 BC and later Jerusalem, Jer. 20.4, but he also sees beyond that to a still future outpouring of God's wrath on the entire planet, Zeph. 1.2, 3, which will accompany the Lord's glorious return to set up His Kingdom. We may call him the prophet of global warning!

The **SILENCES** of the book are interesting. Although historically the Chaldeans were God's instrument of discipline, they are not named, ct. Hab. 1.6, so that God's hand alone is seen. We are to learn that 'every joy and trial cometh from above'. Nor is the Messiah mentioned specifically, although 3.15 identifies Jehovah as Israel's King, thus agreeing with those prophets who emphasize both the deity and humanity of

Israel's future ruler, Mic. 5.2. Zephaniah is not quoted in the New Testament, yet one assumes that Paul counted on the Thessalonians knowing his teaching about the Day of the Lord, 1 Thess. 5.1-2.

As to **STRUCTURE**, the book moves from judgement, 1.1-3.8 to joy, 3.9-20, from gloom to glory. It can be outlined thus:

A. Personal Identification 1.1
B. Universal Devastation 1.2-3.8
    1. World 1.2, 3
        2. Judah 1.4-2.3
            3. Gentiles 2.4-15
                (i) Philistia 2.4-7
                (ii) Moab 2.8-11
                (iii) Ethiopia 2.12
                (iv) Assyria 2.13-15
    4. Judah 3.1-7
    5. World 3.8
C. Divine Jubilation 3.9-20

A. Personal Identification 1.1

Biblical introductions are never insignificant. Of the eight names in this verse, three deserve our attention: Jehovah, Zephaniah, and Josiah. First of all, we are informed that the entire book constitutes 'the word of the Lord', for this prophecy, like the rest of scripture, is not man's thoughts about God but God's infallible word to man, 2 Pet. 1.21. This profound assertion of absolute authority permeates the book with the repetition of 'saith the Lord', 1.2, 3, 10; 2.9; 3.8, 20, and 'the word of the Lord', 2.5. Zephaniah, far from being an irrelevant Hebrew document, is the unchanging message of God.

Second, we discover that Zephaniah was the great-great-grandson of Hezekiah (the alternative rendering of Hizkiah). Since the royal title is omitted, some question whether this was the godly king of Judah, but it seems best to accept the identification simply because it is so strikingly unusual for a prophet to have his genealogy traced back four generations. The point is to highlight his royal ancestry. Therefore, when Zephaniah had to pronounce judgement on 'the princes and the king's sons', 1.8, he was dealing with his own family connections. How often in a local assembly has the truth of God been sacrificed on the altar of family loyalty! But Zephaniah was faithful to his trust. Perhaps he appreciated the meaning of his name, 'Jehovah will hide'. The believer who knows that he has a safe shelter in the Living God will find it easier to stand alone for truth, however unfashionable and unpalatable.

Third, the setting of Zephaniah's prophecy is the reign of King Josiah, the godly son of an ungodly father, 2 Kgs. 21.19–22; 22.1, 2. Although no son can entirely escape the influence of his parents, neither spirituality nor wickedness is automatically inherited. Josiah did not follow in his father's evil steps, but, alas, neither did he pass his own godly ways on to his children, 2 Kgs. 23.30–32. Whether we come from good or bad stock, all must stand as individuals before God, and make His truth our own possession.

B. Universal devastation 1.2–3.8

Zephaniah's vision is broad enough to include the entire planet, for though God's judgements may focus particularly on His chosen people, He is still 'the God of the whole earth', Isa. 54.5, 'the Creator of the ends of the earth', Isa. 40.28, and 'the Judge of all the earth', Gen. 18.25. The prophet's announcement of coming punishment therefore begins and ends with world-wide desolation, 1.2, 3; 3.8, while in between concentrating on Judah and her Gentile neighbours. But as we consider this solemn section, we must never forget the overall structural progression of the book, from retribution to restoration. The only route to divine blessing for the nation of Israel and for this sinful world as a whole is through the fires of judgement, 1.18; 3.8, 9. There *is* a glorious light at the end of the tunnel!

1. The world 1.2–3

The language suggests a catastrophic reversal of the work of creation in Genesis 1. There God created, decorated and populated the earth in six twenty-four hour days of ordered activity culminating in the divine verdict, 'very good', Gen. 1.31. But here the work of His hands is to be abruptly swept away as if He can no longer tolerate the sight of it. The reason is man, once upright, now fallen, Eccles. 7.29. And man's sin has brought the whole world under a curse, Rom. 8.20–22. Such a universal clearance happened once before at the flood, Gen. 6.5–7, when man's sin came to a head, and it will happen again, 2 Pet. 3.10. The tragedy of our generation is that men tremble at the thought of nuclear holocaust and global pollution while completely disregarding the real terror of the wrath of God. The believer can rejoice that he does not belong to this doomed planet but is instead a citizen of heaven awaiting his soon-coming Saviour, Phil. 3.20–21!

2. Judah and Jerusalem 1.4–2.3

In this extended section Zephaniah scrutinizes Judah as the object of God's displeasure. In the year 722 BC the breakaway Northern Kingdom of Israel had been carried into captivity by the Assyrians as a result of its continued departure from the Lord. Judah, however, with its Davidic monarchy, had experienced periods of spiritual awakening and blessing under kings like Jehoash, Uzziah and Hezekiah. The recent rediscovery of the Law in 622 BC had stirred up Josiah to root out idolatry and return to divine worship, 2 Kgs. 22.11–23. 25. One might have thought that all was well with the nation. But Zephaniah's prophecy exposes the heart beneath the outward reformation, uncovering the persistent sins which provoked divine anger. The key verse is 1.17, 'because they have sinned against the Lord'. Here is the reason for all judgement: not social injustice, political corruption, or even moral turpitude, but sin against God, Ps. 51.4; Luke 15.18. And since judgement begins with the most privileged, 1. Pet. 4.17, no wonder Judah was subjected to such solemn warnings!

Consider, first, the sins that provoked God's judgement. Zephaniah's analysis of Judah's transgressions is pointedly relevant, for man's heart is as deceitful as ever. The first problem was **idolatry**, 1.4, 5, for Baal was the chief deity of the Canaanites, and the Chemarim were idolatrous priests, 2 Kgs. 23.5. A nation formed by God and for God had over the years drifted into idol worship, 2 Chr. 33.3, 7. An idol is anything that takes the place which belongs to God alone. Idolatry therefore is an insult to the living God, for it robs Him of His worship, and it is an injury to man because it builds its confidence upon a fraud: idols just don't work, Isa. 46.7! Yet it is so easy to let legitimate responsibilities like the business and the family usurp the pre-eminence due to the Lord Jesus. As John says, we must keep ourselves from idols, 1 John 5.21. A particular manifestation of this was **astrology**, 1.5. When people turn from God they inevitably turn to lies, and the star worship of Judah is not far removed from our twentieth-century obsession with spiritism and the occult, lately invigorated by the repackaged paganism of the New Age Movement. Sinful man will believe anything rather than God.

Another error was **ecumenism**, 1.4, 5, 8. Although she had adopted false religions, Judah had not yet outwardly renounced Jehovah. Instead the people paid honour to Jehovah and Malcham (possibly the Ammonite god Molech, Jer. 32.35). But such spineless compromise always involves rejection of truth, for the living God demands nothing less than total and exclusive commitment to Himself. Even the royal family were adopting foreign fashions in clothes, thus discarding their God-ordained Jewish distinctiveness, Num. 15.38, 39. Far from being broad-minded and tolerant, ecumenism resists the word of God in all its fullness. If we have any kind of fellowship with error, even under the name of evangelism, we effectively betray the truth. The call today, as needful as ever, is to separation; anything less is unworthy of God.

Some in the nation were marked by full-blown apostasy, 1.6. To 'turn back' suggests that they had once professed faith. Spiritual reality does not show itself overnight: time is the great test. The proof of genuineness before God is not that we begin enthusiastically but that we continue steadfastly, Luke 9.62; Acts 2.42. Others were marked by apathy, 1.12, a casual indifference to the claims of Jehovah, as if they foolishly imagined that He would not bother Himself with men. The widespread spiritual indifference of our century can so easily infiltrate assemblies of God's people and corrupt our attitude to the Word. Beware of being lukewarm!

Materialism was a special target of divine anger, ranging from the criminal activities of cheats and robbers, 1.9, to the successful merchants of Jerusalem's thriving business community, 1.11–13. However men may obtain wealth, it will all ultimately be swept away, 1.18. Love of money is a potent snare for any who are ignorant of the transience of this world, 1.13; 2 Pet. 3.10–12. Silver and gold cannot save, 1.18, but we have been eternally redeemed at infinitely greater cost, 1 Pet. 1.18, 19!

Second, the prophet announces the swiftness of God's judgement. Having itemized its causes, he also heralds its fast approach. Divine intervention in the lives of men was imminent, 1.7, 14. In 612 BC, the Babylonians annihilated Nineveh so conclusively, 2.13, that it is almost impossible to this day to plot the exact site of 'the rejoicing city that dwelt carelessly', 2.15. And in 605 BC, only 17 years after Josiah rediscovered the Law, and perhaps 15 years after Zephaniah was writing, Jerusalem itself became the victim of Chaldean aggression, Dan. 1.1, 2. God's discipline of Judah was not an event in the remote future.

Yet we must carefully distinguish between the immediate and the long term fulfilment of these prophecies. Like many Old Testament seers, Zephaniah telescopes events so that the Babylonian invasion of Judah blurs with that final eschatological eruption of judgement which will rock the entire planet at the coming Day of the Lord. This period stretches from the Great Tribulation right through the Millennial Kingdom to the final winding up of the present universe. For the Christian, of course, the coming of the Lord to receive His own people is nearer still, John 14.3.

Third, the severity of God's judgement is starkly portrayed. That coming day, anticipated in Judah's history, will be a striking unveiling of God's character, 1.7, so that men will be silenced in the unmistakable presence of His power, glory, holiness, and burning indignation against sin. All too often even believers have an inadequate appreciation of God. How long is it since we heard ministry on God's wrath, holiness, or jealousy, 1.18? If, as A W TOZER has said, 'the essence of idolatry is the entertainment of thoughts about God that are unworthy of Him', then many of us would have to plead guilty. Gospel preachers stand charged with short measure to man and unfaithfulness to God if they soft-pedal the solemn realities of God's character. Our God, remember, is light as well as love.

The unleashing of judgement, 1.14–17 is described so graphically as to make even the saints tremble. Those saved by the precious blood of Christ are, of course, exempt from these terrors, Rom. 8.1, but how we should mourn for a world running headlong into destruction. The Babylonian invasion is likened to a day of sacrifice, 1.7, 8, with Judah as the victim to be slaughtered and devoured, just as at the Lord's glorious return the birds of the air will be summoned to the 'supper of the great God', Rev. 19.17, 18. It is also a day of wrath, 1.15, 18, for God is angry about sin, and unbelievers will receive to the full what is due to them, John 3.36; Rev. 11.17, 18. It is a day of distress, 1.15, 17, a maelstrom of darkness, death and desolation, when even the toughest of men will cry out in anguish, 1.14, and the confused noise of slaughter will reverberate through the city, 1.10. And this, let us remember, is but the earthly prelude to the miseries of eternal torment, 2 Thess. 1.9. It is a proof of divine mercy, however, that this period of vengeance, for all its terrors, is called a day whereas the present season of gospel opportunity is the 'acceptable year of the Lord', Isa. 61.2. Our long-suffering God is 'not willing that any should perish', 2 Pet. 3.9.

This brings us to the final point of the section: the provision of shelter from God's judgement, 2.1–3. Hitherto there has been no hint of escape, because Jehovah will 'search Jerusalem with lamps', 1.12, RV, to root out all the guilty: for the ungodly there can be no hiding place, Rev. 6.15–17. But Zephaniah's words are no counsel of despair. He aimed not to frighten men out of their wits but out of their sins. The nation as a whole was shamelessly hardened in its evil, 2.1, but there were some whose hearts the Lord had touched. 'Seek ye the Lord', is the urgent exhortation to all. Not that such a turning would avert God's coming wrath any more than the presence of righteous Lot in Sodom could save that city. But those who earnestly seek the Lord find their shelter in Him, Ps. 31.1–3; 61.2, 3, for He Himself is the refuge of His people. Zephaniah's very name (Jehovah will hide) was an assurance of divine grace. But let us be clear: to seek the Lord is more than a mere emotional or intellectual exercise. Rather it is a deep purpose of heart, like Daniel's, Dan. 1.8, which will express itself in a lifestyle pleasing to Him – 'righteousness and meekness', 2.3. Zephaniah had no time for cheap professions of faith; where there is spiritual reality there will always also be corresponding godly behaviour.

3. Gentiles 2.4–15

Now the prophet turns his attention to Judah's pagan neighbours, representative nations to the west, east, south and north of the land. This geographical sweep betokened the universal scope of God's intervention in His creation, and was gracious, though unheeded, warning to Judah, 3.6, 7.

The first victim of divine justice is Philistia, 2.4–7, the coastal strip of Palestine, long the enemy of Israel. The chief cities, Gaza, Ashkelon, Ashdod and Ekron are listed for demolition. Gath alone is omitted, perhaps because it had never recovered from Uzziah's attack, 2 Chr. 26.6. History recounts that this area fell prey to a succession of marauders: Egyptians, Scythians and Chaldeans, all unconsciously fulfilling God's purpose revealed as far back as the curse on Canaan, Gen. 9.25. How chilling to hear that 'the word of the Lord is against you', 2.5! Those who despise scripture should note that it is by that very word they will be judged, John 12.48. Judah, however, would inhabit the enemy's lands and enjoy them in tranquillity, 2.7. Such a promise has never yet been fulfilled and awaits its sure vindication when God's ancient people are restored and blessed under the personal reign of Christ.

Moab and Ammon, 2.8–11, the long term consequences of Lot's sin, Gen. 19.30–38, were particularly vicious and malignant foes of the Jews. Balak, King of Moab in the time of Moses, had even gone so far as to hire a prophet to curse Israel. But now all their malice and pride would be requited, 2.10, for to oppose Israel is to oppose God Himself and come under a divine curse, Gen. 12.3; Zech 2.8. Amazingly, the very people God has condemned for idolatry and departure are now described as 'the people of the Lord of hosts', 2.10! Like David, 1 Sam. 17.36, Zephaniah can see that faithless nation as God sees them, in the light of His irrevocable purpose. Truly, 'the gifts and calling of God are without repentance'; Rom. 11.29, and, as He will faithfully keep His promises to Israel, despite their failure, so too will He keep His word to the believer in Christ. All our blessings depend entirely upon sovereign grace. That He is able to fulfil His word to the letter is implicit in the glorious title 'the Lord of Hosts' (one sadly and irreverently mangled by translations like the NIV). 'The Lord of Hosts' reminds us of His ineffable power and the innumerable agencies at His command. Just one believer, with such a God on his side, is sufficient for any foe, 1 Sam. 17.45!

But the divine prediction for Moab and Ammon goes beyond their fall and Israel's eventual possession of their land, 2.9, to embrace an even grander truth. Zephaniah foresees a time when worship will ascend to God from the entire earth, 2.11. Here we get a glimpse past the rigours of the Great Tribulation into the blessings of the Millennial reign. Then will the earth be filled with the knowledge of God as the waters cover the sea, Isa. 11.9, but only after Israel has been disciplined and restored to her proper place. And all that future worship will be as much a result of Calvary as is a local assembly's worship today, Ps. 22.27–29. There is not one blessing which cannot be traced back to the atoning death of Christ.

Ethiopia receives but passing notice, 2.12, being the most southerly nation to have contact with Judah. Nevertheless its mention highlights the vital principle that, behind all judgement, whatever the instrument, is God. Historically, Babylon invaded the Cushite territory in the south of Egypt – but Jehovah identifies the attacker as 'my sword'. The unsaved are blind to the providential involvement of God in the affairs of men, but the believer, alert to divine realities, is constantly learning to trace all his experiences, whether good or ill, to the hand of a gracious God, Ps. 66.8–12.

Assyria, 3.13–15, concludes the summary of God's vengeance on the heathen. God had used this warlike people in the past as His tool in chastising disobedient Israel, but they themselves were by no means guiltless. That great and arrogant city Nineveh, whose overthrow was the burden of Nahum's prophecy, pictures human pride, self-sufficiency and independence. Her boastful joy and self-esteem, 2.15, blasphemously parody the words of Jehovah, Isa. 45.5, and repeat, as do so many of men's actions, the futile aspirations of Lucifer, Isa. 14.13–14. It is always Satan's aim to mould men in his twisted image. But man without God cannot succeed. Created to have dominion over the animal kingdom, Gen. 1.26, he is here reduced to the ultimate ignominy: his thriving metropolis is populated only by sheep, pelicans and hedgehogs, 2.14, NASB, a striking image of emptiness and ruin.

Zephaniah thus emphasizes that divine judgement is not only general, in that it comprehends all, but also specific because it responds to the particular sins of each nation. Everything the Judge of all the earth does is right, Gen. 18.25.

4. Judah 3.1–7

The solemn message has not finished. Zephaniah returns to his own people (always the most difficult to reach), but this time, instead of an inventory of their sins, he gives an analysis of the problem.

If Nineveh was stained by carnal joy and carelessness, Jerusalem was worse still, guilty of wilful disobedience to her God, 3.1. Greater light brings greater accountability, Luke 12.48b. It is sadly possible to possess truth without practising it, and the faithful ministry of the word is today becoming increasingly marginalized by the drift towards entertainment, easy-going compromise (usually paraded under the banner of 'love'), and religious respectability. The four tragic negatives of verse 2 indicate how far Jerusalem had departed from the divine ideal: chosen to be God's dwelling place on earth it had sunk into complacent iniquity. The local assembly is the one place where God's voice should unquestioningly be obeyed, and His correction gladly received; the place where He is the sole object of trust and worship.

Next, Zephaniah scrutinizes the nation's leaders, only to conclude that those who should have been examples of godliness were in the vanguard of defection from the truth, 3.3-4. A company of God's people is only as spiritual as its elders, and it has too often been forgotten that those who exercise spiritual leadership amongst the saints must meet the biblical qualifications, 1 Tim. 3.1-7. Godly elders have the prime responsibility to take heed to themselves before ever they can take care of the church of God, Acts 20.28; 1 Tim 3.5.

This failure of leadership was all the more culpable in the light of Judah's great privilege. Alone of all the nations of the earth she had Jehovah in her midst, Exod. 25.8, and despite her total unworthiness He still maintained His gracious presence, 3.5. That a local assembly today gathers to the name of the Lord Jesus, Matt. 18.20, is no formality but the most thrilling and weighty honour. A righteous God demands righteousness of His people.

Yet Jerusalem persisted in stubbornness. Deaf to all warnings, blind to all signals, she remained coolly indifferent to the dramatic evidence of God's punitive dealings with the countries round about, 3.6, 7. Abraham may have risen up early in the morning to obey Jehovah, Gen. 21.14; 22.3, but his descendants 'rose early and corrupted all their doings', slothful in spirituality but enthusiastic in evil.

5. World 3.8

This lengthy exposition of judgement, taking up the vast bulk of Zephaniah's prophecy, concludes as it began with the earth at large. The entire section has come full circle, but now concentrates on the gathering of the nations for the judgement of God prior to the inauguration of the Kingdom. While John sees this global mobilization before the Lord's return as a climactic expression of human defiance, Rev. 19.19, Zephaniah, like other Old Testament prophets, Zech. 14.2, views it all from the heavenly angle. Therefore the emphasis falls on God's activity: He will 'rise up', 'gather', 'assemble', and 'pour' His judgements on the nations, 3.8. All man's boasted freedom is seen to be but the fulfilment of God's eternal plan. Whether men like it or not, they simply and unwittingly accomplish His sovereign will. It happened at Calvary, Acts

4.25-28, and it will happen again. No wonder the Psalmist could exclaim 'surely the wrath of man shall praise thee', Ps. 76.10!

C. Divine Jubilation 3.9-20

But Zephaniah does not end with gloom. The Day of the Lord extends beyond the judgements of the Great Tribulation and the Lord's return, to include the entire Messianic Kingdom. Thus the prophet reminds us that Israel's future blessings are still part of 'that day', 3.11, 16. And what blessings there are! We may divide them into two categories: restoration, 3.9-13, and rejoicing, 3.14-20.

The restoration wonderfully embraces the Gentiles. As a result of the preceding judgements the confusion of Babel will be reversed so that 'the peoples', 3.9, RV, will call on the name of the Lord and worship Him 'with one shoulder' (literal rendering). At the moment the only thing that unites the nations of this world is opposition to God, Ps. 2.1-3; but in the Millennium true unity will be found in submission to Christ. This, of course, is also the only recipe for oneness in a local assembly today, Phil. 2.2; 4.2.

From world-wide blessing Zephaniah turns his attention to the restored remnant of Israel, 3.10-13. She will be regathered to her land, not simply in a wave of fervent nationalism such as we are seeing in Europe in the late twentieth century, but as a repentant and spiritually awakened people. The sins so honestly described in earlier passages will be blotted out, and she will be marked by genuine worship, 3.10, humility of spirit, 3.11, trust in Jehovah, 3.12, and righteousness, 3.13. Like a well-tended flock, Israel will feed safely, no longer threatened by enemies because under the direct protection of Jehovah, Ezek. 34.29-31. What Israel will experience materially in the kingdom age the believer in Christ enjoys spiritually now, and each local assembly is a testimony to the shepherd care of the Lord Jesus, 1 Pet. 2.25.

Complete restoration leads inevitably to rejoicing 'with all the heart', 3.14. Only those who have experienced the infinite mercy of God have any real reason to sing. Biblical joy is no irrational or hysterical exuberance but an intelligent response to the revelation of the Lord's goodness. If our joy is in God, Rom. 5.11, then it must be worthy of Him. Much so-called 'joy' in Christian circles today seems little more than fleshly excitement instead of a thoughtful delight in the living God.

There is then a solid foundation for Israel's future gladness: judgement has been removed, the enemy destroyed, Jehovah Himself is in the midst, and national peace is eternally secured, 3.15. Jerusalem will become a place of safety and divine service, 3.16, busily engaged in worshipping God. Prophetically this all awaits the Lord's return. For the Christian, however, it is a present possession in Christ, John 5.24; Heb. 2.14–15; Matt. 18.20; Rom. 8.31. But if Jerusalem's joy will be complete in that coming day, so too will God's. Verse 17 excited the comment of SPURGEON, 'I think this is the most wonderful text in the Bible in some respects – God Himself singing!' At creation the morning stars sang together, Job 38.7, but at the repentance and blessing of Israel God Himself will sing. The whole verse throbs with divine pleasure as Jehovah, in the midst of His ancient people, is so moved with joy that He is 'silent in His love' (NEWBERRY margin). Would that our periods of quietness when we gather to remember the Lord were so eloquent! Silence, you see, may indicate a heart so full that it cannot speak, or a heart so empty that it has nothing to say.

The book ends with a sixfold 'I will' of blessing, 3.18–20, just as it began with a sixfold 'I will' of judgement, 1.2–4. Our God is the source of all, be it discipline or deliverance. Hannah's words sum up the teaching of Zephaniah, 'The Lord killeth, and maketh alive: he bringeth down to the grave, and bringeth up. The Lord maketh poor, and maketh rich: he bringeth low, and lifteth up', 1 Sam. 2.6, 7; Deut. 32.39. God's programme for Israel marvellously illustrates this divine principle, for He who says, 'I will utterly consume', 1.2 also says, 'I will gather', 3.18!

It is encouraging to note the objects of God's tender care. He singles out those 'that are sorrowful for the solemn assembly', 3.18, dispersed Jews who grieved at their enforced exile from Jerusalem and its ceremonial. Those who have God's interests at heart, like Daniel in Babylon, Dan. 9.17–19, and Nehemiah in Shushan, Neh. 1.3, 4, find themselves objects of divine love. Further, Jehovah's compassion extends to the weak and feeble, 3.19, for He will save the lame. The local assembly is meant to be a nursing home for sickly saints, a place where Mr Ready-to-halt, Mr Feeble-mind, Mr Despondency and his daughter Much-afraid can find spiritual nourishment.

Jehovah also notes the way the world has treated His saints, 'I will get them praise and fame in every land where they have been put to shame', 3.19. Just as Israel will be universally honoured, so too will the faithful believer of this age. Many of the Lord's dear people have been savagely persecuted, often in the name of apostate religion. Their vindication is announced in the Lord's own words to Philadelphia, 'I will make them to come and worship before thy feet, and to know that I have loved thee', Rev. 3.9.

Zephaniah's prophecy ends, then, with a gladsome hymn of divine love as God takes pleasure in His people. It will do us all good to keep in mind what the redeemed mean to their Redeemer! After all the gloominess of judgement comes the glory of God's own joy. And its fulfilment is sure for this is the infallible word of the God who cannot lie.

THE PROPHECY OF
HAGGAI

by IVAN STEEDS

INTRODUCTION

HAGGAI IS THE FIRST OF THE POST-EXILIC PROPHETS and his message was crucial for God's people of that time, as it is crucial for Christians today. At issue was the building of the temple, God's 'house' and His early sanctuary. From the beginning God had stated His desire to dwell on earth in the midst of His people, and out of necessity on account of their passage through the wilderness, journeying from Egypt to Canaan, the first house was a tent. That form of dwelling did service for many years, even after the nation was established in its own land, in fact until the latter stages of David's reign. Arising out of David's great desire to see a permanent and fitting house erected as God's dwelling-place on earth, vast preparations were made so that Soloman (man of peace, unlike David his father) could complete with utmost facility the task of building. The resultant temple was an edifice of exceeding richness, beauty, and magnificence, entirely suited for its purpose and, like its predecessor the tabernacle, built according to divine instruction. The site of the temple was chosen by God, Ps. 132.13–14.

Destruction of that temple in 587 BC and the people's years of captivity had meant the prolonged absence of any earthly edifice to represent God's dwelling-place. All this was changed by the edicts of ungodly rulers, prompted by God to allow a remnant of people to return from captivity, 538 BC, and rehabilitate themselves in their own land. Their attempts to rebuild the temple are described in the book of Ezra, and there is an account of opposition to the project resulting in cessation of work, 4.23–24. After a lapse of some 16 years the Lord sent His messenger Haggai to deliver a series of challenging messages to leaders and people. Those messages brought home to the people then, as now, the importance to God of their building His house in the place where He has set His Name. Nothing must stand in the way of this holy enterprise.

Outline of Book

A Message to Leaders, 1.1–2.
A Message to the People, 1.3–11.
The People's Response to the Message, 1.12.
The Third Message, Assurance to all of divine support, 1.13–15.
The Fourth Message, Encouragement to leaders, and all the people, 2.1–9.
The Fifth Message, Principles of service, and promise of blessing, 2.10–19.
The Sixth and Final Message, Personal to the leader of God's people, 2.20–23.

A message to leaders, 1.1–2

Each of the messages conveyed by Haggai, the Lord's messenger, is clearly dated. The year is 520 BC and the month August/September according to our calendar. Harvesting of a variety of crops would have been in progress and the pastoral community would have been entirely preoccupied with the amount and value of crops ingathered. At such a time 'came the word of the Lord by Haggai, the prophet'. This is a different expression to that generally used of other prophets, 'the word of the Lord came to'. Its literal meaning is 'by the hand of', and this is an apt description of Haggai's transmission, in terms essentially practical, of God's message to 'his people'. After all, he is described as 'the Lord's messenger' to His people.

Personally addressed in this first message are Zerubbabel, grandson of Jehoiachin, 1 Chr. 3.19, and therefore of princely birth, and Joshua the high priest, see also Zech. 3.1–5; 6.11–12. Zerubbabel's appointment by the Persian king as governor of Judah, and Joshua's high-priestly role, identify these men as the political and religious leaders of the community. God addresses them first, highlighting the extra, onerous responsibility of those aspiring to leadership of God's people. On the other hand, New Testament teaching reveals that handsome rewards are reserved for faithful leaders of the flock, 1 Pet. 5.1–4.

God speaks as the Lord of Hosts. This title He uses many times in Old Testament prophecies, and it must have been to impress a fearful, and often sceptical people, as to His authority, and power to overrule in the affairs of men, to the outworking of His eternal purposes. His reference to 'this people' rather than to 'my people' probably indicates their detachment from Him at this time. They were openly expressing their feelings, so that their leaders would have been made fully aware of their intentions not to take up again the building-work on God's house. That these same leaders were seemingly happy to allow matters thus to slip away without making strenuous efforts to rally the people is something of an indictment against them. Many leaders of God's people in our own time note the lack of urgency to build generally, and rather count the ready explanations offered to account for this lack as excuses. It is their rôle to seek to inspire God's people to build, whatever the circumstances.

The excuse proffered here was that the timing of the operation was not right – an age-old excuse! The next message would seem to indicate that there were other things in people's lives that consistently took priority over the Lord's work. Conceivably, there may have been those who took the view that the full time of judgement (70 years according to Jeremiah's prophecy commencing 586 BC with the final fall of Jerusalem) was not yet completed. Whatever, the universal cry was, 'The time is not come, the time that the Lord's house should be built'.

Ezra's account of these times would throw light on why originally the building-work ceased, Ezra, chapters 4 and 5. Evidently there were adversaries committed to stopping work on the temple, and their determined attempts at intimidation, with involvement of the Persian authorities, had brought about a decree by Artaxerxes that the work be suspended, Ezra 4.23–24.

A message to the people, 1.3–11

Through the prophet, God turns the words of the people to challenge them, with some irony, as to the rightness of the time to build His house. They said, 'The time is not come, the time that the Lord's house should be built', so then God says, 'Is it time for you, O ye, to dwell in your cieled (panelled) houses and this house lie waste?'. In such a way God would expose the falseness and dishonesty of their position. Time for their own things but no time for God's! We are reminded elsewhere that time is a gift from God, and that it is of short duration, Ps. 39.5; Job 7.6; 1 Cor. 7.29. Time represents opportunity. Note the twice-repeated phrase 'redeeming the time', Eph. 5.16; Col. 4.5. The Greek text means literally buying up the opportunity, (see RV margin) and suggests the idea of 'doing business' in time to the advantage of our Master. Alas, in Haggai's day, as later in Paul's, 'all seek their own not the things which are Jesus Christ's', Phil. 2.21. The visible evidence was there to prove where effort had been expended over past years: their own houses panelled in luxurious fashion, while God's house lay waste. Obviously, they showed no compunction for their remiss conduct as David might when living in 'an house of cedar' while 'the ark of God dwelleth within curtains', 2 Sam. 7.2.

Verses 5–6 contain the exhortation, 'Consider your ways', (literally, 'Set your heart on your ways', see RV margin; this indicates the depth of feeling God expects from them in response). God suggests it is time for honest assessment, and this must be a healthy exercise for His people at any time. That He is supremely aware of all our 'ways', and looks for us to engage in honest self-appraisal/acknowledgement of failure, is made clear by the following statements of facts. Apparently all their efforts to succeed in material things had produced meagre returns, and this can only typify the loss suffered by God's people today in their neglect of

God's house. 'Ye have sown much' – great activity but no real spiritual harvest. 'Ye eat, but ye have not enough' – having a spiritual appetite, but suffering spiritual starvation. 'Ye drink, but ye are not filled with drink' – seeking spiritual satisfaction but to no avail. 'Ye clothe you ...none warm' – spiritual coldness. 'Wages ...into a bag with holes' – accumulation of earthly treasures resulting in spiritual poverty. The people's condition warrants comparison with that of the church at Laodicea, Rev. 3.17.

In verse 7, the exhortation is repeated, 'Consider your ways'. If it had a hint of rebuke the first time it is used, it now carries a message of encouragement. It is followed by clear instruction from God as to how the grievous state of affairs can be entirely rectified to the point where He can 'take pleasure in it', and 'be glorified', v. 8. Three directives are given: 'go', 'bring' and 'build'. They embrace the actions and servitude of every believer. As God's servants we must make the effort, and stir ourselves to play an active part in God's work. (Note the first word of the angel's directive to Peter, Acts. 5.20). Thereafter, the fruits of labour should be devoted entirely to God, and concentrated upon the work of God's house. This follows God's statement aforetime as to the attitude, and total approach, of those contributing to the building of the tabernacle, 'That they may bring me an offering: of every man that giveth it willingly with his heart', Exod. 25.2. And the final requirement is that we actively 'build', i.e. constructive, purposeful activity along established lines of construction, and 'according to the pattern'. We note it is said of Bezaleel, a skilled workman contributing to the building of the tabernacle, 'I have filled him with the Spirit of God, in wisdom, and in understanding and in knowledge, and in all manner of workmanship', Exod. 31.3. Not surprisingly the name 'Bezaleel' means 'in the shadow of God'.

Although 'this house', compared to Solomon's exceedingly magnificent house, would be 'as nothing', God says, nevertheless, 'I will take pleasure in it and will be glorified'. Let not any vision we might have for the present be totally overwhelmed by recollections of past glories. God's faithful people today are but 'a remnant', and it is evidently a day of small things. Nevertheless, wholehearted efforts by those who heed God's directives in the field of service must for them lead to divine approbation.

In verses 9–11 God explains why events have worked out so tragically in the immediate past, and at the same time He affirms that He is the One who has absolute control over earthly affairs. Any ideas they might have had that their problems were caused by 'natural' disasters are contradicted by a series of emphatic pronouncements by God. God says that it was He who prevented abundant harvests, the fall of dew, the fruitfulness of orchards. He it was who called for drought over the whole countryside. The paucity of crops was His doing: little corn, little new wine, little oil, little root crops, with men, cattle, and all 'labour' affected. And why? 'Because of mine house that is waste, and ye run every man unto his own house'.

Believers can rejoice in the truth that God is still on the throne, and that He is able to dictate in world affairs, to the outworking of His eternal purposes.

The people's response to the message, 1.12

It would seem there was a swift, unanimous response to God's trenchant utterances through Haggai the prophet. Notably the initiative to respond was taken by the appointed leaders of the people, Zerubbabel and Joshua. Singled out in God's first message, and bearing an extra burden of responsibility for how things stood, they now lead in the response to God's directives. A reminder of the people's weakness, in human terms, is embodied in the phrase 'the remnant of the people'. The phrase is used often in the Old Testament, having the meaning 'the residue of the people after decimation of numbers by whatever means and for whatever reasons'. Isaiah had clearly prophesied that only a remnant would return to the land after captivity, Isa. 7.3 [N.B. 'Shear-jashub' means 'The remnant shall return'.]; 10.21; 11.11, and so now, in the light of the task ahead, their resources would be stretched to the limit. Responding to Haggai's prophetic words, the people reacted in dual fashion, 'they obeyed the voice of the Lord, their God', and 'feared before the Lord'. We might judge the latter reaction as a necessary preface to the former, but the words of Samuel remind us of the necessity of total obedience in God's sight, and that to obey is a necessary antecedent to any demonstration of worshipful fear. Notably at this time is reference to 'the Lord their God', indicating a closer intimacy with God than previously.

The Third Message, Assurance to all of divine support, 1.13–15

The message could hardly be shorter, but what depth of meaning it carries! It comes immediately after the people's right response to the first messages with their devastating statements. 'I am with you', the Lord now says. Any misgivings they might have had in present circumstances must have been swept away by such a promise. A remnant they were, with limited resources and facing a daunting task, surrounded by many adversaries, and with a record of past failure. But now, God's promise to be with them is the answer to every problem, and assures them of every blessing. Many of God's people have clung to this promise in circumstances of deep trial, e.g. Moses, Exod. 3.12; Joshua, Deut. 31.8, 23; Gideon, Judg. 6.16; Jeremiah, Jer. 1.8. It is a promise extended to us, Heb. 13.5–6. Verse 14 gives insight into how any kind of revival is brought about in God's people. Consequent upon their changed attitudes, we are told that 'the Lord stirred up the spirit' of one and all. Should their response have been in any way faltering and uncertain, God's intervention in this respect meant that a great wave of enthusiasm engulfed the people, so that 'they came and did work in the house of the Lord of hosts, their God'. Reference to the 'house' in these terms would remind all of the supreme privilege attached to any kind of service to One so great. It would remind, too, of the vision all must have who would be involved in any revival among God's people. An incomplete, neglected building it might have stood at this point in time, but from now onwards it would be to work 'in the house of the Lord of hosts, their God'!

It will be apparent that there was some lapse of time between the first message and the actual recommencement of the building work, twenty-three days in fact. Obviously, arrangements had to be made to assemble materials for the construction, and to marshal and organize the labour force that was available, identifying particular skills. We have to remember too, that the task of harvesting crops, however meagre they might have been, was bound to have required the people's urgent attention. Taking all these matters into consideration, it would appear the ultimate resultant work in the house of the Lord of hosts was expedited with remarkable speed, indicating the people's complete change of heart and genuine desire to get started.

The Fourth Message, Encouragement to leaders, and all the people, 2.1–9

After the passing of almost a month since work recommenced on the house a message from the Lord is relayed to prince, high priest and all the people. It was calculated to rally everyone to the cause, and to reassure lest any misgivings that showed might slow the momentum. Significantly, it was delivered in the seventh month, and in the twenty-first day of the month, with heavy emphasis of the number seven. Not only would this remind us of the impeccability of God's timing as He intervenes to meet any crisis of confidence in our affairs, but also it would remind us that all God's purposes concerning His house bear the hallmark of perfection.

A look back at past glories, 2.3

God makes comparison of past and present as if to emphasize current limitations and the remnant's ineffectuality of operation as they sought to do His work. Comparison is made between Solomon's glorious temple, so richly appointed, and the basic functional edifice now being built by a weakened and impoverished workforce. Revival at any time is sustained by the enthusiasm of those involved: it might now be thought that such a sharp reminder of present weakness and the prospect of only moderate results to follow all their enterprise would be likely to sap that enthusiasm. Surely the lesson, then and now, is that God would have His people assess their circumstances in realistic fashion. Nothing is to be gained by resting on delusions, and talking in unreal terms. Here was a remnant-people, living in the midst of hostile nations who represented constant opposition to their great enterprise, made conscious of their weakness and inadequacy, and of having to live under the shadow of past glories. What they needed to realize was that God looks for His people to work in connection with His house at all times, whatever the circumstances, and whatever the results of their labours. It is the Lord's work, and by whatever yardstick men might make comparisons, so as to discount present 'results', it is at this point that God says 'Go . . . bring . . . build the house, and I will take pleasure in it, and I will be glorified'.

One point of interest in verse 3 is God's reference to 'this house in her first glory'. He speaks again of 'this house' in verse 7, and while the first reference has Solomon's temple in mind, surely this second reference is to Ezekiel's temple set up in a future day when Christ's kingdom is established on earth. Obviously, God sees the succession of temples as 'one house'. From this we might construe that in His eyes the glories of former and latter days extend over the 'here and now'. Surely this will help to prevent our making any invidious comparisons between past and present, as we contemplate the modest extent of our own achievements.

A look around at present support, 2.4–5

Leaders and people again are addressed. The exhortation to all is to 'be strong', an echo of God's words to Joshua, Josh. 1.6, 7, 9, 18. This is not encouragement to assemble human resources, for it is accompanied by another assurance of the Lord's presence with them, 'I am with you, saith the Lord of hosts'. Full and honest assessment would reveal to them the extent of their weakness, so that they might fully appreciate that all their strength emanated from the Lord. Paul realized this too, in his own experience, and from the Lord's words to him, 'My grace is sufficient for thee, for my strength is made perfect in weakness'. Paul's conclusion was, 'for when I am weak, then am I strong', and his exhortation to others was to 'be strong in the Lord, and in the power of his might', 2. Cor. 12.9–10; Eph. 6.10.

There is reference in verse 5 to God's covenant promises in His word: these are unfailing, and are a sure support at any time. Such power as was demonstrated in Israel's deliverance from Egypt is available for God's people now. What comfort, assurance, and guidance we can find in the inspired word of God, sufficient at all times to ensure 'that the man of God may be complete, thoroughly furnished unto every good work', 2. Tim. 3.17, NEWBERRY.

Further assurance is given in the statement, 'My Spirit remaineth among you' ('abode among you', RV). Apparently, both renderings are permissible, (see *Tyndale Old Testament Commentary*), emphasizing that the presence of God with His people had been a continuous process since first covenant promises were made. All this is reminiscent of Our Lord's words, 'And I will pray the Father and he shall give you another Comforter, that he may abide with you for ever, even the Spirit of truth', John 14.16–17. Believers today should be conscious that the Spirit of God is as much with us, indwelling every true Christian, and dwelling in the midst of each local assembly of Christians, as He was with those of the early church after Pentecost, 1 Cor. 6.19; Eph. 2.22, RV.

Having given assurance of divine support, it is not surprising that the Lord then says to His remnant people, 'Fear ye not' (cf. Zech. 8.13, 15). The words of this section are virtually the same as David's words to Solomon prior to the building of the first temple, 1 Chr. 28.20. What needs to be emphasized, however, is that in Haggai it is God who speaks, and that He speaks to all involved in the work of building!

A look ahead to future restoration and glory, 2.6–9

Here the message becomes one of foretelling of future events, calculated to inspire and encourage the lowly remnant with the glittering prospect of a day when 'the desirable things of all nations' will be brought to the latter house, see RV rendering, and *Tyndale Old Testament Commentary, New Bible Commentary*. No shortage of costly materials then to affect the operation of building the Lord's house: God establishes that all of the world's silver and gold are His anyway, and all will be forthcoming and made available so as to embellish this most glorious house. But it is He who 'will fill this house with glory', and it is He that 'in this place will . . .give peace', vv. 7, 9. As a prelude to this blessed state of affairs, it is His power that will have shaken all nations, in judgement setting aside earthly rulers and kingdoms of men, so as to establish His own 'kingdom that cannot be shaken', Heb. 12.26-28.

The Fifth Message, Principles of service, and promise of blessing, 2.10–19

This came two months after Haggai's previous message, and is interrogative, instructive, and inspiring. It is a statement of moral requirements that God will have in His servants. Their failures in the past can be explained by their low moral state at the time.

Interrogation, vv. 11–13

The priests, as an authoritative source of information, are asked to rule on matters of God's law. They are asked if that which is holy, coming into contact with other mundane substances can render them holy. The answer is an emphatic, 'No'! Holiness cannot be imparted in such fashion. A second question as to whether defilement can be transmitted by contact is answered in the affirmative, Lev. 11.28; 22.4-7.

Instruction, vv. 14–17

These principles, applied to the people's activities over past days, had rendered 'every work of their hands, and that which they offer there' as 'unclean', v. 14. Consequently, in His governmental dealings with them the Lord had disciplined them in various ways. Blessing had been denied them, and all their work had been smitten with 'blasting and mildew and hail', v. 17. Obviously, they had not appreciated the Lord's hand in this, for He says, 'Yet, ye turned not to me'.

Inspiration, vv. 18–19

Here, the Lord's word makes an obvious break with what is past and gone, and turns the people's minds towards what the future can hold for them. Change of heart, repentance for what is past, acting upon the word of the Lord and taking up work upon His house will change matters completely. The Lord says, 'From this day will I bless you'. Surely this entire section illustrates how blessing from the Lord will follow the wholehearted efforts of His people to work at building His house, providing that there is a faithful attachment to principles of service that He has laid down in His word. On the other hand, departure from those principles, and dereliction of our duty to 'serve God acceptably, with reverence and godly fear', Heb. 12.28, must result in barrenness of soul. Such condition must be regarded as the meritable sequel to our indiscipline in service, and of consequent action by God to discipline us.

The Sixth and Final Message, Personal to the leader of God's people, 2.20–23

This last message was given on the same day as the previous message. It was given separately on account of its being addressed personally to Zerubbabel, the officially recognized leader of the community. It is entirely related to future events, although it would have given much encouragement to Zerubbabel and all the people at that particular time inasmuch as it declares how great is God's power to dominate all rule and authority on earth. For them the status quo was only until God, in His own time, and in dramatic fashion, would bring about changes. 'I will shake', v. 21; 'I will overthrow', v. 22; 'I will destroy', v. 22; all emphasize God's omnipotence, and His ability to dictate events according to His will. This He will do with ruthless efficiency whenever it is warranted. Held out as an incentive to the leader of God's people is promise of future honour, authority, and reward, 'I will make thee as a signet, for I have chosen thee, saith the Lord of Hosts', v. 23.

Whatever events followed Haggai's prophecy so as, in measure, to fulfil these predictions for the benefit of Zerubbabel and all the people, this message has to be regarded as far more portentous than that. It extends to another remnant people in a day far future. Zerubbabel must be regarded as type of One who is destined in God's plan for the ages to rule over the nations with absolute authority, Psa. 110.1–2. All hostile powers will have been put down by God's direct intervention, so that His people might recognize Him and acknowledge Him as their Saviour – God. 'In that day', the One elsewhere referred to by God as 'my Servant', will be installed in highest majesty, though He was formerly 'despised and rejected of men'. He is the One ordained by God to rule the nations with all the weight of divine authority, cf. Isa. 42.1; 52.13–15.

CHAPTER ELEVEN

THE PROPHECY OF
ZECHARIAH

by CYRIL HOCKING

Introduction: Behold thy King cometh unto thee

Setting

In Judea within the first century of political 'subserviency' to Gentile 'super-powers'. The politico/historical period therefore is Persian, and Zechariah's dated inputs fall between 520 and 518 BC, 1.1, 7; 7.1; Ezra chs. 5–6, see Table, pp. 192–193. The undated contributions, chapters 9 to 14, most probably are later and belong to his service in the first quarter of the fifth century BC. He witnessed the return of a remnant from captivity and restoration to the land, the re-establishing of a national identity and 'political constitution', and he promoted the rebuilding of Jerusalem's temple.

Servant

He was a priest by birth, and a prophet by divine call, a younger contemporary of Haggai with whom he served the Lord in a constructive and complementary way: ponder the inter-relationships of their service, true unity without uniformity. Zechariah's name (= Yahweh remembers), 1.1,7; 7.1; Ezra 5.1; 6.14; Neh.12.16, has great covenant overtones, and significantly is the most 'popular' name among Israeli families, there being about thirty people so named in the Old Testament. It expresses the faith of parents in the unchanging faithfulness of the Lord.

Subject matter

A substantial contribution to the sweep of God's salvation-historical programme, from the return from exile in Babylon, through the Medo-

Persian, Greek and Roman periods and on to the end of this age and the manifest installation of the Lord as King in the age to come. A huge place is given to the different roles and offices of the King-Messiah, and His first advent grace and second advent glory as the Stone, Servant, Shepherd, Priest and King Messiah is revealed here.

Structure

Contents arranged in two major sections:

A. 1.1–8.23. Present merges with distant	B. 9.1–14.21. Future troubles and triumphs
Visions, symbolism, apocalyptic	More literal, descriptive, messianic, prophetic
Repentance and change	Repentance and cleansing

In both sections large place given to Jerusalem/Zion, 'In that day', the Lord of hosts

---

A. Apocalyptic Panorama, 1.1–8.23	**B. Messianic Projections, 9.1–14.21**
1. A Call to Repentance. 1.1–6	**1. Advent of King-Shepherd. 9.1–11.17**
2. Visions of Restoration. 1.7– 6.15	Enemies destroyed – God's house defended, 9.1–8
1. Rider, Horses among Myrtles, 1.7–17	Advent of Messianic King announced, 9.9–12
2. Four Horns and Four Destroyers, 1.18–21	Peace, prosperity, triumph assured, 9.13–16
3. Man with Measuring Line, 2.1–5	Look to the Good Lord Alone, 9.17–10.2
Direct Prophetic Appeals, 2.6–13	Lord will Strengthen Judah – Save Joseph, 10.3–12
4. High Priest Crowned and Clothed, 3.1–10	Country devastated – Flock decimated, 11.1–3
5. Lampstand, Lamps and Oil Supply, 4.1–14	Rejection of Good Shepherd, 11.4–14
6. The Flying Scroll and its Curse, 5.1–4	Chastised through false shepherd, 11.15–17

7. Woman in Ephah Taken to
Shinar, 5.5–11
8. Four Chariots, 6.1–8
Crowned Priest sits on
Throne, 6.9–15

**3. Your Fasts to be Feasts,
7.1–8.23**
The Question Raised, 7.1–3
Negative – Rebukes
Contemporaries, 7.4–7
Negative – Reflecting on the
Past, 7.8–14
Positive – Oracles concerning
Future, 8.1–17
Positive – Oracles concerning
Feasting, 8.18–23

**2. Advent of Shepherd-King,
12.1–14.21**
**2.1 Defence of Jerusalem,
12.1–13.6**
Lord Guarantor concerning
Israel, 12.1–2
Jerusalem a burdensome stone,
12.3–8
Purpose to Destroy Nations,
12.9–13.1
Idols cut off. Prophets
ashamed, 13.2–6

**2.2 Deliverance of Jerusalem,
13.7–14.21**
Who may abide the day of His
coming? 13.7–9
Behold, a day for the Lord
cometh, 14.1–7
The Lord King of all the Land,
14.8–11
Plague, Panic for enemies of
Jerusalem, 14.12–15
Nations worship the King,
14.16–19
All will be Holy to the Lord,
14.20–21

^ after Scripture refs = all in book referred to.
* all uses of word, phrase or title in OT/NT/Bible.
MBA = *Modern Bible Atlas*, ed. Ahareni and Avi-Jonah/Pub. George
Allan & Unwin.
Jos. Ant. = Josephus, *Antiquities of the Jews*.

Inter-Relationship of Haggai's and Zechariah's Ministries

Haggai and Zechariah commenced their corrective, challenging and constraining work among God's people in the second year of Darius I Hystaspes, i.e. 520 BC. How their contrasting and yet complementary service is dove-tailed together is set out in the following Table.

King	Day/ Month/ Year	Our Date	Prophet	Ref.	Message/Effect	Passage
Darius	1/6/2	Aug/Sept 520	**Haggai**	1.1	First Message: Challenge and Command,	1.1-11
	24/6/2	Sept 520	**Haggai**	1.15	Temple Building Recommenced,	1.12-15
	21/7/2	Oct 520	**Haggai**	2.1	Second Message: Encouragement,	2.1-9
	–/8/2	Oct/Nov 520	*Zechariah*	*1.1*	*First, a Call to Return to God,*	*1.1-6*
	24/9/2	Dec 520	**Haggai**	2.10, 18	Third Message: Promised Blessing,	2.10-19
	24/9/2	Dec 520	**Haggai**	2.20	Fourth Message: Unshakable Kingdom,	2.20-23
	20/11/2	Feb 519	*Zechariah*	*1.7*	*Second, A Series of Visions,*	*1.7-6.15*
	4/9/4	Dec 518	*Zechariah*	*7.1*	*Third, Question and Answers re Fasts,*	*7.1-8.23*

In the mercy of God Haggai and Zechariah saw the completion of the Rebuilding of the Temple at Jerusalem in *the year 516 BC*. It is said that 'the elders of the Jews builded, and they prospered through the prophesying of Haggai the prophet and Zechariah the son of Iddo. And they builded and finished it, according to the commandment of the God of Israel, and according to the commandment of Cyrus, and Darius, and Artaxerxes king of Persia. And this house was finished on *the third day of the month Adar, which was in the sixth year of the reign of Darius the king*: Ezra 6.14, 15. It would appear that Zechariah, being a younger man, considerably outlived this glad day, and was taken up again by God to develop the two prophetic burdens with which his book is closed, Zech. 9-14.

A BIBILICAL HISTORY OF THE EXILIC/POST-EXILIC PERIOD

JUDAH

609–598 Jehoiakim 2 Kgs. 23.34–24.7; 2 Chron. 36.5–8; Dan. 1.1, 2
First Deportation from Jerusalem to Babylon

598/7 Jehoiachin 2 Kgs. 24.8–16; Chron. 36.9–10; Ezek. 17.12

Second Deportation from Jerusalem to Babylon

597–587/6 Zedekiah 2 Kgs. 24.17–25.21; 2 Chron. 36.11–21

Third Deportation from Jerusalem to Babylon
THE FIRST TEMPLE DESTROYED

See Dan.5

First Return under Zerubbabel — History of book of **EZRA** begins here

Ezra 1-2 The return to Judah

Ezra 3 Altar and Second Temple Foundation Laid

BABYLON
Nebuchadnezzar
606/5

598/7

587/6

Belshazzar
BABYLON FALLS TO
MEDO-PERSIA
539

Cyrus (550–530)
537/6

Cambyses (530–522)
Smerdis (522)

Darius (Hystaspes) (522–486)

— 520   Ezra 5 People Encouraged; Work recommenced

Ministries of **HAGGAI AND ZECHARIAH**

— 516   Ezra 6 SECOND TEMPLE BUILDING PROJECT COMPLETED

Xerxes (**Ahasuerus**, 486–465)

Story of *ESTHER* belongs here (483–473?)

Artaxerxes (465–433)

— 458   *Second Return; EZRA'S MISSION — EZRA 7–10 belongs here, 7.7*

— 445   *Third Return; NEHEMIAH'S MISSION — NEHEMIAH belongs here, 1.1; 2.1*

— 397?   Ministry of **MALACHI**

Note that there are six books devoted to the post-exilic period. Three of these are more histories in narrative form. Three record the ministry of the last of the so-called Minor Prophets. The table indicates that they inter-relate in the following way:

536	520–16	458	483	445	397?
Ezra 1–4	Ezra 5–6	Ezra 7–10	Esther	Nehemiah 1–12, 13	
	Haggai and Zechariah				Malachi

Many silent years intervene, often described as the Inter-Testamental Period, between this Spirit inspired sunset-ministry of the Old Testament and the new divine initiative in the visit of the Dayspring from on high with which the NT opens.

A. Apocalyptic Panorama, 1.1–8.23

1. A Call to Repentance Heeded –
Human Responsibility, 1.1–6

The prophetic revelation through Zechariah, vv. 1–6c, results in the people acknowledging its truthfulness, v. 6d–f. For details concerning **the setting and the servant, v. 1,** see the Introduction. This is the first of three timenotes which divide the first section into its three historical parts dated by the reign of a Gentile monarch, 1.1, 7; 7.1. All are set in the times of the Gentiles, during which the 'not my people' indictment obtains for Israel. Yet the prophet and his immediate forebears bear significantly appropriate names; Zechariah – the Lord remembers, Berechiah – the Lord blesses, and Iddo – appointed time. Faith confesses that the Lord is committed to His covenant, and it anticipates a blessing-laden initiative exactly as programmed by the Lord of history. Notice the classical prophetic formula, 'The word of the Lord (that) came unto … saying, 1.1; 4.8; 6.8; 7.1, 4, 8; 8.1, 18; cf. 4.6; 6.8. Another frequent message-opening formula insisting upon the divine authority of the message is, 'Thus saith the Lord (of hosts) … saith the Lord', see 1.3, 4, 16 etc. Such expressions emphasize that it is the Lord who reveals, the wholeness and unity of the revelation (note the singular 'word'), as well as the personal privilege and responsibility of those who pass it on to the people. Where plurals are used, e.g. 'my words and my statutes', it is the minutiae of the Lord's message that are insisted upon, cf. v. 6a–c. The 'word' and the 'words' point to a *verbal revelation* of God.

The substance of the opening revelation, vv. 2–6c, first condemns the past behaviour of the fathers with whom the Lord had been 'displeased with displeasure' (lit.). The verb and noun from the same root open and close the sentence, indicating the strength and all-embracing nature of His anger, v. 2; ct. v. 15, before He challenges the present generation not to pursue the same disastrous course, vv. 3–6. This is done by the double-use of the imperative 'return', vv. 3, 4; cf. 9.12. If for Haggai Judah's first priority is to build God's house, for Zechariah it is to return to the Lord Himself. He woos them positively: 'Return unto me' and the promise is 'I will return unto you', v. 3; cf. v. 16; 8.3. The Lord of hosts is longing to run to meet His returning prodigals. They had returned to the land; this was not enough; they must return to the Lord. Position must be matched by condition! Also the verb is used negatively to warn them in the light of their fathers' deafness to His demand: 'Return ye now from your evil ways' for otherwise discipline and destruction looms ahead as with 'your fathers' (note the distancing tone of this pronoun), vv. 2, 4, 5, 6; cf. 13.7.

The divine name 'Lord' [or yhwh, that is Yahweh or Jehovah; note in Eng. Versions the sole use of upper case letters distinguishes this divine name from other Hebrew words translated 'Lord',] occurs only in the Bible. With the word for 'hosts' added it creates a frequently used combined title, and Zechariah is particularly fond of it (some 47 refs). In chapter 1 alone it occurs ten times. The Lord is the commander-in-chief of the heavenly bodies, of the angelic hosts, and of Israel's armies as of all others; He is the Almighty Warrior cosmically and covenantally, this being a most encouraging truth, particularly in difficult times.

The people's return and confession, v. 6d–f. The call to 'return' was obeyed. They confessed 'Like as . . . so'; what the Lord of hosts had purposed to do conformed exactly with what He had done [lit.same verb in each case]; He is imminent in history, effecting His sovereign purpose in woe and in weal. The justice of His purpose is acknowledged in their confession 'Like *as* . . . *as* our ways . . . *as* our doings' [lit.]. Sins confessed to God are sins forgiven!

2. Eight Visions of Restoration Given in One Night – Divine Sovereignty, 1.7–6.15

Vision 1. Rider and Horses among the Myrtles, 1.7–17. *Message: The Lord's Informed Interest and Promised Involvement in His City and Land*

To verbal revelation in verse one, *visual revelation* has now been added, vv. 7–8. The change to 'I saw, or looked, or beheld, or shewed' alerts us to this. This is frequently followed by the graphic supplement, 'and behold', 1.8; 4.2, the prophet's favourite expression being 'I lifted up mine eyes, and saw, and behold . . . ', 1.18; 2.1; 5.1, 9; 6.1; cf. 5.5. Such God-given *visions call for explanation*, hence the questions, 'What are these?', 1.9, 19; 4.4; 6.4, or 'What is it?' etc., 5.6. Explanations then follow, by *the angel interpreter*, 1.9, 13, 14, 19 etc., who was kept busy dispelling the prophet's ignorance, 'answering and saying' etc, 1.9, 10, 12, 14, 21. Compare the role of the angelic intermediary in Revelation. Divine reserve was meant to be felt by Judah, while assuring the remnant of the glories that will follow.

The re-introduction of **the timenote, v. 7; cf. v. 1**, marks the opening of a new and lengthy sub-section. Haggai's recorded ministry had been completed some two months earlier, see Table on page 191. Now **the scene and the subject of the vision**, v. 8, arrest the prophet's attention. To be able to see in the night is a precious faculty indeed: it cuts short the weeping that would tarry through the night, already apprehending the 'joy (that) cometh in the morning', Ps. 30.5. The 'man' is variously depicted: he is 'riding on a red horse', he 'stood among the myrtle trees', vv. 10, 11, and he is also *'the angel of the Lord'*, vv. 11, 12. Regarding this angel or messenger, he has a singular ministry in the Old Testament, protective, intercessory, 1.12; 3.1-6, and saving, Isa. 63.9, and is often identified contextually with the Lord Himself, see Exod. 3.2-18; Mal. 3.1. He is the theophanic angel, a Christophany, and is to be distinguished here from the interpreting angel, vv. 9, 13, 14. He is seen 'among the myrtles' [lit.], which feature three times here, vv. 8, 9, 10, and elsewhere only at Neh. 8.15; Isa. 41.19; 55.13, which see for their messianic suggestiveness. In form the myrtle is a lowly evergreen shrub, whose leaves have healing properties. It is yet to replace altogether the briar in the age to come, when the evidence of the curse is to be removed for ever. These myrtles were located 'in the bottom', referring probably to where the Hinnom and the Kidron Valleys meet. Shrub and setting depict the lowly condition and depressed spirit of contemporary Judah. The man astride the 'red horse' had 'behind him' three distinctly coloured groups of horses, red, sorrel and white; he was their leader/commander and in control of history, the unseen and seen participants alike; ct. 6.1-8.

Then **the prophet's question, v. 9a**, is resolved by **the answer of the man who is the angel of the Lord, vv. 9b-11**. The interpreting angel *shewed*, but it was the 'man' standing among the myrtles who *answered* the prophet, vv. 9-10. The horses represented the hidden spirit agencies sent to patrol the earth by the Lord, and to report back to the 'man'; ct. 6.5 where the four groups of horses are described as 'the four spirits of heaven, which go forth from standing before the Lord [*'adon*] of all the earth' [here = world] to effect divine judgement. Their 'behold', v. 11, concentrates the mind on their intelligence report; 'the earth' [here = inhabitants of its countries] is laid back and quiet; they sit while 'the man', who cares, stands!, cf. Acts 7.55-56. There is no sign of Haggai's promised shaking of heaven and earth yet!

The angel of the Lord's sympathy prompts his **supplication for them, v. 12**, 'O Lord of hosts, how long'? As long as Jerusalem and Judah have not obtained mercy, Israel is still 'not my people'. The seventy years enforced captivity had come to an end in 537/6 BC, Jer. 29.10-14, and the seventy years of desolations suffered by city and country were virtually ended too, (517/6 BC,) 25.11; 2 Chr. 36.21, indicating the timeliness of the plea. This 'Angel Advocate' has power with God. **The divine answer, v. 13**, the Lord's words, both favourable and comforting, first must be given to the interpreting angel and then they are communicated to Zechariah, v. 13. As 'the Lord answered', v. 12, 'So the angel . . . said unto me', v. 14.

The prophet is now **commissioned to comfort, vv. 14–17**. Note the twofold imperative 'Cry thou . . . Cry yet again . . .' [here = to proclaim with energy as a herald], vv. 14, 17. To those sensing the distancing effect of their sins, and depressed with doubts regarding their future, the prophet's seven-point message was to reassure. None dare question the *ability* of the Lord of hosts to deliver such benefits, vv. 14, 16, 17; dare any doubt the *dependability* of the covenant-keeping, unchanging Lord's return, cf. vv. 3, 4? His return is to be with mercies [plural of intensity] and comfort in fulfilling His promises to Zion, and His making evident that Jerusalem is the city of divine choice, vv. 16, 17. The *Lord* is: 1) exceedingly jealous/ zealous 'for'; He is never jealous 'of' Jerusalem/ Zion, neither is His love simply one that will not tolerate a rival, but it must energetically pursue positive intentions for her, 2) *very* displeased with displeasure against Judah's enemies, cf. v. 2, and their insensitive unconcern, ct. 'for I' . . . but 'they', 3) returned to Jerusalem with mercies. The *Lord promises*: 4) My house shall be built in it, cf. 4.7–9; 6.12–13, 5) a surveyor's line is to be stretched forth over Jerusalem in pursuing its reclaiming and rebuilding, cf. 2.1, 6) My cities through prosperity, cf. v. 13, shall overflow, and He is yet 7) to comfort Zion, and to choose Jerusalem, returning to the place He has chosen to put His name, Deut.12.5; 26.2; 31.11. Zechariah as a priest-prophet is fascinated by Jerusalem (41 refs.) and Zion (8 refs.), inverted references to which, in his opening and closing 'Cry', provide a frame for this sevenfold revelation, vv. 14, 17.

Visions 2 and 3: 1) open with the same introductory formula, **2)** are concerned with more external evidence of God's sovereign interest in Judah/Jerusalem, whether negatively in the *destruction* of opposing political powers, or positively as yet to be seen in the material *construction and expansion*, and the security and splendour of Jerusalem, **3)** develop one of the details of Vision 1, and **4)** project the Lord's prophetic purposes in addressing present problems.

Vision 2. Four Horns and Four Destroyers, 1.18–21[2.1–4]. *Message: Heaven's Control of Earth's Affairs – Terrifying and Casting Down the Scatterers*

'And I lifted up mine eyes, and saw, and behold . . . '. This second
vision designedly expatiates on the statement of 1.15 and is in two parts,
vv. 18b, 20, which prompts the prophet's twofold question, vv. 19a, 21a,
which in turn is answered by the angel's twofold interpretation, vv. 19b,
21b, c. The prophet beheld first *'horns'* which when used metaphorically
refer to physical might and power whether destructive or defensive,
whether of God, 2 Sam. 22.3, or of men, Deut. 33.17; Dan. 8.20, or of
nations and their kings. Here they symbolize those nations which arro-
gantly and terrifyingly oppressed Judah, for 'no man did lift up his
head'. They had 'scattered . . . lifted up (destructively, violently, continually) their horn against . . . Judah', vv. 19, 21, thereby going beyond
God's disciplining purpose in raising them. Note the past tenses, 'prophetic perfects' encouraging confidence in the God who projects the
future as though already completed. Zechariah also saw *'smiths'*,
craftsmen in metal, stone or wood, whose skills guarantee effective
action, vv. 20, 21. The number of the horns and smiths was the same,
each of the latter being raised and equipped first 'to fray' [lit. 'to terrify']
and then 'to cast down' the former. The *'four'* specifically represent the
four Gentile 'superpowers' of Daniel, spanning the 'times of the Gentiles', rather than four of Judah's contemporary petty neighbours, or
universal opposition from the four quarters of the earth. This is supported by there being only three distinct groups of horses sent to
reconnoitre all the earth in the previous vision, for Babylon, and the
spirit-world forces commissioned to oversee it, already had left the
scene.

Vision 3. Man with Measuring Line at Jerusalem, 2.1–5[5–9]. *Message:
Jerusalem; the Measurable and the Measureless*

Here the destruction of the foes seen in vision 2 is followed by the
construction of the city. Vision 3 elaborates the pithy promise 'a line
shall be stretched forth over Jerusalem', 1.16. The details of the vision,
v. 1, lead the prophet to question, v. 2a, resulting in the man's explanation, v. 2b–d, and the commissioning of the interpreting angel by
another angel, vv. 3–5. Observe the change from 'a man', v. 1, to 'this
young man', v. 4. The 'man' was a surveyor equipped with the tool of
his trade, a 'measuring line', who informed the prophet that he was
engaged in the more immediate possession and development of Jerusalem, cf. Nehemiah's later enterprise, 3.11, 19, 20, 21. The 'young man'
however refers to Zechariah, to whom an angel redirected his angel
interpreter, in order that he might be enthused about the population

explosion of the eschatological city, without walls and yet dwelling serenely secure, v. 4; cf. Isa. 49.19, 20; 54.2. 'For *I*, [emphatic] saith the Lord, will be unto her a wall of fire round about, and I will be the glory in the midst of her', v. 5. The nation's abominations had caused the 'glory of the God of Israel' to depart from temple and city in the past, Ezek. 9.3; 10.14, 18. This will change when He will come and 'dwell in the midst of thee', vv. 10, 11, and will be 'the glory in the midst' of the city on earth. Then His glory will return and fill the millennial temple, Ezek. 43.1-5; ct. 'the holy city Jerusalem' to come down out of heaven 'having the glory of God', Rev. 21.10, 11, 23. At last the city's expansiveness and external security will be surpassed by the presence of God who 'will be the glory in the midst of her'.

(Parenthetical) Direct Prophetic Appeals, 2.6–13[10–17]. *Message: Calls to Separation, Song and Silence, 'for, lo, I come'*

The unifying thread of the first three visions is the sovereign character of the Lord's intervention. Following these, the return to direct verbal revelation here provides a 'Selah'. This is evident from: 1) the opening use of the arresting word 'Ho, ho', v. 6, cf. v. 7, 2) the repeated use of the oracular formulae 'saith the Lord', vv. 6(2), 10, and 'Thus saith the Lord of hosts', emphasizing the authority of the direct message, v. 8, and by 3) the authentication of the divine mission of His agent, the messenger who is sent. Only the Lord Messiah's mission can satisfy what is predicated of the sent one here, for He is sent to the nations in the prosecution of God's glory; His hand brandished over them reduces them to subjection, and He is to see many nations join themselves to Him in that day, vv. 8, 9, 11. The interpreting angel is absent altogether, vv. 9, 11. The logic in responding to all of these pleas is supported by the sixfold use of the causal 'for', vv. 6, 8(2), 9, 10, 13.

Appeals to the exiles in Babylon, vv. 6–9, are made in the light of the coming judgements and of the glories to follow, cf. Isa. 52.11-12. These take the form of warnings to flee, cf. 14.5(3), and to escape the judgements directed against Babylon, cf. Isa. 48.20; Rev. 18.4. The land of the north, v. 6, is one with its people, the daughter of Babylon, v. 7, among whom the majority of the nation still dwelt. God had scattered Zion *governmentally* because of its sins, v. 6c. In addressing her as 'Zion', it is *grace* that is beckoning her to respond, v. 7, 'for' 1) it is 'after glory', v. 8a, that is with a view to realizing His purpose to glorify Himself and His people with Him, that His agent has been sent to the nations, 2) he that touches so as to harm them, cf. 1 Chr. 16.22; Ps. 105.15, touches the apple of His eye, that is the pupil, the most informing and sensitive part of His tender Being, v. 8b. Those kept as the apple of His eye are so precious to Him, Deut. 32.10; Ps. 17.8, and 3) the Lord is sent to the nations generally to exert omnipotent power, the diaspora is to be repatriated and the despoilers are to be spoiled themselves, v. 9; ct. v. 11.

Conversely, **the appeals to the daughter of Zion, vv. 10–12,** directed to that part of the nation already returned to the land, encourage her to sing a shout of jubilation to God and rejoice! What cause Zion will have for song in that day, cf. Zeph. 3.14–17. The One who had said to God at His first advent 'Lo, I am come . . . I delight to do thy will', Ps. 40.7, 8[8, 9], promises Zion a second advent, 'lo, I come', not simply that a day of the Lord will come, 14.1, but 'I will dwell' permanently and personally 'in the midst of thee, saith the Lord', Zech. 2.10; 8.3; Ps. 74.2; Isa. 52.7–10; Ezek. 43.9, impossible of realization without their redemption, cf. Exod. 15.17–18. In that day, too, 'many nations shall join themselves unto the Lord' and shall be His people, fulfilling a welcome feature of the Abrahamic covenant that in him 'shall all the families of the earth be blessed', v. 11; Gen. 22.18. Both by the subjugation of the opposing nations and by the glad service of the saved nations the Lord of hosts' Sent One shall be recognized at last, 2.9, 11. This anticipates millennial blessedness. Only then shall the Lord 'inherit Judah as his portion', Deut. 4.20; Isa. 19.24, 'in the holy land', the only place in the Bible where the land is thus described, and truly so because at last the Holy One is in their midst, cf. 8.3; 14.20, 21. His original choice of Jerusalem, and the irrevocable Davidic covenant bound up with it is finally evident and acknowledged by all, v. 12.

Finally, **the appeal to all flesh, v. 13.** The imperative 'Be silent', calls for a universal awesome stillness before the Lord, cf. Hab. 2.20, the reason being that He who has been withdrawn and inactive, cf. 1.11, is 'waked up' and is about to be revealed out of His heavenly sanctuary and to come to His holy land.

Visions 4 and 5 are unique and central to the series for: 1) they are introduced differently, the initiative not being with the prophet, 2) they both are personal yet representative in character, being addressed to the contemporary leaders of the nation, note 'Joshua' (5 refs.) the high priest and 'Zerubbabel' (4 refs) the royal prince, 3) each features a prophetic verbal supplement to the vision.

Vision 4. Joshua, High Priest Crowned and Clothed, 3.1–10. *Message: Priestly People, Cleansed, Clothed, Consecrated. Messiah, the Servant, the Shoot and the Stone.*

The details of the vision, vv. 1–5, are followed by a direct verbal revelation to Joshua, including protest, and promise, vv. 6–10. In this 'priestly' vision alone the interpreting angel has no part, but the prophet, free of questions this time, has his own request granted, v. 5.

In the Vision, vv. 1–5, sadly Joshua here is not interceding but answering for the nation, cf. vv. 4, 9; cf. Exod. 28.12b, 29, 30c, 38. If the land is to become 'the holy land', and the Lord is yet to come out of the habitation of His holiness to dwell in the midst of the nation, cf. 8.3; 14.20, 21, radical changes must be effected, as the frank descriptions of Joshua's state intimate. For in the high priest, the condition of the whole people he represents is exposed. The iniquity of priest, people and land alike has to be dealt with before all may be reconsecrated; God's holiness and righteousness must be satisfied. Judgement must begin at the house of God.

The vision introduces *Joshua, the Angel and the Adversary*, vv. 1–2. J[eh]oshua is one of eight Old Testament characters so named, and is to be identified with Jeshua, Ezra 2.2; Neh. 7.7 etc. The former name is the fuller form of the latter, meaning 'the Lord saves' [cf. Greek '*Iesous* = Jesus]. He 'stands' *before* the angel of the Lord, vv. 1, 3, not as representative intercessor, Deut. 10.8, Ezek. 44.15, nor as privileged servant, Zech. 3.4; 1 Kgs. 17.1, but as offender and defendant in a court before his Judge, Deut. 19.17; Jer. 7.10. The closing phrase of verse one literally reads 'and the Adversary [*Satan*] ... to be his adversary', the appropriateness of his name/title being demonstrated in his nefarious activity, cf. Job 1.2; Rev. 12.10. The Adversary has a strong case against Joshua's suitability for sacred service. But it is the Lord, previously described as 'the angel of the Lord', who silences the Adversary with a twofold restraining 'rebuke' based upon 1) the sovereign and irrevocable choice of Jerusalem, Isa. 41.8–10, and 2) the demonstrated mercy in 'this' despicable fellow being snatched from destruction, Amos 4.11; cf. Jude 23; ct. Exod. 3.1–8.

The Lord's rebuke of Satan is followed by His *removal of Joshua's iniquity and his proposed reclothing in rich apparel*, vv. 3–4. The repulsiveness of Joshua's condition is represented in his 'filthy garments', cf. Isa. 4.4; 64.6. He was in no fit state to serve in the sanctuary soon to be completed. Joshua stood before the Angel condemned until His command 'unto them', heaven's courtiers standing before Him, to take away his filthy 'habit' from upon him. The significance of that symbolic negative act was then explained 'unto him' (Joshua), 'See I have caused to pass from upon thee thine iniquity' [lit.]. That same Angel of the Lord now adds positively 'I will clothe thee with rich apparel' suitable for reconsecration to sanctuary service thus to 'worship the Lord in the beauty of holiness', v. 4; Ps. 29.2; cf. 110.3; Isa. 61.10–11. Divinely provided atonement and adornment in garments of glory and beauty meet the demands of God's holiness, for 'holiness becometh thine house, O Lord, for evermore', cf. Exod. 29.4–5; Ps. 93.5.

Enthusiastically, the *prophet adds his own request*, v. 5, 'Let them set a fair mitre upon his head', see Exod. 28.37; 29.6; Lev. 16.4. Surprisingly, in clothing Joshua, that which the prophet requested is given first place. Of course, this was appropriate for the immediate circumstances, but the Angel also anticipated a future of glory when the crowned Head of the man, the glorified Royal Priest, would be fully revealed for all to see, cf. 6.11–13.

The Verbal Revelation, vv. 6–10, to Joshua follows, featuring characteristic opening and closing phrases, vv. 7, 10. Its first message was delivered in protesting tones stressing *the challenge of present responsibility*, vv. 6–7. Cleansed, clothed and 'crowned', he is now commissioned and charged. Catch the conditional character of the promises, 'If ... and if ... then'. The first condition regulates his personal and official conduct, the course of life; 'If thou wilt walk in my ways', then Joshua would have the privilege of governing, administering, 'my house'. The second condition insists on careful attention to 'keep my charge', a word-play using cognate verb and noun, that is, to keep all the regulations governing the performance of priestly official duties, so that his privilege would be also to 'keep' or have the charge of 'my courts' surrounding the house. To the due reward of faithful conduct and charge-keeping in the service in the temple, the Lord of hosts will 'give' yet more, the inestimable blessing of constant places to walk, that is, unimpeded access for Joshua among the angelic hosts that stand in attendance in the immediate presence of God.

The imperative 'Hear now' opening the second message arrests the attention of Joshua and all the priests 'that sit before thee' with *the comfort at future blessedness*, vv. 8–10. These 'sit' in the good of a work of cleansing completed while others 'stand'; the former still await the privilege of serving when the temple is rebuilt. 'For' [3x here] they are 'typical men', they foreshadow the re-institution of the temple priesthood in messianic times, Ezek. 41.6, 11, the promise being 'for, behold, I will bring forth [cause to enter] my servant the Branch', v. 8. This title combines two glories of the Messiah, namely, that of God's *Servant*, 'the most prominent personal, technical term to represent the Old Testament teaching on the Messiah', Isa. 42.1; 49.6; 50.10; 52.13; 53.11; Acts 3.13, 26; 4.27, 30, and that personal dignity of His as the *Branch* which grows, sprouts, springs up, whether as 'my servant', v. 8, 'the man', 6.12, 'a king', Jer. 23.5; 33.15; cf. Isa. 11.1; 2 Sam. 23.5; Ps. 132.17; Ezek. 29.21, 'the Lord', Isa. 4.2; cf. Luke 1.78, 'the branch/ dayspring from on high'; Rev. 5.5; 22.16, and the allusion suggested by His being called 'the Nazarene', Matt. 2.23. To further engage their attention concerning the promised One He says, 'For, behold, the *stone* that I have set before Joshua', v. 9, directing to *the* foundation, the chief corner-stone already supporting the temple being built, 4.9; Hag. 2.15, 18; Ezra 3.10, 11, 12, this in turn pointing to the Lord God's work at the Messiah's first advent when He laid Him 'in Zion for a foundation a stone' which was to prove 'a sanctuary' for some, Isa. 28.16; 8.14; Matt. 21.42; 1 Pet. 2.6. That 'one (unique, only) stone', yet another title for Messiah, is indeed a tested and precious corner of a sure foundation, the all-engaging Object of divine attention and affection (hence the seven eyes upon it). Yet the Lord of hosts declares 'I will engrave the graving thereof . . . that they may be accepted before the Lord', Exod. 28.36, 38; though Zion feel forsaken, it was graven on the palms of His hands, cf. 12.10; Isa. 49.15, 16. The Lord is yet to 'remove the iniquity of the land in one day', v. 9, the day in question being Israel's divinely appointed day of atonement when 'there shall be a fountain opened . . . for sin and uncleanness', 13.1; cf. Isa. 66.8. 'In that day' of the nation's justification and sanctification, that sabbath rest that remains for the people of God, every man shall call his neighbour to share the shade and sustenance of the vine's joy and the fig's sweetness and fruitfulness, v. 10; Mic. 4.4; cf. 1 Kgs. 4.25; 2 Kgs. 18, 31.

Vision 5. A Lampstand, its Lamps, and Oil Supply, 4.1–14. *Message: Limitless Oil of the Spirit From Priest and Prince Before the Lord of the Whole Earth*

This second of two personally directed visions, has the prince/governor rather than the high priest in view. The two olive trees here designedly point to both of these anointed offices as the unending source of oil for the lamps. The interpreting angel returns and is busy throughout, both addressing and answering questions.

The exhausted prophet is stimulated by **the Vision of an Exhaustless Lampstand, vv. 1–3,** through *the interpreting angel's action* in waking him, v. 1; ct. 2.13[17]; 13.7; 9.13. This is the only occasion in the whole series where the weight of revelations had taken such a toll of his spirit and emotions. Now alert, he is faced with *the angel's question*, v. 2a, which further promotes the concentration of his mind. The *prophet's* *detailed description* is evidence enough for that, vv. 2b–3. He sees a lamp-stand, a familiar and quite the most glorious item in the holy place. However, it is the differences that most fascinate him. This all gold lampstand with its seven branches each supporting a golden lamp, features also a bowl above it acting as a supply reservoir for all the lamps, and seven conduits connecting it to each of them, see JND footnote. Additionally, there were two olive trees on either side of the bowl, living, limitless sources of golden oil. The differences emphasize the directness, the prodigality and the perfection of the sources and supply lines.

Consequently, **the prophet seeks help in understanding the vision, which is duly supplied by the angel, vv. 4–7.** The angel's expressed surprise at the prophet's ignorance increases the suspense element, vv. 4–5; cf. v. 13, and heightens the interest in his reply, vv. 6–7. 'This is the word of the Lord unto Zerubbabel'. Neither the military force of the many, nor the power of the individual is sufficient to see the temple building completed against all odds and obstacles, see Ezra chs. 4–6. The unfailing ministries of the Spirit of the Lord of hosts alone in those already sanctified will prove sufficient for these things. Only thus will a great mountain become a plain, an insurmountable obstacle become a level place (note 'Who?', a great political personage or power gives an equitable decision in the Jews' favour). God ever chooses the weak to confound the mighty, 1 Cor. 1.26–29. Zerubbabel would yet 'bring forth the headstone with shoutings of Grace, grace, unto it', v. 7; cf. Ezra 3.11–13, that is amid shouts of jubilation at the evident divine favour, cf. 12.10. If the image of the foundation stone or corner stone points to Messiah's first advent, Isa. 8.14; 28.16; Rom. 9.32–33; 10.11; 1 Pet. 2.6; ct. 1 Cor. 3.11; Eph. 2.20, then the headstone, or top stone, here alludes to Messiah's second advent, joyously acknowledged as the crowning of God's favour to the nation in the fulfilment of all His promises to her, Ps. 118.22; Matt. 21.42–44; Mark 12.10; Luke 20.17, 18. Note how salvation and judgement, grace and government are strangely blended in the stone imagery in the scriptures.

Next a **direct verbal revelation to the prophet, vv. 8–10**, assures him that Zerubbabel's hands which had commenced the temple project also would complete it, cf. Ezra 3.10; 6.15.

The prophet challenges those of his contemporaries who dismiss with contempt the present enterprise, though he acknowledges sadly the smallness of things when compared with yesterday's greatness, cf. Ezra 3.12, 13; Hag. 2.3. However, if the omniscient Lord is cognizant of all that is going on throughout the whole earth, and has revealed that His consuming joy and attention are found in Zerubbabel's ongoing concern for perfection in his testing use of 'the plumbline' on His house, how can any despise what is patently so dear to Him? Such is the import of 'these seven', that is the seven lamps of the lampstand in the vision, v. 10.

Finally, **the prophet's questions and the Angel's answer, vv. 11-14,** are recorded. Zechariah no longer seeks information about the vision as a whole as he had done in verse 4. Rather, he asks 'What are these two olive trees?', and then 'what be these two olive branches, in the hand of [lit.] the two golden spouts, that empty the golden (oil) out of themselves?', vv. 11-12. Notice that 'the two golden spouts' have not featured in the prophet's previous description, neither have the olive branches. The more complete picture therefore includes two olive trees to right and left of the golden lampstand, two olive branches abiding in their respective trees which apart from human intervention pour their 'liquid gold' out of themselves through the golden tubes into the golden bowl-reservoir, from which forty-nine golden pipes convey an unfailing supply of oil to the seven golden lamps. This is stylized symbolism at its most glorious!

Small wonder to us, even if a cause for surprise to the interpreting angel, that the prophet is unable to explain these details. Help is available for those who ask! Again the angel is concerned to identify 'the two sons of oil', themselves occupiers of anointed offices and who stand by the universal Lord ['adon = owner, possessor] as His mediating branch-supply-lines to the remnant returned from Babylon. Joshua the high priest and Zerubbabel the royal prince were graced with these roles in the sixth century BC, which later are united in Joshua alone, 6.12-13. In that day when Israel is yet once more 'my people' to their God, the saved and sanctified nation will respond to the call 'Arise, shine; for thy light is come, and the glory of the Lord is risen upon thee', see Isa. 60.1-3. Her glorified King-Priest will be her limitless source of the 'liquid gold' ministries and energies of the Holy Spirit, when 'the Lord shall be unto thee an everlasting light, and thy God thy glory', cf. Isa. 62.1-2.

Visions 6 and 7. unlike visions 2 and 3 which are more external, political and material in their emphasis, portray more internal, ethical and 'ecclesiastical' motifs. Unlike visions 4 and 5 which are gracious in tone, we sense in these a governmental tone. All concern Israel in the land in unbelief. The establishing of God's righteousness and peace, the realizing of His grace in the land, calls for the prior judgement and removal of all that offends Him there. 'Behold then the goodness and severity of God'.

Both visions 6 and 7 relate to the visible heavens and earth, vv. 1, 2, 9; both affect the land of Israel, the second however ends in another land, Shinar, vv. 3, 6, 11.

Vision 6. The Flying Scroll and its Curse, 5.1–4. *Message: The Lord's Curse to Purge Transgressors from Land*

Once again it is the prophet's own initiative in lifting up his eyes to see that is noted, cf. 1.18; 2.1. He proceeds to describe the vision, in answer to the angel's question, vv. 1–2, after which a comprehensive interpretion of its features is provided, vv. 3–4.

As to **the vision, vv. 1–2**, he saw a peculiar scroll in that it was 'flying', describing its swiftness and uniqueness of movement. It is still the heavens which rule, and to its inflexible demands those in the land of Israel must be exposed. For Gentile rebel rulers the writing is on the wall; Israel is exposed to what has been written on the tablets of stone. Further, the truly massive dimensions of the scroll registered with him, for it was completely unrolled. It was approximately thirty feet long and fifteen feet wide, measurements familiar enough to the priest-prophet because they matched exactly those of the internal Holy Place of the wilderness tabernacle, Exod. 26.1–3, and more to the point those of the external porch which stood before the temple, 1 Kgs. 6.3. The holy and righteous claims of the God of the house issued forth from that porch, as did the curse upon all households which repudiated them.

The angel's interpretation is supplemented by a direct **divine revelation, vv. 3–4**. The angel equates the flying scroll with 'the curse that goeth forth over the face of the whole land', indicating its extensiveness, v. 3, cf. v. 6. The scroll exposed every transgressor and executed the appropriate curse, 'according to it', so as to purge the apostates out of the land, cf. Deut. 27.26 = Gal. 3.10; Deut. 28.15; ct. Gal. 3.13. Whether his offence be that of stealing, proving him unjust, or of falsely using God's name, proving him ungodly, that is, whether he breaks the second or the first table of God's law respectively in neither loving his neighbour nor honouring God as he ought, his sins would find him out inevitably. The whole law indeed hangs upon just these two central requirements inscribed upon the two tables of stone, cf. Mark 12.28–34. The inescapable and comprehensive character of the curse is conveyed by its contents being written on both sides of the scroll, v. 3; cf. Exod. 32.15.

To this the word of 'the Lord of hosts' adds the fact that He is to cause the curse to go forth, providing a second confirmation that it is the porch of the temple, the place of the going forth, that provides the imagery to explicate the proportions of the scroll, vv. 2, 3, 4. Judgement issues from the house as also it begins at the house of God, that is, among those who claim to be His own people. The claims of the Lord's house are yet to enter into 'the house of the thief', not simply with the purging out of every transgressor from the whole land, but to extend even to his house, as though blighted with the leprous evidence of his own sin in its timber and stones, which must be utterly consumed from the holy land, 2.12; cf. Lev. 14.33–47. To some then the Lord's visitation will prove a savour of death and of disaster, cf. 13.8. The day of His longsuffering will soon expire!

Vision 7. Woman in Ephah Transported to Shinah, 5.5.–11. *Message: Land Rid of Apostate, Commercialized Religion*

On this occasion, it is the interpreting angel who encourages the prophet to observe and to grasp 'what is it' and the significance of a preliminary vision, vv. 5–8. Helped through this, he lifts up his own eyes and sees a supplementary vision, being puzzled not by the 'what' but by the 'whither' of its movement, and he is provided also with the angel's explanation of this, vv. 9–11. Both visions 6 and 7 dilate upon divine judgements yet to fall upon the land of Israel. However, the former insists that all transgressors among the nation are to be purged out of the land, while the latter informs us that all false religious trappings trespassing in the land are to be transplanted in Shinah. These things, as indeed all of those imparted in the whole series of visions, are yet to find their complete fulfilment within the period of Daniel's seventieth seven, and more particularly in the latter half of it, namely the much-referred-to closing three and a half years of this age. Only then can the threshold into the millennial reign of piety, peace and plenty be crossed, and that promised and longed for age-to-come be enjoyed.

    The preliminary vision, vv. 5–8, opening with *the angel's command* that he should 'see what (is) this goer-forth'(lit) only made *the prophet mystified*, vv. 5b–6a. To the priest-prophet a scroll was familiar enough, but he made no sense of an ephah, hence his 'What is it?', v. 6a. His question draws out *the angel's explanations and interpretations*, vv. 6b–8. What the prophet saw in fact was 'the ephah', a very large commercial amphora with a standard dry-measure capacity equivalent to a modern 22 litre/5 gallon container. Externally 'This is their eye in all the land' [lit.], that is 'how they appear through eye-gate', their appearance. The tantalizing 'their' is left undefined, who they are that appear thus! The prophet's attention is then drawn to a talent [lit. 'A round', and 'a stone(weight)' in v. 8] of lead, the largest Jewish weight used in commercial transactions being about 30 kilos. In this instance the talent weight was acting as a lid to cover the mouth of the ephah. As this lid is mysteriously lifted up, seemingly by being thrust up from within, the angel points out that *This is a certain specific woman'[lit.]* dwelling within it. A last vigorous attempt on her part is made to brazenly exhibit her seductive, adulterous, and to this time hidden influence which has been permeating an externally dominant commercial system throughout the whole land. The truth is out, and the interpretation is supplied; *'This is Wickedness'*; and the angel casts her down again into the ephah and casts the lead lid back in place.

Zechariah, fascinated to see more, 'lifted up his eyes', and saw **a supplementary vision, vv. 9–11**. This time *the prophet identifies the new elements*, v. 9, which include the appearance out of the enveloping darkness of two women with wings as those of the stork, and borne more swiftly still by the wind in their wings symbolizing providential influences which lend their assistance. Storks are unclean birds in the dietary catalogue, Lev. 11.19, and an angel from heaven will yet declare of fallen Babylon that she is become a habitation of demons, and a hold of every unclean spirit, and a hold of every unclean and hateful bird, Rev. 18.2. These came forth, and 'lifted up the ephah between the earth and heaven' in order to bear it away, v. 9. Then follows *the prophet's second question*, v. 10; 'Whither' the ephah? Certainly the days of its influence throughout the land are over, but where is it being taken? Vision 6 revealed that *transgressors* and their houses were to be destroyed in the land. Here, the prophet, relieved by the revelation of the removal of the ephah and its evil occupant from the land, cannot imagine why it, too, was not destroyed in the land, and wherever could this wickedness be destined, v. 10. His appointed helper, *the interpreting angel provides the answer*, v. 11. Her destruction is not yet. The unclean not only are to bear her to, but they are to build her an house in the land of Shinar. Once her house, her own idolatrous temple, is set up there, the ephah with its Woman who is Wickedness, 'shall be set there in her own place', concretizing her claim to be the gateway to God, v. 11. Clearly therefore, the ephah and its occupant do not belong to 'the holy land'; they are *trespassers*, and are to be air-lifted out of it prior to their final destruction. They had, in fact, represented in the land that 'great harlot ... MYSTERY, BABYLON THE GREAT, THE MOTHER OF THE HARLOTS', Rev. 17.5; ct. the Man of Sin, 2 Thess. 2.3–5. The harlotry in question is that of idolatrous, apostate, oppulent, seductive, corrupting, defiant man-made religion symbolized when first it raised its head in that 'plain in the land of Shinah', Gen. 11.2-4. At the end, such centralized religious corruption of the true is not simply to be dispersed from the land but is to be destroyed 'in her own place', cf. Rev. 16.19; 18.1-24. Her final doom is not Zechariah's brief!

Vision 8. Four Chariots and their Horses, between Two Bronze Mountains, 6.1-8. *Message: Heaven's War-Chariots Establish Quiet on Earth*

In the last vision of the series, Zechariah, through the symbolism of horses, is re-directed to the first vision providing a topical inclusion, 1.8(2); 6.2(2), 3(2), 6; in fact among Old Testament writers he majors on horses! 9.10; 10.3,5; 12.4(2); 14.14.15, 20 [20x of total 138x]. This provides a significant link with John's Apocalypse, where, apart from James chapter 3 verse 3, all of the New Testament references are to be found [16x]. Horses feature biblically as creatures of commerce, 1 Kgs. 10.28, of conveyance, Esther 8.10, and of conflict, terrifyingly strong and triumphant in war, Job 39.19, 20. Horses therefore symbolize swiftness and strength under the control of the rider. The rider of the red horse who stood among the myrtles 'in the bottom', 1.8, is the same One though in a different role whom John describes as sat upon a white horse, and followed by the armies of heaven on white horses, coming out of heaven to judge and make war, Rev. 19.11-16. God Himself is depicted as the divine warrior who treads the sea in *wrath* with His horses, and who drives chariots of *salvation*, Hab. 3.8, 15. The sixth century BC reconnaissance feed-back provided by the horse patrols of chapter one assures us of an encouraging beginning: the mobilizing of chariots and horses for the final conflicts which are to bring in the messianic age, guarantee the triumphant end. By this means will Israel be redeemed by power and the universal messianic kingdom be established by the Lord, the possessor and rightful owner of the whole earth, 6.5.

The details of the vision, vv. 1-3, draw out the prophet's question and the angel's answer, vv. 4-7b, to which is added a direct word from the Lord, vv. 7c-8.

The Vision, vv. 1-3. A highly mobile military task force is seen coming out from between two massive bronze mountains. The horse-drawn chariots of the ancient world were manoeuvreable and menacing firing platforms akin to the armoured tanks used by modern armies. Their number, four, compares with the four craftsmen of vision two, and represents heaven's control of political power during the prophesied Times of the Gentiles, v. 1; 1.20–21. The chariots were distinguished by four differently coloured pairs of horses, vv. 2–3.

The prophet's question, v. 4, '*What* are these . . . ?' is explained in **the angel's answer, vv. 5–7b.** The differently coloured horses drawing the war-chariots symbolize 'the four winds (spirits) of heaven, which go forth', cf. Ps. 104.4; Heb. 1.7–9. These four spirit-world agencies, described as coming out 'from standing between' the two bronze mountains until the divinely appointed time, were ready to go forth [same verb] 'from standing before the Lord of all the earth', and to do His bidding in judgement when once it was made known to them!, v. 5; cf. Rev. 9.14–15. They were standing before the Lord ['*adon*] of the whole earth, as did the priest when he stood between the two massive bronze pillars in the porch of the temple [Boaz = 'in Him is strength' and Jachin = 'He will establish']. From between the constraints of these two aspects of God's unyielding righteousness, judgement and salvation, shall truth spring out of the earth, for righteousness has looked out of heaven, see Ps. 85; 89.8–18. The horses' different colouring suggests the variety of forms of divine intervention by means of which all opposition to the Lord's purposes will be almightily overcome, cf. Rev. 6.1–8. Three of the four coloured groups were involved already in reconnoitering under the direction of the Rider on the red horse, that colour there representing the then dominant political power, Medo-Persia, see 1.8, 10–11.

Then the angel makes known *where* the chariots went: the two drawn by the black and white horses went toward the north, the grisled went toward the south, v. 6. Nations to the north and south of Israel have been its most consistent and cruel enemies. Their final debacle at the end of this age is accurately though briefly presented here, in that the northerner is the greater threat, while the southerner is all but effortlessly removed, cf. Dan. 11.36–45. Consequently, the bay (or strong) horses, which are equated with the grisled in verse 3, aptly sought an extension to their initial commission so that their role might take on more universal proportions, that they might walk to and fro generally, v. 7a–b. Evidently, the four groups of horses do not represent the four points of the compass, ct. Rev. 7.1. The chariot drawn by the red horses has no role allocated to it here. Charioteers are not mentioned; the Lord alone controls all.

The Direct Word from the Lord, vv. 7c–8. The Lord's command, authorized the request of the bay horses. His 'Get you hence' was uttered and their obedience was immediate, 'So they walked to and fro',

v. 7c–d. The Lord's triumphant cry heralded the quietening of His spirit in the north country, v. 8, the compass point so frequently associated with divine judgement in the scriptures. Vision 1 depicts the Lord disturbed at the report of the nations sitting still, at rest, at ease, totally unmoved by Israel's plight, 1.11, 15. All this is changed in Vision 8, climaxing as it does with the Lord's spirit quieted by His agents of judgement against Israel's northern implacable foes, 6.8.

(Climactic Goal) Prophet Symbolically Crowns Joshua, the High Priest. Crowns Placed in Temple, 6.9–15. *Message: The Man, the Branch, God's King-Priest Rules*

Visions 1 to 3 end with a parenthetic *appeal* in the light of the Lord's coming out of His heavenly sanctuary and to His holy land. Visions 6 to 8 are climaxed by the prophet's *action* in crowning the high priest, symbolizing the combined official glories of priest and king yet to be seen in One who is to build the temple, to bear the glory and to be a priest upon His throne. The combination in one person of these normally distinct offices has already been anticipated in the two central visions, 4 and 5, which focused upon the high priest and the Davidic prince, respectively. The exhilarating new day which follows the preceding night of eight exhausting visions has come at last!, v. 10. At the beginning, at the divine word 'Let there be light . . . there was evening and there was morning, one day', Gen. 1.3–5. At the end of this age, 'that day' which is 'not day, and not night' and which befits the mixed nature of God's searching and sifting judgements, will conclude with bright millennial glory for 'at evening time there shall be light'.

First, **the symbolic action is prescribed and prosecuted, vv. 9–11.** The word of the Lord was obeyed. The incident concerned some of those carried away to Babylon, and who had returned to Jerusalem with silver and gold. Both metals are precious, and are associated with redemption and glory. Those who returned were 'typical men', anticipating that great regathering of the elect who will have spoiled those who had previously spoiled them, cf. 2.9; Exod. 12.35–36; Isa. 11.11–16. The Lord's instructions were simplicity itself: 'take . . . make . . . set them upon the head of Joshua', vv. 10, 11. Zechariah took the silver and gold which had been brought, and made distinct silver and golden crowns which, fitted together, produced a 'crown of crowns' [note plural in vv. 11, 14, though the verb '(it) shall be' used in connection with 'crowns' is singular, v. 14]. This was no high priest's mitre nor a usual royal crown. Neither was it to be placed upon Zerubbabel's head, but upon Joshua's

[Hebrew equivalent of Jesus], who in turn is to 'sit and rule upon his throne'. How strange this uniting of district offices in one person wearing a two-tier crown made of a silver circlet representing redemption completed as the basis of all, and a golden circlet the glory that rightly accrues to a royal redeemer.

Secondly, **the significance of the symbolism is explained, vv. 12–13.** Joshua the high priest is chosen to foreshadow the greater than Joshua, and than Melchizedec before him, the king of Salem, priest of the Most High God, cf. Heb. 7. It is the Lord of hosts whose almighty will cannot be thwarted, and there is none He delights more to honour than 'the man whose name is the Branch', see on 3.8–10. This is the first of seven distinguishing characteristics, which itself guarantees all the others: who He is supports what He will achieve, and it is to Him that Joshua's attention is directed: 'Behold, the man . . . '. This One 'shall sprout, spring up from beneath [lit.]', referring to His resurrection and not simply to His lowly incarnation, v. 12b. As the risen One He 'shall build the temple of the Lord', a fact twice repeated for emphasis and to distinguish His future millennial temple project from that contemporary enterprise in Zerubbabel's hands, vv. 12c, 13a; see also John 2.18–22. This One 'shall bear the glory' who once bore our griefs, Isa. 53.4, 12, for He will be seen as the 'King of glory' excelling Solomon in all his regal glory, v. 13b; Ps. 24.7–10; 45.3[4]; ct. 1 Chr. 28.25. Divinely installed in office He 'shall sit (permanently and judicially) and rule (sovereignly and administratively) upon his throne', v. 13c; Luke 22.28; Rev. 3.21. Uniquely in Israel's long history He 'shall be a priest upon his throne' after the order of Melchizedec, Ps. 110.1, 2, 4. And finally, in Him the claims of sympathetic, merciful priesthood and of fair and firm kingly justice will be reconciled. All will enjoy the boon of 'the counsel of peace', the true *shalom* which makes people whole, fulfilled, and in harmony, with God, His creatures and all creation.

Finally, light is provided on **the sign and the sharers in the reign of the Sent One, vv. 14–15.** The symbolic coronation of Joshua was short-lived. But God instructed Zechariah that the significant typological event, prompted by the generous giving of those who had travelled from afar with their silver and gold, should be kept alive in the memory, maintaining a yearning for symbol to become reality. The crowns should be kept 'for a memorial in the temple of the Lord', v. 14. In fact, those who had come from afar were themselves typical of many whose sympathies will move them to 'come and build in the temple of the Lord', Isa. cf. 60.3–22, and the whole nation would know then that the Lord of hosts had indeed sent Joshua-Jesus the Messiah to them, v. 15a-b; 2.11.

Of course, the purpose of God to establish His kingdom under Messiah the King-Priest will be fulfilled. But not all of the nation will live or be raised to have part in it, cf. 13.8–9; Dan. 12.1–3. God's earnest appeal to this day is 'Hear ye him', for entry to His kingdom is reserved for those who 'diligently obey the voice of the Lord' their God, v. 15c.

3. Your Fasts will become Feasts, 7.1 – 8.23. God is with you

This new sub-section is opened by Zechariah's third and last historical time-note, 1.1, 7; 7.1, and records an incident set in the fourth year of Darius, nearly two years after the visions sequence, and about two years before the temple rebuilding was completed, Ezra 6.15. Here then we rest midway to reflect upon the lessons of the past, and find stimulation for the present in the projections of the glories that are to follow. A problem raised with the priests and prophets by a deputation from Bethel, 7.1–3, is addressed by Zechariah in four distinct revelations by means of 'the word of the Lord (of hosts)' coming to him, 7.4, 8; 8.1, 18. The message of the chapters may be summarized under two broad titles:

Past Disobedience the Cause of Present Distress, ch. 7
Future Hope for Israel and the Nations upon the Earth the Stimulus for Present Obedience, ch. 8

The Question Raised, 7.1–3

It all started with the arrival of a deputation to the house of the Lord in Jerusalem from Bethel (= House of God) some twelve miles to the north. No longer was it a rival centre of calf worship, vv. 2b–3. Two reasons are given why they came: 1) 'to intreat the favour of the Lord' by means of the appropriate propitiatory sacrifices, so that the frown of His disfavour might be changed into the smile of His favour and prosperity, and 2) to enquire whether their weeping over the past destruction of Jerusalem by the Babylonians was really necessary now the rebuilding was well under way, 2 Kgs. 25.8–9. This fifth-month fast was not one of the divine appointments for the nation. Nazarite separation to God is one thing, but self-imposed fasts, and 'separating myself' from things in which the flesh takes pleasure, become irksome and the carnal confess wearily 'these so many years'!, v. 3.

The priests have no answer, but the priest-prophet Zechariah is equipped by the Lord to comprehensively address the issues both negatively and positively, delaying a direct answer however until the end of chapter 8.

The First Revelation – Negative – Rebukes Contemporaries, 7.4–7

The question might appear parochial; the response is *an authoritative word* of the Lord. His is *a salutary message* addressed to the nation, including 'all the people' and the priests as a class, v. 5a–b. He brings *a searching message*, exposing the superstition, and selfishness behind all their religiosity when they 'fasted and mourned', v. 5c. In addition to the fifth month fast, recalling the destruction of city and temple, there was the seventh month fast commemorating their bloodguiltiness in the murder of Gedaliah their own governor, v. 5c; 8.19; Jer. 41.1. If introspection saw only self-pity and the privations of 'these many years', the Lord would remind them of 'these seventy years' of prescribed desolations which should soon be completed, Jer. 25.10–12. Mourning for sorrows is not mourning for the sins that brought them.

Their superficial question is countered with three penetrating questions from the Lord, vv. 5b–7. The first is 'did ye fast at all [intensified by word-play] unto me, even to me?', v. 5, for earnestness is no guarantee of correctness, and correctness is not necessarily acceptable. God appointed only one fast in the nation's religious calendar, the Day of Atonement of which no mention is made in these two chapters, and yet it is one which the nation will truly keep when it looks upon the One whom they pierced, 12.10–14. However the flesh may find pleasure in fasts of its own creation; it is these that the Lord questions here. Godly sorrow that works repentance rends the heart and not simply the garments!, Isa. 58.3–4; Joel 2.16. The Lord next questions their feastings and condemns them as occasions of satisfying physical appetites and not occasions of thankfulness sanctified by the joy of fellowship with Him, v. 6. The 'whether' or the 'when' of fastings and feastings were their chief concerns; the God with whom all have to do knows the heart, and He is most concerned with the 'why' that prompts everything. Motive matters! The third question is rhetorical, and calls for a resounding 'Yes' to the wisdom of returning to the detailed 'words which the Lord hath cried by the former prophets', v. 7. Then, Jerusalem and its satellites were peopled and prosperous as was the land of Judea as a whole; proving that to obey is better than sacrifice, and is the true basis of enjoying peace and plenty in the inheritance.

The Second Revelation – Negative – Reflecting on the Past, 7.8–14

It opens with a *statement of the unchanging demands of the Lord*, vv. 8–10; cf. 8.16–17. He had made known these four typical moral requirements, do's and don'ts, in the Law in the past and He still insisted on their practice in Zechariah's day. To 'judge true justice [lit.]' is to administer justice equally and impartially, influenced only by truth, 8.16. To practise 'mercy and compassion' is to be steadfast in love and tender in inner feelings to one's brother (fellow). The dangers facing the defenceless through the perverting of true justice call for the warning 'oppress not', and the antithesis of mercy and compassion shown to one's brother calls for 'let none . . . imagine evil against his brother' in the heart.

Israel's determined disobedience and rebellion in the past is rehearsed, vv. 11–12c. Their increasing obstinacy is traced to an initial refusal to hear, which led them to reject, like an incalcitrant animal, the constraints of the yoke; then to deliberately make heavy their ears so as to prevent any further message getting through to them; and finally determining to harden their hearts (more than flint, Ezek. 3.9) against even that already lodged in it. Their determined purpose was to steel themselves against the law and then against the many convicting words which the almighty Lord of hosts sent by His Spirit, and by the hand of the former prophets.

The awful consequences of hardening themselves against God's will and words followed the exhausting of His longsuffering and patience. Zechariah writes 'therefore came there great wrath from the Lord of hosts'. How great that wrath proved to be is described in terms of *Israel's Dispersion from the Land, and the Desolation of the Land itself,* vv. 12c–14. The rebellious nation is made to reap what it has sown. As when He had cried to them they had refused to hear, so when they cried He did not hear, cf. Isa. 1.15. Furthermore, He would scatter them in whirlwind judgements among foreign nations, and would desolate and depopulate the land of delight, cf. Dan. 11.16, 41. The prophet's message concludes with the salutary warning to his contemporaries that it was the sins of their rebellious fathers that had brought the pleasant land to ruin; still it waits to become 'the holy land' of promise, 2.12.

Zechariah turns now from his rebuke of the present generation, and his review of the refusal of the past generations to hear and obey God's word through the law and the former prophets, and addresses the deputation's question regarding the appropriateness or otherwise of continuing with the fasts. In chapter eight he does so on a positive note by means of two further divine revelations, both of which are taken up with the glorious future. The separate parts of each are prefaced by an oracular formula, 'Thus saith the Lord' (of hosts), 8.2, 3, 4, 6, 7, 9, 14/

8.19, 20, 23, complemented in some cases by a pithier formula more usually used to close an oracle, 8.6, 11, 14, 17. Within the parameters of these ten oracles the message of hope is expressed with great variety and authority.

The Third Revelation – Positive – Seven Oracles Concerning the Future, 8.1–17

The declaration of God's sovereign intentions (oracles 1 to 5), vv. 2–8, is followed by an exhortation calling for the people's response (oracle 6), vv. 13–17, the basis being that the Lord's active goodness demands a change in their behaviour (oracle 7), vv. 14–17. God's promises are still made conditional upon obedience.

Oracle 1 – declares *the Lord's love that will not let His people go*, v. 2, and which is determined to mightily deliver her. The Lord of hosts' great jealousy for Zion, the city of His choice, is the guarantee of this, see on 1.14, 17.

Oracle 2 – *the Lord will return to Zion and will dwell in the midst of Jerusalem*, v. 3. The glory indicating His presence will yet take up residence there again, see Ezek. 43.2–5. Then it will be indeed the city of truth, cf. Isa. 1.21, 27, for the God of truth will be there, Zeph. 3.18. The mountain on which it will stand will elevate both the Lord of hosts' universal sovereignty and the sanctity of His sanctuary.

Oracle 3 – *Jerusalem is to be joyfully inhabited*, vv. 4–5. Its crowded streets will be safe and socially friendly areas where the elderly may enjoy restfully the blessings of community life, and where the aged, 'every man', will be free of the fear of death, cf. Isa. 65.19–20; ct. Gen. 5. Methuselah's record nine hundred and sixty nine years will be exceeded by all who enter the millennial reign at its inception. Jerusalem's youth bursting with energy will also find space to express its carefree happiness there.

Oracle 4 – *the Lord's intervention and its effects are to be marvellous in His people's eyes*, v. 6. God's promises seem incredible to Zechariah's contemporary harassed and helpless remnant, v. 6, and for the remnant which is to pass through that awful day of Jacob's trouble in the future. But all things are nonetheless possible with the Lord of hosts. Amazed at seeing their rejected and returning Messiah, that saved generation will cry 'This is the Lord's doing; it is marvellous in our eyes', Ps. 118.22–24.

Oracle 5 – *the diaspora is to be saved and to come to dwell in Jerusalem,*

vv. 7–8. The Lord arrests their attention with three 'I wills', two of which open and one closes the oracle. Of those scattered to east and west (not only those from the north, ct. 2.6–7) He says 'I will save' them, and 'I will bring them' to Jerusalem. Only then will they be able to 'dwell in the midst of Jerusalem'. Then their covenant relationship will be realized, for 'they shall be my people (no longer 'not my people'), and I will be their God', cf. 13.9. Only the new covenant of which the Messiah is the mediator will prove an unbreakable 'everlasting covenant', and its relationships will reach beyond externals to satisfy the holy and righteous claims of God and the deepest needs of Israel 'in truth and in righteousness'. For the nation the everlasting covenant must be in reality not formality, in righteousness not simply fleshly relationship and privilege, if the city is to be 'the city of truth', the city of righteousness, the faithful city, Isa. 1.26.

Oracle 6 – promises a dramatic change, '*as ye were a curse . . . so will I save you, and ye shall be a blessing*', vv. 9–13. This salvation oracle is framed by the exhortation 'Let your hands be strong', vv. 9, 13. 'Before' the ministry of Zechariah and Haggai, encouraging resumption of the work on the temple, was heard among them, conditions were appalling. There was no wealth nor work, neither safety because of the dissensions disrupting society, all of which were evidences of the Lord's chastisement, v. 10; cf. Hag. 1.2–6; 2.16–17. 'But now' things were to be so different, vv. 11–12. Nature's yield and heaven's dew are indivisible, and their harmony reflects the removal of the sin which disrupted it, Hos. 2.21–23.

Oracle 7 – *the Lord's intention to do good unto Jerusalem*, vv. 14–17, was addressed to the contemporary situation. As the Lord had 'thought to do evil' (in the form of judgement of city and land and people) and had carried out His purposed punishment in due course, 'so again have I thought in these days to do good' to them. He would be true to His blessed promise; His salvation purpose was equally sure, they had no cause to fear, vv. 14–15, cf. v. 13. However, their realization of divine blessing was conditional upon their return to Him, and those ways that please Him; 'These are the things that ye shall do'. Human responsibility and divine sovereignty are mysteriously intertwined! The four imperatives urging a morality demanded by God, are arranged in positive and negative pairs, regulating genuineness in private relationships and the impeccable administration of public justice, vv. 16–17. Those who belong to God must hate the things which the Lord hates, 7.9–10; cf. Prov. 6.16–19. 'Truth' and 'peace' are part of a broad semantic field of covenant morality terms.

The Fourth Revelation – Three Further Positive Oracles – Judah's Feasting and Many Peoples come to enjoy and acknowledge God's Favour, 8.18–23

Oracle 8 – Your fasts shall be turned into feasts, vv. 18–19. The number of fasts specified here is increased to four, and they are all of the people's devising, commemorating a variety of judgements which were really divine chastisements for their sins. They are: 1) the seventeenth of the fourth month, the siege of Jerusalem by Nebuchadnezzar, and the breaching of its walls (today it recalls also Titus' entry), Jer. 52.6–7; 2) the ninth of the fifth month, and the burning of the city and temple (also today Titus' destruction of Herod's temple in AD 70, and defeat and destruction associated with Hadrian's suppression of the Bar Kochba revolt in AD 135, M. *Taanit* 4.6), 7.3; Jer. 52.12–13; 3) the third of the seventh month (immediately following the feast of trumpets, the beginning of the civic new year), and the murder of Gedaliah the governor, 7.5; 2 Kgs. 25.25–26; Jer. 41.1–3; 4) the tenth of the tenth month, and the beginning of Jerusalem's siege, 2 Kgs. 25.1. Yet all of the nation's troubles are not only to be forgotten, Isa. 65.16, but these man-appointed fasts are to be made occasions of 'joy and gladness, and cheerful feasts' [= divine appointments]. Once again, the moral conditions required are love for the truth and peace, cf. vv. 7–8, 16–17.

Oracle 9 – Many peoples are to come to Jerusalem to seek and entreat the favour of the Lord, vv. 20–22. Attention here is switched from Judah to the many peoples [read the plural in vv. 20, 22 JND] and strong nations who, witnessing Judah's blessedness, wish to entreat the favour of the Lord and benefit from His gifts, as well as to seek the Lord of hosts, the Giver Himself, in Jerusalem. Evidently an amazing change has been wrought in Gentile attitudes toward the covenant-keeping Lord of Israel here. The genuineness of the peoples' *intentions* is evidenced in the response of whole city populations to travel to adjacent cities with an urgent *exhortation*, 'Let us go speedily' [lit.'Let us go to go'], and the determined *action* expressed in a typical individual's 'I will go also'. The *realization* of their goals is already assured for 'many peoples and strong nations shall come . . .' to Jerusalem indeed!, Isa. 2.2–4. However the inversion (or the chiasm, a, b, b', a') of their stated goals properly gives the pre-eminent place to their seeking of the Lord Himself, ct. vv. 21, 22.

Oracle 10 – there will be an international determination to go with the Jew for God is with him, v. 23. The tenth oracle tells of the response of a group of ten men out of all the languages of the nations. The number ten embraces the range of numbers, and is therefore comprehensive and representative in character. It also symbolizes man's responsibility before God as suggested by the ten commandments. The many tongues exist as a token of God's confounding judgement on man's co-ordinated rebellion, and yet here men of all languages shall 'take hold of the skirt of him that is a Jew'. The rebellious are to be reconciled at the end, and will desire a share in the enterprise of bringing diaspora Jewry home to their land. Upon the Jew's skirt was a border of tassles which was bound by a blue cord. This was to remind him of God's judgement without mercy upon the sabbath law-breaker, and of his own commitment to remember and to do all God's commandments, Num. 15.38; Matt. 23.5. Grace and truth here meet together, and righteousness and peace kiss each other, and the nations bow to grasp this for themselves, Isa. 56.6–8. Another ancient sign was given to rebellious Judah in the virgin who should 'conceive and bear a son' and should call His name Immanuel [God with us], Isa. 7.14; cf. 8.8, 10; Matt. 1.21–23. The nations will carry the Jew shoulder high, and express their determination to 'go with you, for we have heard that God is with you', v. 23; cf. Isa. 45.14–15, 23–24. Then Jerusalem's temple will realize the hope its court of the Gentiles represented, namely, that God's house 'shall be called an house of prayer for all nations', Isa. 56.7; cf. Matt. 21.13.

B. Messianic Projections, 9.1–14.21

Here *a change in setting* is involved. The immediate issues regarding the temple building project which extended over some four years as in chapters 1–8 and Ezra chapters 5–6 are all now behind them. Rather the prophecies of chapters 9–14 spring out of their different circumstances during the sixty years of the Persian Period slotted between the close of Ezra 6 and the opening of Ezra 7, see Table. Jerusalem as a city during those years was still far from secure, it had a governor but no Davidic King, and the people were surrounded by local hostile power groups who opposed the restoration of the state and sanctuary. The dispirited and the anxious needed fresh revelations to reassure them that the great hopes fostered through Isaiah and Ezekiel were a little more distant but no less definite than they had believed. The messianic King and His kingdom of peace and power would certainly come.

The contents of chapters 9 to 14 are grouped into two distinct blocks by means of the twice repeated prophetic formula, 'The burden of the word of the Lord', 9.1; 12.1. Already by this a *change in style* is signalled from the formula 'The word of the Lord' which has dominated the first eight chapters. These 'burdens' are not simply 'an uplifting of a voice', 'an utterance', but here they relate to delivering a divine sentence as a heavy weight, prophesying woes, disaster, judgement which is to rest 'upon' peoples and places. These 'burdens' are prophetic, and more specific in character, in contrast to the more apocalyptic and general visions of the earlier eight chapters.

Then there is *a change in substance* evident between the two sections of the book, in that chapters 9 to 14 paint the full-length portrait of the messianic King-Shepherd. The first burden has Israel's rejection of its King-Messiah at His first advent in lowly grace as its major though not sole constituent, and has as its backcloth the Greek and Roman periods of history. The second, a 'burden concerning Israel', majors on the final assaults of the nations yet to be mounted against Judah and Jerusalem, and on the Lord's empowering, purifying, and final delivering of His own at His second advent in glory. The troubles that are prophesied here are but the portal to that final triumph.

1. First Advent of the King-Shepherd, 9.1–11.17

Classically this sub-section presents the peculiarities of prophetic perspective. The imagery of Zechariah chapters 9 and 11, used in the New Testament to describe the first century AD appearance of Jesus of Nazareth, establishes that the forecast lowly and loving ministry of Jerusalem's King, and Israel's rejected Good Shepherd, are proof enough that Jesus the Messiah's advent has embodied and 'fulfilled' these predictions. But a cursory examination of Zechariah's other contextual forecasts will demonstrate that there still remains much that has not been fulfilled. The messianic King has entered Jerusalem, 9.9, but the Lord has not as yet 'cut off the chariot from Ephraim, and the horse from Jerusalem', v. 10; cf. 10.3; 12.4; 14.15, 20. The Good Shepherd has appeared, He has been betrayed for thirty pieces of silver, and His own people rejected Him, yet the Worthless Shepherd, the False Shepherd-Messiah who is to be raised up in the land has still not emerged, 11.15–17; cf. John 5.43; Rev. 13.10. Separating verses 9 and 10 of chapter 9 and verses 14 and 15 of chapter 11, God's work of grace through the church has pursued its course through nearly two millennia about which the Old Testament reveals nothing. Only after this are Zechariah's 'end of this age' prophecies to be fulfilled to the jot and title in all those events bound up with the Messiah's second advent, and with His kingdom of peace and glory. Preparatory to this Zechariah views Israel's place in history during the rise of Gentile world powers, the Greek in chapters 9–10, and the Roman in chapter 11. These chapters prophesy highlights of some five hundred years of what is to us now history, through the inter-testamental period to the first century AD. And even this is but a harbinger of other verities which are yet to be historicized!

Enemies destroyed, God's house defended, 9.1–8

The removal of Medo-Persia by the Greeks under the brilliant leadership of Alexander the Great, paved the way for the military successes of 332 BC anticipated in these verses. Man in general, and all the tribes of Israel, would see the Lord in these events, either with fear or amazement. Syria, vv. 1–2a, Lebanon (Tyre, Zidon), vv. 2b–4; cf. Isa. 23; Ezek. 27–28, and the lush coastal plain south of modern Jaffa (Philistia; note four of the five city-kingdoms of the Philistines named), vv. 5–7, fell before this daring conqueror. The haughty sins of these petty states, their vaunted wisdom, v. 2, confidence in their impregnable security and power, vv. 3a, 4, incalculable wealth, v. 3b–c, false confidences, v. 5, pride, v. 6, and idolatry, v. 7, were ripening fast for the judgement of the Lord [*Adonai*], the owner of the earth, v. 4. Perhaps most remarkable, however, is the forecast conversion of idolatrous Philistines from their past abominations to become 'a remnant for our God' among the divisions of Judah's remnant, v. 7. Clearly nothing the equal of this resulted from the Greek campaigns. Verse 8 gives credit for the protection of Jerusalem and its temple, and its deliverance from the oppressor passing through and returning [lit.], to the seeing eyes of God's caring omniscience, and providential intervention. JOSEPHUS records a remarkable and peaceable appearance of Alexander at Jerusalem after his successful seige of Gaza, *Ant.* 11.8.4, 5; *Modern Bible Atlas* 172–4. However Jerusalem still awaits the complete fulfilment of the promise 'no oppressor shall pass through them any more', v. 8; ct. 12.2–9; 14.1–15. Only the coming of Jerusalem's meek and mighty king can effect the end of all invasion of the land.

The advent of the messianic King announced, 9.9–11

The opening sentence is so familiar to us through the evangelists' citation of it in the setting of Jesus' public and official approach to Jerusalem, Matt. 21.4; John 12.14–15. This was indeed 'the city of the great King', Matt. 5.35, and our Lord intended that this public approach, for those with eyes to see, should register as an official, messianically significant event, though even the disciples were slow to grasp it, John 12.16. Already the arresting word 'behold', found in each of the references, suggests this. For Zion/Jerusalem it was 'thy king (that) cometh unto thee', and it was to recognize *His regal title and calling*. Its King was not simply coming to the city, but His coming was for the city's blessing. For the prophet therefore the occasion called for great rejoicing, for Matthew it provided glad tidings which all should 'tell', and for John it was a salvific sign which should put fear to flight (the Isaianic prophecies conflated with Zechariah in the Evangelists' citations give to them distinctive and instructive supplements, see Isa. 62.11; 40.9). Next it is *the character of the king* that is described. He is just, and God's king must be so, Isa. 11.4–5; Jer. 23.5–6 (as also His Servant, Isa. 50.8; 53.11–12). He is the unshakably dependent One, who had no liberty to say 'Father, save me from this hour', but who already during His life had been 'saved' often [lit. = a Heb. passive participle form only elsewhere at Deut. 33.29; Ps. 33.16]. In the garden He directed His prayers to the One able to save Him out of death, and His submission, dependence and piety had their reward in resurrection. The LXX here replaces the passive with an active participle, meaning 'One who saves, who is saving, Saviour'. This close association of justice and salvation features frequently in Old Testament contexts, cf. Isa. 45.21, and informs the righteousness/salvation thesis of the Epistle to the Romans. The death that Jesus the Messiah died was essential to obtain and provide salvation for the nation and the nations. The very mode of transport He chose befitted His lowly condescension, while demonstrating paradoxically His penetrating comprehension and sovereign control of the events others were slow to grasp, v. 9.

The citations in the New Testament end here most appropriately. For verse 10 patently remains unfulfilled to this day. Jerusalem's King entered His city riding upon an ass's colt in the first century AD; the only person in Jewish history to do so. He must appear 'a second time, apart from sin, to them that wait for him (in the nation of Israel), unto salvation', Heb. 9.28. Only then 'all Israel shall be saved', when 'there shall come out of Zion the Deliverer; he shall turn away ungodliness from Jacob: and this is my covenant unto them, when I shall take away their sins', Rom. 11.26–27. For Zechariah the *consequences of the King's coming* shall be enjoyed by Israel and the nations. Chariots, war-horses and battle-bows alike, all the accoutrements of aggression, or stockpiled deterrents to discourage it, are to be destroyed by their King, Mic. 5.10–11. Ephraim and Jerusalem will be no longer parts of rival kingdoms, and the Lord Himself will be their protection, 2.5. Israel's messianic Prince of peace is to 'speak peace unto the nations', Mic. 4.3; Isa. 2.4. The extent of Messiah's 'dominion shall be from sea to sea, and from the River to the ends of the earth', cf. Ps. 72.8. The lowly One will be the universal emperor, King of kings and Lord of lords. To yet another group of exiles, incarcerated in dried cisterns as Joseph and Jeremiah had been, divine liberation is assured. The basis of such intervention is the propitiatory 'blood of thy covenant' by which it is sealed, v. 11; cf. Exod. 24.5-8; Heb. 9.11-14, 18-21, 25-28; Matt. 26.28-29; Mark 14.24-25; Luke 22.20. To those true 'prisoners of hope' [lit. 'the hope', only here in OT with the article = the Messiah], to those waiting for redemption, Luke 1.77-79, the appeal is 'Turn you to the strong hold' [a participial divine title] . . . (and) 'I will render [lit. return, turn, the same verb] double unto thee', that is theirs shall be the firstborn's portion, v. 12; ct. Isa. 40.2

Peace and prosperity to come, triumph assured, 9.13-16

The Greeks are the designated oppressors in this and the following chapter, though they were a people showing no sign of emerging as a world power in Zechariah's time. The Lord as the divine warrior would take up a united nation. He would bend Judah as a bow, set Ephraim as an arrow in it, and finally close in for hand-to-hand encounter stirring up Zion as a sword of a mighty man against the sons of Greece occupying the land. Already in the second century BC the almost superhuman success of the Maccabees against impossible odds represented by the Greeks has provided a harbinger of what is yet to happen 'in that day', v. 13; cf. 12.2-8. Storm imagery is then used to describe the Lord's terrifying part, intervening 'over them', with the clouds as His chariot, the lightning as His arrow. The Lord God [Adonai Yahweh] will sound the thunders as His trumpet blast, and blow upon the opposition with His tempests, v. 14. After all, it is the Lord of hosts, mighty in battle, who shall defend them, cf. 12.8, a verb used solely of divine activity. With Him as their shield and defender, they shall be invincible overcomers too, v. 15. The fourth distinctive divine title used in this paragraph, revealing that it is 'the Lord their God (who) shall save them in that day as the flock of his people', is the most thrilling of all, expressing a restored relationship more excellent than all His promised mercies. Their King shall have come to them bringing salvation! And their political deliverance as a nation will be excelled by their spiritual salvation as 'the flock of his people', see 13.7-9; Isa. 40.10-11. Only then shall His people be exalted over His land, as precious stones glittering with glory, cf. Isa. 54.11-14; 62.3.

Let them look to the good Lord alone, 9.17–10.2

In all that He promises His people and His land, there is an unfolding
of *what He is*! The prophet's outburst of praise does not dwell simply
upon His greatness, but on 'how great is his goodness', Ps. 31.19;
Exod. 33.19, 'and how great is his beauty', v. 17a–b; Ps. 45.2; Isa.
33.17. *What He will give* the young men and the maidens therefore will
cause them to bear fruit by means of 'the old corn of the land', the
Passover-time cereal, Josh. 5.10–12, the staff and strength of life, and
the new wine of joy and satisfaction which at last will be acknowledged
as better than the old at tabernacles-time, v. 17c–d; ct. Luke 5.38–39.
Glory, peace and plenty will be their portion as they fill the face of the
earth with fruit, Isa. 27.6. But *they must ask*, hence the imperative to
intercession. 'Ask ye of the Lord rain in the time of the latter rain . . .
and he shall give showers', more than they ask!, 10.1; cf. Matt. 7.7–11.
The nation's hope is in God alone, and in His promised latter day
showers of blessing which symbolize so much more than the physical
reversal of their lot in exile, ct. v. 11; cf. 12.9; Joel 2.18–27. Their
turning to false household gods, and the black arts of diviners and
dreamers had fostered vain, unrealized hopes. As a result, the flock of
the house of Judah had gone astray like sheep because there was no
true shepherd to lead them in the past, referring to their kings or
rulers, v. 2; Isa. 44.28. God's anger was kindled against their own
uncaring shepherds therefore, and He would punish also 'the he-
goats', referring to foreign (Greek) kings/rulers who had afflicted them,
v. 3a–b; cf. Ezek. 34.1–10; Isa. 14.9 marg; Dan. 8.5, 19–25.

The Lord of hosts will visit, strengthen Judah, save Joseph, 10.3–12

The hope for the helpless is with the almighty Lord of hosts who is to
visit 'his flock', the house of Judah, to deliver it, like a good and caring
shepherd. His intervention will transform a fearful flock into a fearless
war-horse which He rides to victory!, v. 3c–d.
    The Lord of hosts visiting Judah is then expressed in other terms. For
it is out of the royal tribe [note 'from him' 4x] that the promised ruler, the
Messiah is to 'come forth', and to us 'it is evident that our Lord hath
sprung out of Judah', Heb. 7.14. In Him and His unique glories, the
tribe will reach its pre-eminence, v. 4. From him (Judah) shall be *'the
corner (stone)'*, a most significant metaphorical title of the Messiah. When
the term stands alone as here, or in a context containing the word
'stone', it refers to the foundational work of the Messiah laid in Zion at

His first advent, which represents also the messianic means of joining together two distinct 'house' walls, Isa. 28.16; Rom. 9.33. The rejection of the One who was 'for a stone of stumbling and for a rock of offence to both the houses of Israel', Isa. 8.14, which 'broke the brotherhood between Judah and Israel', 11.14, is Himself the only sure foundation for the re-united nation in the future. However, when the word 'head' appears with the word 'corner', it refers to a 'key' or 'crowning' stone by which a building is completed architecturally, Ps. 118.22; cf. Matt. 21.42; Mark 12.10; Luke 20.17; Acts 4.11; 1 Pet. 2.7, and points on to the finalizing of God's messianic promises for the nation by the coming in glory of Israel's Messiah. From Judah too has come forth Messiah '*the nail/[or 'tent peg']*, upon whom all the messianic glories promised for 'the tabernacle of David', will be draped and displayed, Isa. 22.23–24; 55.3–5, and who also will bear all weight of 'government . . . upon his shoulder', Isa. 9.6–7. From Judah, the Davidic Warrior Messiah comes 'to break oppression' as '*the battle bow*', and victoriously to subdue all to the will of God, Ps. 45.5. And then, not only will chieftains of Judah devour all the enemies who come against Jerusalem, 12.5–7, but from Judah an unbroken line of princes and administrators will serve in His kingdom, Ps. 45.16.

Judah's response in the day of His power shall indeed be that of 'mighty men', victorious over all their foes despite the might of the trained cavalry which they face, 'because the Lord is with them', and because He has promised '(I) will strengthen the house of Judah', vv. 5–6a; cf. Ps. 18.31–50. Judah is strengthened in the land, v. 6a, but the divine promise to the dispersed northern kingdom (Joseph and Ephraim) only strikes a similar chord after concluding a series of other reassurances of the Lord to bless them, in the words 'I will strengthen them in the Lord', v. 12a. This is the eighth 'I will' of divine future intention, filling up the octave of a completely new start for Joseph and Ephraim. The other seven irrevocable promises are: **1)** 'I will save (them)', involving spiritual and political elements, which is where all must commence for the diaspora, v. 6b; **2)** 'I will bring them again', v. 6c; though in Zechariah's day they were still cast off, all causes of alienation and exile were to go forever. Only thus would there be tangible evidence of an established covenant relationship again, see number **3)** they would know again that 'I am the Lord their God', with its covenant corollary 'and I will hear them', v. 6b–g; cf. 13.9; **4)** 'I will hiss for them, and gather them (with the shrill signal given by the shepherd in collecting his sheep); for I have redeemed them', yet another reminder that meeting their spiritual need is fundamental, v. 8; **5)** 'I will sow them among the peoples', an initial scattering in judgement which He will make a blessing to them, v. 9; Hos. 1.4, 10–12; 6). 'I will bring them again also out of the land of Egypt, and gather them out of Assyria', a second exodus-event style deliverance from bondage and exile, v. 10a–b, 7). 'I will bring them into the land of Gilead (in the east as under Moses) and Lebanon (to the north, as not even achieved under Joshua); and place shall not be found for them', vv. 10c–d, 11. The proportions of their inheritance and the increase of posterity promised to Abraham at last materialize for them, Gen. 15.18–20; cf. Jer. 30.19; Ezek. 48. Undeniably, the Lord demonstrates the bases for all this, which are in Himself and in His work for them, 'for I have mercy upon them', 'for I have redeemed them', vv. 6d, 8. In chapters 9 and 10 the blessings of the new covenant as they affect the house of Israel and the house of Judah inform everything, Jer. 31.27–37.

The house of Joseph's response to all of these boons will be confidence in their restoration and renewed practice of the presence of their God, v. 6. By God's enabling they become 'like a mighty man' in battle, and rejoice as with the wine of victory, which even their posterity acknowledges to be the Lord's doing and causes them also to 'be glad in the Lord', v. 7. Their very scattering will bring them to remember the Lord and to return to Him, v. 9. Thus strengthened in the Lord, all that He has revealed Himself to be to them will motivate them to walk worthy of Him and that vocation to which He has called them, v. 12b.

Chapter 11 opens with a frightening poetic stanza of judgement, describing in literal, geographical terms the country desolated and the 'flock of slaughter' decimated by a foe from the north pouring through the land, vv. 1–3. The closing paragraph describes in more enigmatic terms the raising up of a shepherd whom the people deserve, a worthless, false shepherd/ruler in the land, vv. 15–16, whose judgement is described in a poetic woe-stanza, v. 17. Both paragraphs present the judgemental *consequences* for a nation described as 'the flock of slaughter', vv. 4, 7, that is the one already destined for destruction, and to which Zechariah is sent. His instructions are to feed such a flock as a representative shepherd until his soul was weary of them, and their soul loathed him, vv. 4–14. It would be the rejection of a good shepherd by their own pitiless shepherds and by the flock, which would be the *cause* of the destruction of the land by the Romans, as history would endorse in 66–70 AD, while the nation's future scourge by the appearing of the false shepherd Messiah still awaits its fulfilment, cf. Dan. 11.36–39.

The country devastated, the flock decimated, 11.1-3

The unstoppable advance of the invader from north to south of the land commences in Lebanon, which is invited to 'Open thy doors' that the glory and loftiness of its cedars may be devoured as by a forest fire, v. 1. The lesser 'fir trees' must howl at their inevitable fate, as also the strong oaks of the Golan [Bashan] to the south who mourn their own exposure, v. 2. And what hope remains for the defenceless Jordan Valley pasturelands and the impenetrable thickets which are 'the pride' of that river's banks; shepherds must howl and young lions must roar at the devouring of all that is dear to them, v. 3. Whether symbolic or literal, the poetry strikes ominous notes; the threatened judgement will 'devour', all is 'fallen', 'spoiled' [3 x], or 'come down', and the howling [3 x] and roaring add to the pathos.

The Rejection of the Good Prophet/Shepherd, 11.4-14

Shepherds and flock here, as so often in scripture, are used figuratively of leaders in Israel and of the nation itself, 10.2, 3; 11.3, 5, 8, 15, 16; 13.7(2) [participle of verb for 'feed']. By means of an acted allegory, the causes of the nation's judgement are dramatically presented. Zechariah is chosen and called by 'the Lord my God' to the representative role of a *Good Shepherd in contrast to that of the nation's own Shepherds*, vv. 4-7a; cf. Matt. 9.36. The Lord's imperative to him is 'Feed', a word embracing the many-faceted service of a true shepherd, vv. 7(2), 9; cf. John 21.15-17; 1 Pet. 5.2; Ps. 23; 78.70-72. In describing the sheep as 'the flock of [i.e. already destined for] slaughter', the prophet is forewarned of the largely fruitless character of his true shepherding work. The discouraging overtone serves only to magnify Zechariah's unhesitating obedience; 'So I fed the flock of slaughter', vv. 4, 7a. How different is his motivation from that of the flock's 'own shepherds', who buy, butcher and make merchandise of the sheep without any sense of guilt or pity, v. 5; cf. Ezek. 34. Pitiless profit-makers only add to their guilt by piously praising the Lord for their ill-gotten gains! And yet the flock had the shepherds that it deserved; the Lord's longsuffering had run out. 'For' He would 'no more pity the inhabitants of the land' and would 'not deliver them again'. The Lord's chastisement would be evident in the fearsome factions destroying the body religio-politic by internecine strife, and the Gentile emperor whom it acknowledged as 'his king' would smite land and people alike, v. 6; cf. John 19.15. One glimmer of hope is represented in 'verily [better "for your sakes" or "because of"] the poor of the flock'. These are a remnant within the nation who gave heed to the prophet and who knew that his 'was the word of the Lord', vv. 7b, 11b; cf. Luke 12.32.

A Survey of the Good Shepherd's Ministry, vv. 7b–11. First, he took, named and cut asunder two staves. These 'two staves' were a shepherd's essential equipment, a rod for defending the flock from foes, and a staff for delivering those who needed to be extricated from impossible difficulties, Ps. 23.4. Equipped with these the good shepherd was God's instrument to beautify and unify the nation. Thus he named the staves. The one, 'Beauty', vv. 7d, 10, represented that well-being which the nation delights in, and which all others appreciate as divine favour toward them. It is the very antithesis of those evil days when the Lord afflicts them for their sins. Moses' plea is yet to be fully realized by Israel; 'let the beauty of the Lord our God be upon us', Ps. 90.13–17. When the shepherd cut that staff therefore as God's agent, God Himself was breaking His unwritten covenant by which He constrains all creation with Israel's peace in view, ct. Hos. 2.18, so that He ceased defending and protecting the nation from the onslaughts of the peoples of the earth. The Roman destruction of city, temple and land in the first century AD terrifyingly demonstrated this. In cutting the second staff called 'Bands', the prophet interpreted this as God 'breaking the brotherhood between Judah and Israel', so that the division between those returned to the land and those scattered in the diaspora was to be continued and exacerbated, vv. 7e, 14; ct. the promise of Ezek. 37.15–28. Second, he 'cut off the three shepherds' clearly referring to the religio-political leaders in the nation. In Zechariah's day, these would be the representatives of the three anointed offices of God's kingdom, namely those of prophet, priest and king, cf. Jer. 2.8. Because of their abuse of these theocratic responsibilities God's true shepherd announced their cutting off [better, 'being effaced'] 'in one month', cf. Hos. 3.4. In the first century AD, compare our Lord's authoritative setting at nought the nation's leaders and His opponents in one month, and the Passover/ Firstfruits month at that, namely the Sadducees, the Pharisees and the Herodians, see Matt. 21.12–23, 36. Remarkably, in himself Zechariah embodied all of these offices for he was a priest by birth, a prophet by divine call, and now he had been called additionally to fulfil the shepherd role. This good shepherd admits 'my soul was weary of [short with] them' and that 'their soul also loathed me', v. 8. They saw no beauty in Him that they should desire Him, cf. Isa. 53.1–2. At the Lord's command he responded with 'So I fed' them; upon their loathing and wilful rejection of the good shepherd and his ministry he said 'I will not feed you', but this did not include 'the poor of the flock' who gave heed to him, and who knew that his was 'the word of the Lord', vv. 7a, 9a, 11. Governmentally, the leaders and the people were given over to the consequences of their own wilfulness; they were hardened, a condition which continues in part for the nation to this day, cf. Isa. 6.8–13; John 12.36c–50; Rom. 11.25.

The Goodly Price at which the Good Shepherd was Prized, vv. 12–14. The good priest/prophet/shepherd asks for the wages due to him for services rendered them in his God-anointed ministry. Their utter repudiation of him is reflected in the paltry price which they weighed out so carefully. Their evaluation was insultingly calculated, amounting only to the damages awarded to a slave injured by an ox, v. 12; Exod. 21.32. The Lord who commissioned the prophet/shepherd originally, now directed him to cast the thirty pieces to the potter, which may be a proverbial idiom for 'the lowliest', for potters were one of the lowest paid among the artisans. The fact that this was to be done 'in the house of the Lord' underlined that their insult had risen up to heaven itself, v. 13. Matthew's quotation is a composite one, drawing from Jeremiah's prophecy as well as from Zechariah, v. 13; cf. Matt. 27.9–10; Jer. 18.2–3; 19.1–13; 32.6–15. Division and dispersion were inevitable for the nation guilty of rejecting God's shepherd, v. 14.

The New Testament quotations drawn from chapters 9 and 11 demand a messianic interpretation. Zion's King who entered His capital city is 'the prophet, Jesus from Nazareth of Galilee', 9.9; Matt. 21.5, 11. He, too, 'is the shepherd of the sheep', sent by God to the nation who were as sheep without a shepherd, and sent specifically to the lost sheep of the house of Israel, Matt. 9.36; 10.6. He was despised and rejected, His ministry was repudiated and a derisory betrayal price was weighed and paid for Him, 11.12–13; Matt. 26.15; 27.9–10. To these facts we may add those prophecies fulfilled in Messiah's first advent and revealed elsewhere in Zechariah. He is described by the Lord of hosts as 'my shepherd', against whom the sword of divine justice was awakened, 13.7; Matt. 26.31; Mark 14.27; as 'my servant the Branch' and 'the Stone', for in Him and His cross work the foundation has been laid for removing the iniquity of the land, 3.8–9. After His expiry on the cross, His side was pierced by a Roman soldier's spear, and at His return from heaven the nation will recognize Him by this and mourn for their part in His wounding, 12.10; John 19.37; Matt. 24.30; Rev. 1.7; Isa. 53.4–6. Of course this assumes His resurrection from among the dead, the Man whose name is the Branch who should spring up from beneath, 6.12, and who is to return soon for the second time!

Divine chastisement through a False Shepherd, 11.15–17

Zechariah was commissioned next to personate a wicked shepherd, the tools of whose trade would remain idle or be unfeelingly misused, v. 15, and so the Lord will yet 'raise up a shepherd in the land', that is a politico-religious ruler, whose neglect and rapacity will be experienced by all, v. 16. The nation's rejection of the true Messiah and good shepherd would inevitably result in their acceptance of a false Messiah, an evil shepherd, as the Lord Himself warned His contemporaries, John 5.43; cf. Rev. 13.11–18; Dan. 11.36–39. God is to send them 'a working of error, that they should believe a lie: that they might be judged who believed not the truth', 2 Thess. 2.8–12. God's 'woe' has been already pronounced upon him who 'leaveth the flock', v. 17; John 10.11–14. The arm that was used, not to protect and heal but to tear so as to satiate gluttony will be withered, and the right eye that should have been ever watchful in overseeing the flock and seeking the scattered, shall be darkened forever.

2. The Second Advent of the Shepherd-King

The Lord King over all the Land, 12.1–14.21

This final 'burden' majors on Messiah's second advent in government and power, when He will go forth as a warrior King to fight against nations, and be installed as King over all the land. This and the earlier 'burden' present Him as the antitypical greater than David, God's anointed who was rejected by His own people before finally being exalted and enthroned over them as a united nation, see p. 219. David and his house are referred to only here in Zechariah, 12.7, 8(2), 10, 12; 13.1. Jerusalem, the city of David, and 'the city of the great King' is specially prominent too (21 x), as is Judah the royal tribe (9 x). Everything is 'concerning Israel', 12.1, as the theocratically privileged people, whom God now owns as 'my people' while the nation too confesses 'The Lord is my God', 13.9; also at 8.7; 9.16.

One peculiarly dominant feature of this final sub-section is the use of the phrase 'in that day', which has appeared earlier in Zechariah only three times, 2.11; 3.10; 9.16. But here in chapters 12 to 14 it is used eighteen times, providing one literary feature by which to consider the Lord's future programme. Like the phrase 'the day of the Lord', it is not to be restricted to a twenty-four hour span, but more often it refers to *a climactic period of world history*. In fact, 'that day' concludes 'this age', and is the portal into 'the age to come'. Further, 'in that day', *judgements are to be abroad in the earth and heavens*, the Near East especially being like a magnet attracting not only the interest but the suicidal intervention of all nations. Israel, Judah and Jerusalem are to be the scenes of spectacular victories, siftings, and sad defeats. And yet 'in that day' *God's intervention will be sudden and discriminating*, spelling disaster for the godless and deliverance for the godly. Further *the great goal* 'in that day' is the establishing of the kingdom of God where 'the Lord shall be king over all the land[or 'earth']', 14.9. For many millennia it has been 'man's day'. But God's longsuffering is running out; man's rebellion is to be subdued. Through wrath and judgement the authority, power, majesty and glory of God is to be vindicated; 'the Lord shall go forth, and fight against those nations', 14.3.

At least two distinct enemy engagements against Jerusalem and their aftermath are described in which the Lord's role differs. In the first, 12.1-13.6, 'shall the Lord defend the inhabitants of Jerusalem' *indirectly* in its seige by empowering those of Judah and Jerusalem to gain the victory over 'all the peoples round about'. We understand these to be Judah's age-old antagonistic neighbours who will choose to attack her when the King of the North passes on through the coastal plain in order to attack Egypt in the south. Judah and Jerusalem will withstand and devour these offended 'brothers' who take advantage of Judah's political weakness. These 'peoples round about' are likely to include Syria (Damascus), Jordan (Moab, Ammon, Edom), and Arabia (Kedah), see e.g., Ps. 137.7; Isa. 15-17; 21.13-17; 34; Jer. 48-49.33; Obad.; Mal. 1.2-5. Conversely, in the second engagement, 13.7-14.21, the Lord shall *directly* intervene only after part of the city has fallen to a much stronger foe, and 'Then shall the Lord go forth, and fight against those nations'. These we judge to be under the leadership of the King of the North, who having heard tidings of developments behind him, shall return from Egypt and North Africa to attack Jerusalem with some success before the almighty intervention of the Lord and His hosts, cf. Isa. 10.12-27; 14.24-27; Dan. 11.10-12.1; cf. 9.27; Zech. 14.1-7.

Yet a third campaign may be intended by the brief 'interruption' in the post-war flow of events to describe an apocalyptic style destruction of an invading coalition against the land and its capital city in chapter 14.12-15. As numbers of the details match those used in the detailed account concerning the invasion of Gog of Magog from the uttermost parts of the north, we understand Zechariah's account to describe this final campaign which comes to its doom through the divine intervention alone, cf. Ezek. 38-39.

2.1 The Defence of Jerusalem indirectly, 12.1–13.6

There is no mention here of the 'worthless shepherd', the false messiah/ prophet with whom chapter 11 closed. The divine involvement with Israel here, the nation's empowering, their contrition, their cleansing, and the cutting off of all idolatry among them, requires the prior removal of the Beast and the False Prophet with their unrivalled apostasy blasphemously represented at Jerusalem's temple, 2 Thess. 1.7–9; 2.3–12; Rev. 16.12–16; 19.11–16, 19–21.

The Lord the guarantor 'concerning Israel', 12.1–2. These verses act as a title to a piece heavy with judgement and yet vibrant with hope, and truly eschatological. The oracular 'word of the Lord . . . saith the Lord' assures the theocratically privileged Israel. Their covenant-keeping Lord reveals Himself in His majestic activities in creation, providence and history to encourage confidence in His projections. He 'stretcheth', 'layeth', and 'formeth', the present participles being used metaphorically to insist on, not simply the once-for-all act, but His ongoing ordering of all and His ownership rights over all that He initiated. He is the One who: 1) 'stretcheth forth the heavens' in the celestial sphere as we might draw a curtain, a verbal noun not infrequently used to describe God's activity with the heavens, Job 9.8; Ps. 104.2; Isa. 40.22; 42.5; 44.24; 51.13*; 2) 'layeth the foundation of the earth' in the terrestrial sphere, Isa. 51.13; as a past completed act, see Ps. 24.2; 78.69; 102.25; 104.5 emphasizing stability and permanence. Where the heavens and earth occur together, the whole universe and its order is comprehended; 3) 'and formeth the spirit [or 'breath'] of man (not simply that 'of Israel') within him', the potter's control and creative genius informs the imagery here [the identical participle is translated 'potter' in 11.13(2)]. God is the 'former', not only of man's body from the dust, Gen. 2.7–8; 3.19; Ps. 103.14, and of his heart and eye, Ps. 33.15; 94.9, but also He breathed into him the very breath of life, Gen. 2.7; cf. Job 10.12; Eccles. 12.7; Isa. 2.22; 42.5. Further, the very disposition of man, his ability and desire to seek God diligently, is of God who 'formeth the spirit . . . within him', see Isa. 26.9–10; cf. Heb. 12.9. The God who made the worlds is the One who makes the ages also; He is the God of history. Verse two articulates this sovereignty with an emphatic 'Behold, I myself will set aside for a special purpose, or appoint' [lit.] Jerusalem. Jerusalem has many special appointments in the purpose of God. But this appointment is to have a most disconcerting effect on 'all the peoples round about' determined to swallow it up; it will become 'a cup [bowl, goblet] of reeling' for all, cf. Isa. 51.17–23. Yet that city's disasters, deliverances and future delights are all part of the divine 'I wills'.

Jerusalem a burdensome stone for all the peoples, 12.3–8. This is the first of seven paragraphs opened by the extended phrase 'And it shall come to pass in that day', v. 3a. With poetic justice, the Lord has appointed all (3x here and 1x in verse 2) those implacable foes who are their immediate neighbours, cf. v. 2, to be crushed. In a show of weight-lifting strength, they discover too late that they have over-extended themselves, so that Jerusalem will become 'a burdensome [same root] stone' which they cannot support and which will crush and injure them. The 'in that day' supplements provide further details on how this unexpected reversal is to be achieved, vv. 4, 6, 8. Simply put, He will remove the enemy advantage by confusing their cavalry, v. 4, and resource Judah and Jerusalem in such a way that they shall acknowledge their success to have been of the Lord. He will enable the one to devour, as also He will defend the other so as to make the feeble mighty, vv. 6, 8. Even the ordering of their victory over the invading hordes is designed to outlaw any glorying in their own achievements. Judah will confess that its strength was mediated through Jerusalem's apprehending the resources in 'the Lord of hosts their God', v. 5. But the Lord also 'saved the tents of Judah first' to safeguard against Jerusalem being 'magnified above Judah', v. 7. He says 'I will smite' the enemy cavalry, horse and horseman alike, with panic, v. 4b–c, e. Their enemies sustain a staggering blow! Also He adds 'I will open mine eyes upon the house of Judah', being favourably cognizant of all their needs and supplying them in an appropriate and timely way, v. 4d; cf. 9.8. Of Judah's chiefs the Lord says 'I will make (them) like a pan of fire . . . like a torch of fire', v. 6, similes of scorching destructiveness. First Jerusalem and now Judah successfully confront 'all the peoples round about' representing such implacable 'kinsmen' as Syria, Jordan, and Arabia, vv. 2, 6.

Purpose to destroy all the nations that come against Jerusalem, 12.9–13.1. Patently, this had not been achieved when the Lord had defended Jerusalem, and Judah had devoured the armies to their right and left. The time had come at last to give undivided attention to destroy all Gentiles bent upon attacking Jerusalem, v. 9. But first the Lord will deal with those He purposes to save. To effect this, the Lord who had defended the inhabitants of Jerusalem and the house of David, v. 8, must deluge upon them 'the spirit of grace and of supplication',

v. 10a–c. Their controlling disposition must be dramatically changed to 'a right spirit', to a 'free spirit', and after all it is God who 'formeth the spirit of man within him', 12.1; Ps. 51.10, 12. The Lord will flood them with His realized divine favour, and this in turn will prompt that intensity of 'supplication' [the plural form derived from the same root as 'grace'] to which the Lord responds. Only then will they 'look unto me, cf. Num. 21.9, whom they have pierced' [thrust through, 13.3], the nation's true Passover, Exod. 12.46; John 19.36–37; Rev. 1.7. The discernment of two advents of the one Messiah, alone satisfies the full range of biblical revelation, v. 10d. What depths of condescending grace this displays, for it is the Lord who is seen as the pierced One. This must be the most moving and soul-transforming revelation that the nation 'born out of due time', that is, at the second Passover, Num. 9.6–14, will ever be granted. Through it, it will follow the pattern conversion of Saul of Tarsus who learned through the revelation of the glorified Lord from heaven to him that he was indeed 'the chief of sinners', 1 Tim. 1.12–17. National repentance follows (note the references to 'land', v. 12; 13.2), their deep grief and bitter sorrow expressing itself as one would for one's only true messianic son, or for one's firstborn to whom the double portion belongs. Had the pierced One not risen from the dead, the nation's hope and the covenant with David would have died with Him. What hope is there except in Judah and in David's greatest Son risen from the dead, v. 10e–h. That day the nation will be brought to its only divinely-appointed fast, the true fulfilment of the obligatory Day of Atonement, Lev. 16; 23.26–32, confessing its sins, Isa. 53.1–12.

Another 'in that day' addition to the theme, vv. 11–14, compares their 'great mourning' with that expressed nationally at the calamitous and premature death of king Josiah in the Megiddo Valley. And yet though their mourning is corporate in character, and 'the land shall mourn', it will be an occasion when each person within every family, male and female apart, will have their own peculiar reason for confession and mourning. The family of the house of David and the family of the house of Nathan represent the main and subsidiary regal lines, see 1 Chr. 3.5; Luke 3.31. The house of Levi and the family of the Shimeites (a descendant of Gershom), represent the priests and Levites. All with responsible office give an exemplary lead here, and the common people follow. Princes, priests and people alike need to get alone with God; 'each will find his own sin, and all will deplore their common sin against the Messiah'. The final 'in that day' contribution to this paragraph adds to their godly sorrow, their cleansing from that sin and consequent uncleanness, 13.1. The 'fountain opened' [participle] is a living spring of water (not blood), a perennial source of daily cleansing by the washing of water by the word. This 'fountain' is emphatically for the same ones upon whom the spirit of grace had been poured in chapter 12.10, and who had looked unto the pierced One, namely the royal house and the inhabitants of the royal city. How that city particularly needs, and shall yet have, moral cleansing from blood-guiltiness and spiritual adultery, see especially Ps. 51.2-4, 7, 10-11, 17; Ezek. 36.25-31.

Idols to be cut off, Prophets to be ashamed, 13.2-6

Two further 'in that day' pronouncements develop the themes. First the promise is *I will cut off the names of the idols out of the land*, 13.2-3. However the whole land and not just Jerusalem must be rid of all that is offensive to the Lord of hosts. Initially, by His almighty power He will cut off the very names of false gods and they will be remembered no more, v. 2. Also false prophets and the unclean spirit which ever seeks to deceive will have no place in the land at all. Nonetheless, some will dare to prophesy without any divine revelation given them, and they will be cut off without mercy shown even from their own parents. Thus these evils which have plagued the nation's past, and have encouraged all manner of unclean practices, will be allowed no quarter after the first rays of light pointing to the perfect day.

Then the *prophets will be ashamed every one of his vision*, 13.4-6. These verses view the complete embargo on the rantings of those without a revelation while the King's arrival is awaited. Capital punishment will be the lot of any offender, restraining the peddling of false prophecy and the claim of visions authenticating the lies propagated. Such a 'prophet' will fabricate all manner of explanations to cover up his dabblings in the disallowed when questioned about his vision source, his dress, his occupation or the visible self-inflicted wounds between his sides [lit. not 'in thine hands'], all trappings of his trade. Sooner or later the sins of all such deceivers will find them out.

2.2. The Deliverance of Jerusalem directly, 13.7-14.21

Still 'a day of the Lord cometh', 'the Lord my God' must come, and His feet (how great indeed is the mystery of godliness!) must stand upon the mount of Olives. Jerusalem must yet be exposed to man's last futile attempt to prevent the setting up of God's kingdom. A confederacy of the nation's remaining erstwhile foes, the biblical northerner (see p. 231), is to sing its swansong there, for the Lord of hosts is 'jealous for Zion with great jealousy', 8.2; 1.14. But that which results in *ruin* for the foe is used with divine skill for the *refining* of those who will enjoy the irrevocable relationship and blessing of the new covenant in the millennial kingdom.

Who may abide the day of His coming?, 13.7–9

In the aftermath of the Lord's defence of Jerusalem its inhabitants looked unto their Lord Messiah and were faced with *their responsibility* in His unjust piercing. Here, it is the ramifications of *God's judicial smiting* of His Shepherd Messiah that is in view, 13.7–9; Acts 4.28, and that the One whom justice smote with the sword suffered its judgement vicariously, v. 7; Isa. 53.4–6; 2 Cor. 5.21; 1 Pet. 3.18; ct. Zech. 13.6 (wounded); Isa. 50.6. The drawn sword of the Lord in scripture represents the execution of His inflexible judicial power, and here particularly in judgement of sin, cf. 1 Chr. 21.13–27.

God commands His sword to 'Awake' against 'my shepherd', not a foe but Israel's God appointed caring King, John 10.11, 14–15. He is also 'the man that is my fellow', cf. Ps. 80.17. What canons of Christology are here! The Hebrew word translated 'my fellow' is used only of the closest of ties, whether of family or relationship [11 × in Lev.*]. One translator captures this with the phrase 'the man, my equal', cf. John 10.30. Already the same mystery of His person has been before us in that the pierced One is in fact the Lord, 12.10.

In all the land . . . two parts therein shall be cut off and die; but the third shall be left therein, vv. 7c–9. In Zechariah's constant interplay of first and second advent elements, the flock indeed did repudiate the Good Shepherd's selfless service for them, and the consequence for them latterly will be God's raising of a False Messiah, 11.15–17. However, since God has smitten His Shepherd judicially, the sheep necessarily were scattered; and He said 'I will turn mine hand against the little ones', v. 8; cf. Isa. 1.24–26. Persecution, oppression and dispersion were inevitable, involving the early disciples, Matt. 26.31, 56, 'the poor of the flock', and later involving Israel's widest and longest diaspora. Judgement must begin at the house of God. Such will be the discriminating nature of divine righteousness however, that while two parts of the land's population will be cut off and die justly, a third part will remain, cf. Mal. 3.4–5. And that very remnant itself, He declares, 'I will bring . . . through the fire' of affliction, promising that I 'will refine them as silver is refined' with their redemption in view, and 'will try them as gold is tried' with their glory in view, v. 9a–c; Isa. 1.25–26; Mal. 3.2–3. For 'Zion shall be redeemed with judgement, and her converts with righteousness', Isa. 1.27.

God's ways will bring them to 'call upon my name', and whoever does so will be saved, Joel 2.32. The divine promise goes further; 'I will hear them: I will say, It is my people', 13.9e–f. This element of the new covenant formula on the divine side will be reciprocated in that day by the saved nation's confession 'The Lord is my God', v. 9g. Like Thomas, their seeing and believing would draw forth a similar exclamation of awed wonder and worship, 'My Lord and my God', John 20.24–29.

Behold, a day for the Lord cometh, 14.1–7

To effect this covenant blessing of Israel, the Lord of history will gather a second confederation of foes 'against Jerusalem to battle', who will be encouraged by their success in taking the city, and trigger off another deportation of its population, though a remnant will be left, 14.1–2.

'Then', when all hope is lost, the Lord as 'a man of war' will 'go forth' from heaven, Isa. 26.20–21, and He shall 'fight *against* those nations' as 'the Lord mighty in battle', Ps. 24.8. But He shall 'fight *for*' Jerusalem's remnant also. The One who trod the sea with His horses at the exodus, Hab. 3.15, will 'stand . . . upon the mount of Olives'. Those looking for the rising 'Sun of righteousness' will see Him on that mountain 'on the east', cf. Mal. 4.1–3. The mountain which had witnessed the departure and return of David to his capital, that mountain from which our Lord went up to heaven, is the same one on which His promised return is here realized, 2 Sam. 15.30; 20.2–3; Acts 1.11–12; see on 2.5. Cleaving 'the mountain' will thereby open up a transverse escape valley from west to east between 'my mountains', which will remain a permanent witness to divine power in deliverance, in contrast to the short-lived dividing of the sea in the great exodus event, vv. 3–5b; cf. Exod. 14.14, 25; Ps. 136.13–15. The recognition of divine power will produce the kind of fear that once gripped the people who fled 'before the earthquake (in mid-eighth century BC) in the days of Uzziah', a tragedy still alive in the hearts of Zechariah's contemporaries some two hundred and fifty years after the event, v. 5c; Amos 1.1; Jos. Ant. 9.10.4; 2 Chr. 26.16–21. The mighty exploits of the Warrior Lord leave no option here except a fleeing to safety!

In yet another 'in that day' pronouncement that the *Lord my God shall come*, vv. 5d–7, Zechariah briefly switches from speaking *of* Him to directly expressing *to* Him his wonder at the Lord's coming and 'all the holy ones with thee', v. 5d–e. That alone would set apart that day, but also it shall come to pass in that day that *the light shall not be with brightness and with gloom*, but appear a peculiar combination of the two, a kind of soft evening twilight, 'not day and not night' and which brightens into day at evening as the forerunner of the promised 'morning without clouds'!, vv. 6–7; 2 Sam. 23.4. The days of Israel's mourning will be ended, cf. Isa. 60. 18–22; Rev. 22.5. Such disturbances of the 'laws of nature', and spectacularly those of the stellar heavens, regularly feature in the forecasts relating to that day, Joel 3.9–16.

The Lord King of all the land, Jerusalem secure, 14.8–11. *'And it shall come to pass in that day that living waters shall go out from Jerusalem*, v. 8, and the refreshment of the Lord's victory is first enjoyed by His own. From Messiah's capital His limitless life-giving waters will line its approaches with paradisaic fruitfulness summer and winter, and link the seas to east (Dead, Salt Sea) and west (Mediterranean, Great Sea), Ezek. 47.1–12; Joel 3.18; Rev. 22.1–2. As King over a unified land and people, King over all the land, He fulfils the messianic promise to Israel that 'Thine eyes shall see the king in his beauty', Isa. 33.17. Of course, His personal greatness is such that He is to be universal King of kings over all the earth too, but that is not what is being developed here, cf. Luke 1.32–33. In that day too the Lord shall be the one and only One Israel loves, and shall recognize at last that all He has revealed Himself to be is 'in his name one', 'uniquely one' incomparable Lord, their Messiah King who is the incarnate Lord who reigns, v. 9; Pss. 93.1; 96.10; 97.1; 99.1–2. The Eternal is the goal of history! The geographical configuration of 'All the land' from the northern limit of Judah, Geba six miles north of Jerusalem, to Rimmon some thirty-five miles south west of the city, is to become a level plain, 'as the Arabah' rift valley. This will leave Jerusalem 'lifted up' plateau-like above it and standing 'in her place' alone, beautiful indeed for elevation is the city of the great King, Ps. 48.1–3. The topographical notices of verse 10 demand a literal fulfilment of these promises. No longer will it be 'As the mountains are round about Jerusalem, so the Lord is round about his people', Ps. 125.2. But now the Lord Himself will be there! With all traces of the curse of destruction removed forever, Rev. 22.3, Jerusalem will realize the oft-repeated divine promise at last and 'dwell securely' in their year of jubilee, v. 11; Lev. 25.18–19; Jer. 33.16.

Plague and Panic for the enemies of Jerusalem, 14.12–15. This somewhat 'intrusive' paragraph describing the judgement of peoples who have taken up arms against Jerusalem, is usually construed as supplementing the more positive details affecting the deliverance of Jerusalem

THE PROPHECY OF ZECHARIAH

in verses 3–7. Incontrovertibly, the opening and closing reference to 'the plague' affecting peoples and animals, marks the boundaries of a separate paragraph, vv. 12, 15. As previously intimated, however, the reference to God's people 'dwelling securely', and taking account of the men and animals, the plague and the confusion leading to internecine slaughter among the soldiery, and the huge spoils collected by God's people after God alone had destroyed the foe, a better parallel is to be found in the last desperate invasion of the land by forces from the far north referred to in Ezekiel 38–39. Gog of Magog and the confederated foes from 'the uttermost parts of the north' and other parts embraced in this description, devise evil against the land because it was full of 'unwalled villages', 'dwelling securely' and possessing great wealth. By storm, and shaking that affects the heavens, the sea and the earth, by pestilence and panic that causes every man's sword to be against his brother, the Lord God will slay them upon the mountains of Israel, and call up birds and beasts to devour their carcases, see Ezek. 38–39. First then here, it is God's plague that takes enormous toll of 'all the people mustered' [lit., noun often in title Lord of hosts], on the mountains of Israel with a view to attacking Jerusalem eventually, v. 12. In that day *a great tumult from the Lord shall be among them*, v. 13, so that in the confusion the enemy forces shall kill one another at close quarters. Judah joins 'with'[rather than 'at'] Jerusalem in the fight, though this involves them mostly in 'gathering up the wealth' as spoils of war from the fallen foes, v. 14. Only following upon this enemy invasion will the Lord God 'bring again the captivity of Jacob, and have mercy upon the whole house of Israel; and I will be jealous for my holy name'. Then shall the whole nation 'dwell securely in their land, and none shall make them afraid', see Ezek. 39.25–29.

Nations worship the King, the Lord of hosts, 14.16–19. At last the privilege and responsibility of the (non-militarised) remnant of all those nations which 'came against Jerusalem' is described. These are the 'sheep' among the living nations who will be separated by the Shepherd's rod when gathered before the Son of man, the King, sitting upon 'the throne of his glory' upon earth, Matt. 25.31–40. These had demonstrated their sympathy with those precious to the Lord in the day of Jacob's trouble, and will rejoice to hear His call, 'Come, ye blessed of my Father, inherit the kingdom prepared for you from the foundation of the world', 'the righteous' who enter into 'eternal life'. They *'shall go up from year to year to worship the King, the Lord of hosts, and to keep the feast of tabernacles'*, v. 16. For these to be in His kingdom will be mercy indeed.

But to worship the Lord in the beauty of holiness as the King's subjects is their highest service! Isaiah describes Zion as 'the city of our solemnities', 33.20. And Tabernacles is that seventh month feast and the seventh divine appointment in the course of the salvation history of His people, the 'harvest-home' seven day assembly of joy, to be realized in its fulness in the age to come. For great David's greater Son, who is his Lord, that festival of Tabernacles alone gathers up in its folds all the threads of the tapestry of time in joy unspeakable and full of glory! And yet He Himself chose to major on the great day of that feast, the eighth day which looked beyond the millennial kingdom to the eternal state, John 7.

But commensurate with *privilege*, the spiritually elevating experience of 'going up' to Jerusalem, v. 16, to worship the King, there is increased *responsibility* for the families of the earth, vv. 17-19. The Shepherd who rules does so in righteousness and with a rod of iron; disobedience is disallowed! No attendance, no going up, no rain; no rain, no harvest, v. 17. However Egypt, whose fertility depends not on rainfall directly, but on the annual inundation of the Nile, will suffer the consuming plagues designed to recall the judgements of God leading up to their release of Israel, v. 18; cf. Exod. 9.14. Note the punishment order is inverted in verse 19, and that the first case of non-attendance is bound up with not going up to worship the King, but the other non-attendance cases have no desire even to 'keep the feast'.

All will be Holy to the Lord, 14.20-21. Thankfully, the closing two references to 'in that day' in this chapter insist, positively and negatively, on the holiness that becomes the Lord's house, His land and His people. The golden plate on the high priest's mitre alone had inscribed upon it 'Holy to the Lord', Exod. 28.36-38. But the very bells of the horses and every cooking pot in the homes of the inhabitants of Jerusalem and Judah, and all that is part and parcel of everyday secular life in home, city and country, are alike Holy to the Lord of hosts, vv. 20, 21. Heaven is 'his (God's) holy habitation', 2.13. But in that kingdom day truly the land will be described as 'the holy land', and Jerusalem 'the mountain of the Lord of hosts, The holy mountain', 2.12; 8.3, and its ordinary citizens a 'holy people' to the Lord, Deut. 26.19, a 'holy nation', Exod. 19.6. Every pot in the Lord's house, for cooking the portion of a sacrificial meal for priest and people, will be as holy as those catching the sacrificial blood at the altar. Such will be the increase in demand for cooking utensils in the house of God for the constant stream of visiting worshippers, that the local residents will put their own

secular cooking vessels at their disposal, v. 21b. As in the strong believer's case today, every day and everything is alike holy to the Lord,
for artificial distinctions between secular and sacred undermine the
healthy practice of all-embracive holiness. On the other hand what does
the trader, the mercenary spirit, have in common with God's temple?,
v. 21. As our Lord said to those trespassers in His day, 'Take these
things hence; make not my Father's house a house of merchandise'. He
maintained a consuming zeal for God's house and holiness. So must
we. Paul anticipates the completion of God's present *universal* programme, 'the fulness of the Gentiles ... come in ... and so all Israel
shall be saved', Rom. 11.25-27. To effect this, Israel's people and land
must ultimately be faced with the claims of the Pierced One so that
genuine contrition and divinely provided cleansing might become
theirs; a national Day of Atonement is destined for them, 12.10-13.1.
The day of Jacob's trouble must be sanctified to their refining, and the
unique new covenant relationship between the Lord and His people
must be righteously realized, 13.7-9. Otherwise, how will they become
clothed and consecrated to serve as a holy and royal priesthood?, ch. 3.
The saved nation must diffuse its ministry of glory and light throughout
the whole earth, as the Lord's lampstand, ch. 4. The Lord/King/
Messiah/Priest must build the temple, bear the glory, sit and rule upon
His throne in equity and with sympathy, 6.11-13. The nations must
make their annual pilgrimage to Jerusalem to worship the King at the
feast of the Tabernacles, 14.16.

In conclusion then, such comprehensive coverage of God's messianic
prophetic programme is unmatched in any of the Minor Prophets or in
all of them put together. Zechariah is essential reading for all students of
prophecy, and the most excellent pithy primer on Old Testament messi-
anism. Praise God, this prophet has served us through the Spirit of
Christ who was in him, testifying both 'the sufferings of Christ, and the
glories that should follow them'.

CHAPTER TWELVE

THE PROPHECY OF
MALACHI

12

by DAVID WEST

NOTHING IS KNOWN CONCERNING MALACHI beyond what we may glean from the prophecy that bears his name; his parentage, his birthplace, his occupation and the time when he prophesied are all omitted. However, it would appear by a comparison of his prophecy with the closing chapter of the book of Nehemiah that Malachi could have been contemporary with Nehemiah's second visit to Jerusalem.

Malachi differs from Zechariah, who is an encourager; Malachi himself is a rebuker yet, in the wisdom of God, both have their place among the Lord's people. A spirit of moral indifference and even religious scepticism had fallen upon the nation, affecting the priests and the people alike. At such a time Malachi sounded forth his call to repentance. He lived in a corrupt age and there is an atmosphere of gloom over the book.

Malachi was the last of the three post-captivity prophets; his name means 'my message', and like Haggai he was 'the Lord's messenger in the Lord's message', Hag. 1.13. After Malachi the voice of God was not heard through a prophet for some 400 years. Because of the failure of the nation, the Old Testament ends (so to speak) with a closed heaven, although the Lord speaks of the possibility of opening the windows of heaven and pouring out a blessing, 3.10.

The prophecy itself is characterized by personal reasoning, with the use of question and answer. The Lord through the prophet makes a statement to the various groups of people; this is immediately refuted by those concerned. The Lord then answers and vindicates the charge. This rebuttal is expressed by the words 'yet ye say', 1.2; 2.14, 17; 3.8, 13; 'ye say,' 1.6, 7; 'but ye said,' 3.7; and in each instance they are the translation of the same Hebrew word. Then follows the characteristic question of the book, 'wherein?' (in chapter 2 verse 14 the same word in the Hebrew is translated 'wherefore?' and in chapter 3 verse 13 'what?').

These eight occurrences form a most interesting study, setting forth the Lord's accusations against His people; they suggest an eight-fold division of the contents of the prophecy between the introduction, 1.1, and the epilogue, 4.1–6:

1 1.2–5, The Nation's Denial of God's Love.

2 1.6, The Priests' Despising of God's Name.

3 1.7–14, The Priests' Pollution of God's Altar.

Chapter 2. 1–9 forms a parenthesis where the Lord speaks directly to the priests.

4 2.10–16, The People's Defilement of God's Holiness.

5 2.17–3.6, The People's Criticism of God's Judgement.

6 3.7, The People's Rejection of God's Invitation.

7 3.8–12, The People's Robbery of God's Tithe.

8 3.13–18, The People's Refusal of God's Service.

Introduction, 1.1

The opening words of Malachi's prophecy reveal that his mission was of God, 'the burden of the word of the Lord to Israel'. His was a heavy burden – Malachi felt the weighty impact of the message which he brought to Israel. Although most of the exiles who returned from the captivity of Babylon were of the Kingdom of Judah, nevertheless the prophet viewed the nation as one in the divine purpose.

1) The nation's denial of God's love, 1.2–5

'I have loved you, saith the Lord,' v.2. The prophecy opens with words just as appropriate as those with which it closes, 'lest I come and smite the earth with a curse', 4.6. His attitude had not changed; whatever the state of His people, the Lord never forgets and never hesitates to declare His love for them. The heart of God for His people is invariably displayed before the needed warnings and corrections are given.

Here we see God's love (i) *declared*, 'I have loved you, saith the Lord', v. 2.; (ii) *denied*, 'Yet ye say, wherein hast thou loved us?' v. 2.; (iii) *defined*, 'I loved Jacob', v. 2.; (iv) *demonstrated*, 'your eyes shall see', v. 5. So far as the nation of Israel was concerned, God had made it perfectly clear that His love was not based upon their merits, 'The Lord did not set his love upon you, nor choose you, because ye were more in number than any people; for ye were the fewest of all people: But because the Lord loved you', Deut. 7.7-8.

We cannot be too often reminded that we do not belong to the Lord because we loved Him, but because He first loved us and made us what we are, 'Herein is love, not that we loved God, but that he loved us', 1 John 4.10, 'we love him, because he first loved us', 1 John 4.19.

The state of the people in Malachi's day is immediately evident from their response, 'wherein hast thou loved us?' v. 2. The sheer impertinence of the question is astounding. If the nation questioned the fact of the Lord's love for them, it was but a reflection of their lack of love for Him.

However, here in Malachi's prophecy the Lord proceeds to give His own proof of His love. He might have recounted the numberless examples of His goodness in the experience of the nation, but instead He chose the one outstanding example which was irrefutable, 'was not Esau Jacob's brother? saith the Lord: yet I loved Jacob, and I hated Esau', vv. 2-3.

The primary reference here, no doubt, was to the two races of Edom and Israel, but the words plainly alluded to their progenitors, Esau and Jacob themselves. Esau was the firstborn, Gen. 25.25; to him belonged the birthright (i.e. a double portion of the inheritance, Deut. 21.17). Nevertheless God made choice of Jacob in preference to Esau and this divine choice operated prior to their birth – this we learn from Romans 9.11–13.

God loved Jacob from the first, but He never pronounced hatred towards Esau until that was made manifest which utterly rejected Himself, and that with contempt. When the Lord said, 'I hated Esau', He waited until the last moment, when Esau had shown what he really was. Thus, the first book of the Bible unfolds to us His sovereign choice of Jacob; only the last book of the Old Testament tells us of His hatred of Esau.

Paul discloses that the Christian was chosen in Christ 'before the foundation of the world', Eph. 1.4; the Lord explicitly stated that He had chosen His own 'out of the world', John 15.19. That election Peter declares was 'according to the foreknowledge of God the Father,' 1 Pet. 1.2. Those to whom such favour has been shown should surely respond in gratitude and devotion; yet how many believers there are today who are found questioning God's love as much as did the people of Malachi's day.

Ill health, unemployment, lack of material benefits, an unappealing environment, the unsympathetic attitude of the world may cause some to question God's love, 'wherein hast thou loved us?' However, in the light of Calvary, the question is almost blasphemous.

2) The priests' despising of God's name, 1.6

The basic reason for the attitude of the people was their complete lack of reverence for God and this affected their conduct. His honour should have been the supreme object of their life.

The Lord was described as the Father of Israel in the song of Moses; 'is not he thy father that hath bought thee?' Deut. 32.6; The prophets designated Him in a similar way; thus Isaiah said, 'Thou, O Lord, art our father, our redeemer', Isa. 63.16. If He were their Father, where was the respect due to Him?

God was their sovereign ruler; if He were their supreme master, (a plural form of the word is used, implying royalty), then homage and reverential awe ought to be paid to Him. However, on their part there was a complete lack of loyalty and devoted obedience. But what is our attitude of heart towards the One who is our Father and the One whom we have owned as Lord of all?

Here in Malachi's prophecy the word is directed to the priests. The reason for Israel's condition was to be found in the declension of those who should have been their spiritual leaders. They had failed to teach the character and claims of God and this was largely the reason for the deplorable condition of the nation. The priests despised God's name, (N.B. Malachi places emphasis upon the importance of the name in his prophecy), yet so blind were they to the significance of their behaviour that they said 'wherein have we despised thy name?'

3) The priests' pollution of God's altar, 1.7–14

The priests were accused of offering polluted bread upon the altar, v. 7. 'Bread' is used here for the offering of animals; this is referred to as 'the bread of your God', Lev. 22.25.

If the sacrifice on the altar was the bread of God, it had to be necessarily perfect and the law repeatedly emphasized that such offerings had to be unblemished and free from any defect. Yet the priests evidently were accepting from the people and offering to God sacrifices which did not meet the divine requirements – 'the blind . . .the lame and sick', v. 8. They had thus defiled the altar by their polluted sacrifices.

A sad feature was that the priests had lost all sense of right and wrong and said, 'wherein have we polluted thee?'; v. 7. They saw no evil in what they were doing. However, Malachi sought to bring home to them that they would not have presented such to their governor as a gift.

The RV rendering of verse 10 suggests that the Lord was expressing the desire that the temple doors should be closed against all the false worship of the priests; it would be far better if the whole of their empty ritual was stopped altogether.

Although the priests of Malachi's day had despised His name, there was a day coming – that glorious Millennial age – when the name of the Lord would be 'great among the Gentiles', v. 11. He shall have His portion then, for 'in every place incense shall be offered unto my name, and a *pure* offering', v. 11.

The service of the priests in the temple brought them no joy; it should have been their greatest delight to be engaged in such ministry towards God. Instead they found it utterly wearisome, 'Behold, what a weariness is it!' v. 13. They now lacked the zeal that characterised the temple worship when the remnant had first returned from the captivity of Babylon.

And what of the application to ourselves? We have been constituted 'an holy priesthood, to offer up spiritual sacrifices, acceptable to God by Jesus Christ' 1 Pet. 2.5. Worship ought to be the highest expression of spiritual devotedness to God and whatever is devoted to God must not be polluted – He deserves the very best that we can bring. How sad if we find such spiritual sacrifices irksome!

A parenthesis, 2.1-9

These opening verses of chapter 2 form a parenthesis in which the Lord of hosts speaks directly to the priests, warning them of the consequences of their actions.

It has already been noted that the reason for Israel's condition was to be found in the declension of those who were her spiritual leaders. In making the application to present day circumstances, it has to be borne in mind that the priests, in this respect, have their counterpart in the elders of the assembly: those who take a spiritual lead among the people of God. The assembly is largely reflected in its overseers; the *general* spiritual tone of an assembly cannot rise above the level of spirituality of its elders.

4) The people's defilement of God's holiness, 2.10-16

The divine complaint was not only against the priests, but against the people as a whole, and now Malachi deals with the outstanding sins of his day, viz:-
    (i) false dealing with brethren, 2.10;
    (ii) unholy marriages, 2.11-12;
and (iii) unlawful divorces, 2.13-16.

(i) false dealing with brethren, 2.10.

The first sin mentioned is that of dealing treacherously every man against his brother, 'why do we deal treacherously every man against his brother?' The word 'treacherously' is from a root word meaning to cover (with garment), to deal deceitfully. It would apply to all dealings with our brethren which are less than upright and honest.

Note the truths that the prophet cites as proof to expose the evil conduct of the men of his day: (i) their common standing before God. On the ground of His covenant, 'Have we not all one father?'; (ii) their common relationship to God as their Creator, 'Hath not one God created us?' Knit by common ties to God, both in creation and redemption, they were knit together by common relationships, interests and blessings, the knowledge of which should have guarded them from sinning against their brethren.

As to ourselves, we need to realize that we are bound together with our fellow-believers by imperishable ties as members of the body of Christ; we should therefore look upon their welfare and interests as our own.

(ii) unholy marriages, 2.11–12.

Judah was accused of dealing treacherously, and the prophet declared that an abomination, (a term frequently used almost as a synonym for 'idolatry',) was being committed in Israel and in Jerusalem, 2.11. Thus the two divisions of Judah and Israel were mentioned to indicate that the sin was common to both.

The people had been separated from the Gentile nations and had been set apart to God, 'I am the Lord your God, which have separated you from other people', Lev. 20.24. They had been forbidden to intermarry with the nations of Canaan, 'Neither shalt thou make marriages with them', Deut. 7.3, but now God accused them of profaning His holiness by marrying those who were worshippers of false gods.

We hear Paul's warning, 'Be ye not unequally yoked together with unbelievers', 2 Cor 6.14. The apostle visualized the possibility of a situation arising in which a believer and an unbeliever were rigidly fixed together in a common commitment. A yoke is very different from being 'conformed to this world', Rom.12.2; copying the world is one thing, but joining with it is worse. A yoke is a very powerful influence; human nature being what it is, it is almost certain that the controlling influence of the unbeliever will take precedence.

Many varieties of unequal yoke tempt the child of God into a pathway of disobedience and disaster, e.g. political, religious, social, business and marriages yokes. Any diverse union is wrong for the believer, yet the most serious is the matrimonial one, since one cannot get out of it until death breaks the tie.

In Malachi's day, if there were no repentance, swift and certain judgement would be visited in such a case, and there would be no respect of persons, 'the master and the scholar, etc', 2.12.

(iii) unlawful divorces, 2.13–16

The people's sin was not confined to intermarriage with foreign women who were idolaters; it was coupled with the divorce of existing wives to enable such marriages to take place.

It was clearly the original purpose of God that marriage should be permanently binding, thus Paul says 'the woman which hath an husband is bound by the law to her husband so long as he liveth', Rom. 7.2. The law made provision for divorce in particular circumstances, Deut. 24. 1-4, but the Lord Jesus Himself affirmed, 'For the hardness of your heart he, (i.e. Moses) wrote you this precept', Mark 10.5. He went on to say, 'Whosoever shall put away his wife and marry another, committeth adultery against her. And if a woman shall put away her husband and be married to another, she committeth adultery', Mark 10. 11-12.

There can be no place in the fellowship of a local assembly for a divorced person who has remarried and continues to live with the second partner; likewise there can be no such fellowship for one who is married to a divorced person.

'The Lord, the God of Israel, saith that he hateth putting away', Mal. 2.16; if His people are in communion with His own mind, they will do also.

5) The people's criticism of God's judgement, 2.17-3.6

The people in general had departed from the Lord. 'Ye have wearied the Lord with your words', 2.17; they drew near to Him with their mouth and honoured Him with their lips, but their heart was far from Him. However, in their ignorance of their own condition, they were surprised to hear that they had wearied the Lord, 'wherein have we wearied him?'. They were seeking to justify themselves, but at the same time they were criticizing the judgement of God.

They were maintaining that the evil doer was deemed good in His sight, 'Every one that doeth evil is good in the sight of the Lord, and he delighteth in them'. Perhaps they pointed to the prosperity of the heathen as proof of the Lord's biased judgement. If the Lord were really just, where was the God of judgement?

As a prophet, Malachi was one who not only *forthtold* the mind of God but who also *foretold* future events. So what of Malachi's *foretelling*? The unbelieving people had sarcastically enquired, 'Where is the God of judgement?' 2.17. The reply came in the opening verses of chapter 3.

Firstly the Lord of hosts was to send a messenger to prepare the way before Him, 3.1. Long before, Isaiah had referred to the same messenger, 'The voice of him that crieth in the wilderness, Prepare ye the way of the Lord', Isa. 40.3. The Lord Jesus Himself stated plainly that this prediction was fulfilled in John the Baptist, 'For this is he, of whom it is written, Behold, I send my messenger before thy face, which shall prepare thy way before thee', Matt. 11.10. The forerunner of whom Malachi spoke was to prepare the way 'before me', i.e. the Lord of hosts. In applying the prediction to John the Baptist as His own forerunner, the Lord Jesus was clearly implying His own personal identification with Jehovah of hosts.

The people had asked where the God of judgement was. The One whom the people sought or about whom they enquired was described as 'the Lord', 3.1 (i.e. Adon – the Sovereign Lord of the whole earth). That One 'shall suddenly come to his temple', but although one of the Lord's last public actions was that of the purging of the temple, Matt 21.12, it is evident that this prophecy awaits its future fulfilment. As was the case with several of the Old Testament prophets, Malachi spoke in one breath of the two advents of the Messiah.

The Lord Jesus Himself is 'the messenger (angel) of the covenant', 3.1, the greatest messenger of all – the One promised by God in His covenant with Israel. 'Behold, he shall come', 3.1 – the reference here is not to His first advent which was potentially in blessing, but to His second advent in judgement. Indeed verses 2–6 tell of the character and consequences of His coming.

'He is like a refiner's fire', 3.2; fire symbolizes the holiness of God. The baptism of fire (see Matt. 3.11) at His appearing will effect the purification of His people; 'and like fullers' soap' that day will serve to purge away the uncleanness of Israel.

6) The people's rejection of God's invitation, 3.7

Here the condition of the people is again dealt with. 'Even from the days of your fathers ye are gone away from mine ordinances and have not kept them'. Surely this is a summary of Israel under law.

'Return unto me' – the Lord of hosts pleaded for their repentance – He always gives opportunity for recovery. His heart of love still yearns over the genuine backslider, as well as the sinner. However, the people indignantly enquire, 'wherein shall we return?' – as if to suggest that they were not aware of any departure.

We do well to bear in mind that the path of backsliding is often so gradual that the individual concerned is often unconscious of his departure from the ways of God.

7) The people's robbery of God's tithe, 3.8–12

One of the ways in which the people had departed from Him was that they had robbed Him, 'will a man rob God? Yet ye have robbed me',

3.8 – for they had withheld from Him the tithes and heave-offerings that were His due.

Was it possible that men would deliberately defraud God? The tithe was His as of absolute right. Gifts and freewill offerings were rendered voluntarily from glad hearts in addition, but the tithe was not a gift – it was God's undeniable right. The tithe was holy, (or sanctified, set apart,) to the Lord, 'And all the tithe of the land . . . is the Lord's: it is holy unto the Lord', Lev. 27.30 – and yet the people of Malachi's day had dared to retain it.

Because of this they had been cursed with poor harvests and with locusts destroying their fruits: 'Ye are cursed with a curse: for ye have robbed me', 3.9. But God had a proposition to put to them, 'Bring ye all the tithes into the storehouse', 3.10, i.e. let them bring the whole tithe, even of thin harvests, and see if He would not bless them with abundant harvests and undamaged fruits, 'if I will not open you the windows of heaven and pour you out a blessing, that there shall not be room enough to receive it', v. 10.

A similar charge might be laid at the feet of some of the people of God today; for even as far as material possessions are concerned there is a defrauding of God.

The principles enunciated by Paul concerning giving to God are often overlooked. According to 1 Cor.16.2 we are to give (1) *regularly* – 'upon the first day of the week'; (ii) *individually* – 'let every one (RV reads 'each one') of you', whether male or female, rich or poor; (iii) *systematically* 'lay by him in store' – this would point to the setting aside of God's portion at home; our giving is not to be done haphazardly, the amount that we give is not to be determined by our presence or absence from certain meetings or by the appeal of the moment; (iv) *proportionately*, 'as God hath prospered him' (or 'as he may prosper' – RV).

Sadly there is no longer an exercise of heart among some of the Lord's people about the tithing of income, but rather the bland assumption that the requirements of the law have been annulled and are no longer applicable, as if the giving to God under grace could conceivably be *less* than it was under law.

Are we guilty of defrauding God? This may be in material things, but it may be in the time that we give to Him, the energy which we devote to His service, or the priority which we give to His claims. We live in times of shorter working hours and longer holidays. Yet in general terms, less is being done in His service than believers did in previous generations.

The pleasant state of things promised in verses 11–12 of chapter 3 will be realized only in the golden age of the Millennium, when Christ personally returns and takes up the reins of government, for only then will God be fully acknowledged and His claims fully met. The land of promise will then be holy, set apart for God, 'ye shall be a delightsome (or pleasant) land'.

8) The people's refusal of God's service, 3. 13–18

The Lord again accused the people of speaking boldly against Him, 'Your words have been stout against me', 3.13. Of course they disputed this charge, 'what have we spoken so much against thee?', only to be informed, vv.14–15, that they had blamed God for dealing unfairly with those who served Him.

Centuries earlier, God had quoted the wicked as saying, 'what is the Almighty, that we should serve him? and what profit should we have, if we pray unto him?' Job 21.15. These were the words of *sinners*, but they were virtually what the professed people of God were saying in Malachi's day, 'It is vain to serve God: and what profit is it that we have kept his ordinance?', 3.14. They complained that humbling themselves and walking mournfully, (i.e., they had behaved as mourners, putting on the garments of penitence and humbling themselves as a means of making amends for their transgressions,) had brought no relief from their afflictions. They even said that men who in pride tempted God by doing evil were in fact favoured by Him, 'we call the proud happy; yea, they that work wickedness are set (or built) up; yea, they that tempt God are even delivered', 3.15.

Men still take up Israel's complaint and say, 'It is vain to serve God ...what profit is it?' They measure profit by the standard of worldly prosperity, being forgetful of the Lord's advice to 'lay up for yourselves treasures in heaven', Matt. 6.20. In this present age our blessings are spiritual, not material.

However, in that day there was a remnant within the returned remnant. It is most encouraging to know that God has always had a remnant of faithful ones in every age. 'They ... feared the Lord', 3.16; they lived in reverential awe of Him and walked in godly fear; we too should be marked by a reverential fear of the Lord. 'They ... spake often one to another' – this was their fellowship; their fellowship on earth was not with the mass of people, but with others who were likeminded. It became a characteristic feature of life for them to commune with one another – it was their habitual practice and not merely a casual conversation. Do we speak often one to another of the things that concern His interests?

'The Lord hearkened, and heard it', 3.16: as they conversed their subject matter was so pleasing to Him that the Lord listened intently. Indeed so intent was He to hear the conversation of those who were loyal to Him that the whole of His attention is graphically depicted as being focused upon them.

'And that thought upon his name', 3.16; they certainly did not despise His name (cf. 'O priests, that despise my name', 1.6), nor bring it into disrepute.

In Solomon's day Jehoshaphat, the son of Ahilud, was appointed as the King's recorder or remembrancer, 1 Kgs. 4.3. The remembrancer recorded events of particular significance and noted the names of those who had rendered special service to the King. Thus record was made in the days of Esther of the noble deed of Mordecai which he did on behalf of King Ahasuerus, Esther 6.1-2.

God also has His records, 'and a book of remembrance was written before him', Mal. 3.16, and in His book of remembrance were inscribed the details of the faithfulness and conduct of the loyal remnant of Malachi's day. Such would be honoured with His public recognition, in the day of His glory. They would be His own peculiar treasure, (N.B. 'jewels' – special treasure); this shows the preciousness of the saints to God in any age.

In the day to which the Lord of hosts referred, judgement would be poured out on a guilty world, but He promised that the remnant who had maintained their allegiance to Him would be spared from judgement, 'as a man spareth his own son that serveth him', 3.17.

These words are prophetic and presumably anticipate those days of tribulation which still lie ahead. God is never unmindful of His own and He will take special steps in that day to protect the godly remnant of the Jews who will have been loyal to Him.

As there were those who cleaved to the Lord in the closing phases of the dispensation of the law, so now at the end of this present age of grace, in spite of the general departure and downgrade movement of the church, there are faithful ones who cleave to the Lord with purpose of heart and hold fast to the truth. Such will receive rewards at the judgement seat of Christ when 'every one of us shall give account of himself to God', Rom. 14.12.

Conclusion, 4.1–6

The verses of chapter 4 form the conclusion to the book and are truly prophetic in character.

Verse 1 speaks of *the coming day* – that day which is referred to as 'the . . . day of the Lord', v. 5, that day which extends from the opening of the first seal, Rev. 6. 1, to the setting up of 'new heavens and a new earth', 2 Pet. 3. 13. 'The day . . . shall burn as an oven', 'the day . . . shall burn them up' – these expressions are figurative of divine judgement. Remember, 'our God is a consuming fire,' Heb. 12. 29.

Verses 2–3 tell of *the coming Lord*; it is in the character of 'the sun of righteousness', v. 2, that He will be manifested to Israel. To the church He is 'the bright and morning star', Rev. 22. 16, the One who will shine forth at the darkest hour of the night. To the world at large and to religious profession, He will come as a thief, 'the day of the Lord so cometh as a thief in the night', 1 Thess. 5. 2, 'if therefore thou shalt not watch, I will come on thee as a thief', Rev. 3.3.

The wicked will not always prosper; in that day the brief prosperity of the wicked will be reversed, Mal. 4.3. Thus whilst verse 2 sets forth mercy to the righteous, verse 3 tells of judgement to the wicked. However, there is no treading down of the wicked yet.

Verse 4 sets forth *the challenging law*. 'Remember' (look back) – the law was the test to judge their course; contrast verse 5 where they were bidden to look forward. There were thus two ways of judging the present aright in the light of (i) the past and (ii) the future.

Verses 5–6 speak of *the coming of Elijah*. Whilst Moses, v. 4, was the *giver* of the law, Elijah was the *restorer* to the law.

Whilst this prophecy received a partial fulfilment in the ministry of John the Baptist the word of the angel of the Lord to Zacharias was 'he shall go before him (i.e. the Lord) in the spirit and power of Elias', Luke 1. 17, nevertheless, Elijah himself will actually precede the Messiah when He comes again in power and in great glory.

The closing words of the Old Testament are 'a curse', v. 6, whilst the New Testament concludes with those comforting words 'The grace of our Lord Jesus Christ be with you all', Rev. 22.21. How thankful we should be that we live in this age of grace!

BIBLIOGRAPHY
INTRODUCTION

This Bibliography, has been compiled with a view to giving help for further reading and study. It is not exhaustive and contains some of the books consulted and quoted by the contributors. Books both in and out of print have been included, although time constraints precluded the very detailed search necessary to distinguish them. It may be possible to obtain some of those not in print from dealers in second hand Theological books. Books can be borrowed from Public Libraries through the national interlending scheme. operated by the Public Libraries. There are specialist libraries such as the Evangelical Library, 78a Chiltern St, London, W1M 2HB, with good collections, who will lend to members.

A note has been included on books which give useful help on matters such as word studies but which otherwise should be treated with care, as they give a different approach to that taken by this book. Absence of comment neither means complete approval nor is it an indication that care is not to be taken. In reading any author the infalliability, authority and teaching of the word of God must be paramount.

The place of publication is London unless stated. Some books were either published or were available on both sides of the Atlantic. In some instances it is a later edition rather than the first which is listed

A helpful Bibliographical guide is C. J. BARBER, The Minister's Library, Baker Book House.

* Denotes book noted by contributor.

GENERAL STUDY AIDS AND REFERENCE WORKS

*AHARONI, Y. and AVI YONAH, M. Macmillan Bible Atlas. Macmillan. New York. 1968. An excellent work by Jewish scholars.
*BULLENGER, E. W. (ed). The Companion Bible. Lamp Press. 1964. Also published by Kregel. Grand Rapids. Helpful for grammatical insights, less so in some of the comments.
*HARRIS, R. (ed). Theological Wordbook of the Old Testament. (2 vols). Moody Press. Chicago. 1980. Coded to Strong's Concordance. Invaluable for the serious Bible student.
*INTERNATIONAL STANDARD BIBLE ENCYCLOPAEDIA. ORR, J. (ed). (5 vols). Eerdmans, Grand Rapids. 1939.
*SMITH, W. Smith's Dictionary of the Bible. Revised by H. Hackett and E. Abbott. (4 vols) Baker Book House, Grand Rapids. 1972. Is reputed to be excellent despite its age (first published 1868).

UNGER, M. ed. Unger's Bible Dictionary. 3rd ed Moody Press. 1961.

*WIGRAM, G. V. The Englishman's Hebrew and Chaldee Concordance of the Old Testament. Coded to Strong's Concordance. Baker Book House. Grand Rapids. 1980. Excellent for seeing the occurances of a word in the original and showing the different ways translated in the AV/KJV.

*WILSON, W. Old Testament Word Studies. Macmillan. 1870. Kregel. Grand Rapids. 1978.

INTRODUCTORY TO THE PROPHETS

ARCHER, G. L. A Survey of Old Testament Introduction. Moody Press. Chicago. 1964. Considered the definitive work against the Modernist tendency in OT studies.

*ELLISON, H. L. The Prophets of Israel. Paternoster Press. Exeter. Eerdmans. Grand Rapids. 1969. The Northern Kingdom, with stress on Hosea and Amos. Amillennial.

*FYFE, G. B. Prophetic Profile. Precious Seed Publications. Neath. 1992.

*HARRISON, R. K. Introduction to the Old Testament. IVP. 1970.

HENGESTENBERG, E. Christology of The Old Testament. (4 vols) rpr Kregel. Grand Rapids. 1956. Also available in 2 vol abridged.

LOCKYER, H. All the Messianic Promises of the Bible. P. and I. 1973.

LOCKYER, H. All the Men of the Bible. Zondervan. Grand Rapids. 1983.

*MORGAN, G. C. Studies in the Prophecy of Jeremiah. Oliphants. 1963. A great expositor but an Amillennialist.

STALLAN, F. E. Things Written Afore Time, John Ritchie. Kilmarnock. 1990.

*UNGER, M. Introductory Guide to the Old Testament. Zondervan. Grand Rapids. 1951.

*WOOD, L. The Prophets of Israel. Baker. 1979.

*WOOD, L. A Survey of Israel's History. Zondervan. Grand Rapids. 1970.

*YOUNG, E. J. Introduction to the Old Testament. Eerdmans. Grand Rapids. 1960. rev ed. An important treatment of the problems facing students in their OT studies.

COMMENTARIES ON THE WHOLE BIBLE

These obviously may not all be of the same standard throughout, especially where there are several contributors.

*BAXTER, J. Sidlow. Explore the Book. Zondervan. 1977.

*DARBY, J. N. Synopsis of the Books of the Bible. Many editions eg: Loiseaux Bros. Canada. 1942, rpr Chapter Two. 1992. Also Believers Bookshelf. Kingston, Ont.

*GAEBELEIN, A. C. The Annotated Bible (9 vols) originally printed 1913. Moody P. Chicago. Recently reisssued.

*JAMIESON, R., FAUSSET, A. and BROWN, D. A Commentary, Critical, Experimental and Practical on the Old and New Testaments. Various eds eg: Collins. (6 vols) (nd) and Eerdmans. (3 vols). 1973.

*KEIL, C. and DELITSCH, F. Commentary on the Old Testament. (Minor Prophets are vol. 10) rpr Eerdmans. (10 vols) Grand Rapids. 1971.

*LANGE, J. P. Commentary on the Holy Scriptures (24 vols) rpr Zondervan. Grand Rapids. 1960. Has been called particularly helpful on the OT.
MACDONALD, W. Believers Bible Commentary Vol 1. Old Testament. Nelson. Nashville. 1990.
*NEW BIBLE COMMENTARY (DAVIDSON, F. ed) IVP and Eerdmans. Grand Rapids. 1954. 2nd edition was published as NEW BIBLE COMMENTARY REVISED (D, GUTHRIE. ed). 1970.
*UNGER, M. UNGER'S BIBLE HANDBOOK. Moody Press. Chicago. 1966.
*WALVOORD, J. and ZUCK, R. Bible Knowledge Commentary Vol 1. Old Testament. Victor Books. Wheaton. 1983. Based on NIV.

There are a number of series of commentaries, by various authors, four are given to show the range and some volumes are excellent, but care is needed in certain cases.

*BIBLE SPEAKS FOR TODAY SERIES. Tyndale. IVP.
*CAMBRIDGE BIBLE FOR SCHOOLS. CUP. A standard old work, but uneven. AV used in the earlier editions, RV in the later.
*STUDY GUIDE SERIES. Zondervan.
*TYNDALE OLD TESTAMENT COMMENTARIES. IVP. Longer and more recent than CUP but uneven in interpretation.

ALL OR PART OF 12

*BARKER, H. P. Christ in the Minor Prophets. P. and I. nd.
BELLETT, J. G. The Minor Prophets. John Ritchie. Kilmarnock. nd.
*ELLISON, H. L. Men Spake from God. Studies in the Hebrew Prophets. Paternoster P. Exeter. 1958, Eerdmans. 1958. Good, but tends to compromise on certain issues.
FEINBERG, C. L. Major Messages of the Minor Prophets. American board of Missions to the Jews. New York. (5 vols). 1947/52.
*FREEMAN, R. E. Introduction to the Old Testament Prophets. Moody Press. Chicago. 1968.
GAEBELEIN, F. Four Minor Prophets, (Obadiah, Jonah, Habakkuk and Haggai). Moody Press. Chicago. 1970.
HAILEY, H. Commentary on the Minor Prophets. Baker Book House. 1972.
*HARLOW, R. E. Twelve Minor Prophets. Everyday Publications. Toronto.
*HEWITT, J. B. Outline Studies in the Minor Prophets. Precious Seed. Birmingham. 1968.
HOLE, F. B. Rebuilding Zion. Central Hammond Bible Trust. 1972.
IRONSIDE, H. A. Notes on the Minor Prophets. Loiseaux Bros. New York. 1909.
JENSEN, I. L. Minor Prophets of Israel. Bible Self Study Guide. Moody P. Chicago. 1975.
JENSEN, I. L. Minor Prophets of Judah. Bible Self Study Guide. Moody P. Chicago. 1976.
*KELLY, W. Lectures Introductory to the Study of the Minor Prophets. W. H. Broom and Rouse. 1897. Central Hammond Bible Trust, 5th ed nd.

*MORGAN, G. C. The Minor Prophets and Their Messages. rpr Fleming H. Revell Co. Old Tappan NJ. 1960. Amillennial.

*PUSEY, E. B. The Minor Prophets with a Commentary. Explanatory and Practical Introductions to the several books. (8 vols). James Nisbet. 1860. Extensive and Exhaustive. Amillennial.

STEVENSON, H. Three Prophetic Voices (Hosea /Amos) Marshall Morgan and Scott. 1971.

*TATFORD, F. A. The Minor Prophets. Reprint (3 vols). Klock and Klock. USA. 1982. See also individual books.

YATES, K. M. Preaching from the Prophets. Orig. Pub. Harper Bros. New York. 1942.

THE SPECIFIC BOOKS

In several of the prophets, the majority of the suggested reading is covered either in the previous section, the commentaries or in the series of commentaries.

HOSEA

HUBBARD, D. A. With Bonds of Love: Lessons from the Book of Hosea. Eerdmans. Grand Rapids. 1968.

*KIDNER, D. Hosea, The Bible Speaks Today series. IVP. US edition entitled as 'Love to the Loveless, The Message of Hosea'. IVP. Downers Grove. 1981.

LOGSDON, S. F. Hosea, The People who forgot God. Moody P. Chicago. 1959.

MORGAN, G. C. The Heart and Holiness of God. Marshall, Morgan and Scott. 1934. Fleming H. Revell. Westwood. 1967—Often regarded as one of his best, but Amillennial.

*TATFORD, F. A. Prophet of a Broken Home, an Exposition of Hosea. Prophetic Witness Publishing House. Eastbourne. 1974.

JOEL

CALVIN, J. Commentary on the Prophet Joel. Banner of Truth Trust. Edinburgh. 1958.

DI GANGI, M. Joel. Shield Bible Study series. Baker. 1970.

GAEBELEIN, A. C. The Prophet Joel, An Exposition. Our Hope. New York. 1909.

*ROWLEY, A. C. Joel, A Metrical Translation. Hamilton Adams. 1867.

TATFORD, F. A. Prophet of Judgement day. An Exposition of the Prophecy of Joel. Prophetic Witness Publishing House. Eastbourne. 1974.

AMOS

CLEMENTS, R. When God's Patience Runs Out. IVP. Leicester. 1988. Applied for today.

HOWARD, J. K. Amos Among the Prophets. P. and I. 1966. Baker. Grand Rapids. 1967.
KELLY, P. H. Amos Prophet of Social Justice. Baker. Grand Rapids. 1966.
TATFORD, F. A. Amos, Prophet of Social Injustice. Prophetic Witness Publishing House. Eastbourne. 1974.

OBADIAH

HILLIS, D. The Book of Obadiah. Baker Book House. Grand Rapids. 1968.
TATFORD, F. A. Obadiah, Prophet of Edom's Doom. Prophetic Witness. Eastbourne. 1974.

JONAH

BANKS, W. L. Jonah, the Reluctant Prophet. Moody Press. 1966.
BLAIR, J. A. Living Obediently. A Devotional Study of the Book of Jonah. Loiseaux Bros. NJ. 1963.
BULL, G. The City and the Sign. An Interpretation of the Book of Jonah. Pickering and Inglis. 1970.
DRAPER, J. T. Jonah, Living in Rebellion. Tyndale House pubs. Wheaton. 1971.
EXELL, J. S. Practical Truth from Jonah. Kregel. Grand Rapids. 1982.
FAIRBAIRN, P. Jonah, His Life, Character and Mission. Rpr. Kregel. Grand Rapids. 1964.
*FEREDAY, W. Jonah and His Experiences. J. Ritchie. Kilmarnock. nd.
FERGUSON, S. B. Man Overboard. Pickering and Inglis. 1981.
KENDALL, R. T. Jonah. Zondervan. 1981.
*MARTIN H. A Commentary on Jonah. Banner of Truth. Edinburgh. 1958.
PALMER ROBERTSON, O. Jonah, A Study In Compassion. Banner of Truth. Edinburgh. 1990.

MICAH

TATFORD, F. A. Prophet of Messiah's Advent, an exposition of the book of Micah Prophetic Witness Publishing House. Eastbourne. 1974.

NAHUM

MAIER, W. A. Book of Nahum. Concordia Publishing House. St Louis. 1959. Reprint. James Family. Minn. 1977.
TATFORD, F. A. Prophet of Assyria's Fall. The Message of Nahum. Prophetic Witness Publishing House. Eastbourne. 1973.

HABAKKUK

LLOYD JONES. D. M. Faith, Tried, and Triumphant. IVF. 1987. Originally published as 'From Fear To Faith'. IVF. 1966.
STOLL. J. H. The Book of Habbakkuk. Baker. Grand Rapids. 1972.
TATFORD, F. A. Prophet of the Watchtower, An Exposition of Habbakuk Eastbourne. Prophetic Witness Publishing House. 1973.

ZEPHANIAH

*TATFORD, F. Prophet of Royal Blood, an exposition of the prophecy of Zephaniah. Prophetic Witness Publishing House. Eastbourne. 1973.

HAGGAI

TATFORD, F. A. Prophet of the Restoration. Prophetic Witness Publishing House. Eastbourne. 1973.

ZECHARIAH

ADAMS, J. The Man Among the Myrtles. Charles Scribners Sons. NY. 1913.
BARON, D. The Visions and Prophecies of Zechariah (1918). Reissued. Kregel Publications. Grand Rapids. 1972.
DENNETT, E. Zechariah the Prophet, and Malachi. rpr Bible Truth Publishers.
FEINBERG, C. God Remembers. American Board of Missions to the Jews inc. New York. 1965.
GAEBELIN, A. C. Studies in Zechariah. Francis E. Fitch. NY. 1911.
LUCK, C. Zechariah. Moody P. 1957.
MEYER, F. The Prophet of Hope. Studies in Zechariah. Marshall, Morgan and Scott. 1952.
TATFORD, F. The Prophet of the Myrtle Grove. An Exposition of the Prophecy of Zechariah. H. E. Walter. Worthing. 1971.
UNGER, M. Zechariah, Prophet of Messiah's Glory. Zondervan. Grand Rapids. 1962.

MALACHI

DENNETT, E. see Zechariah.
LOGSDON, S. F. Malachi, or Will a Man Rob God. Moody Press. 1961.
*MORGAN, G. C. Studies in Malachi. Ritchie. Kilmarnock. nd.
MORGAN, G. C. Wherein Have We Robbed God? Revell. NY. 1898.
*TATFORD, F. A. Prophet of the Reformation. An Exposition of the Prophecy of Malachi. Prophetic Witness Publishing House. Eastbourne. 1972.